GRAVES
of our
FOUNDERS

Volume IV

Their Lives, Contributions, and Burial Sites

JOE FARRELL • LAWRENCE KNORR • JOE FARLEY

Mechanicsburg, PA USA

Published by Sunbury Press, Inc.
Mechanicsburg, Pennsylvania

www.sunburypress.com

Copyright © 2025 by Joe Farrell, Joe Farley, and Lawrence Knorr.
Cover Copyright © 2025 by Sunbury Press, Inc.

Sunbury Press supports copyright. Copyright fuels creativity, encourages diverse voices, promotes free speech, and creates a vibrant culture. Thank you for buying an authorized edition of this book and for complying with copyright laws by not reproducing, scanning, or distributing any part of it in any form without permission. You are supporting writers and allowing Sunbury Press to continue to publish books for every reader. For information contact Sunbury Press, Inc., Subsidiary Rights Dept., PO Box 548, Boiling Springs, PA 17007 USA or legal@sunburypress.com.

For information about special discounts for bulk purchases, please contact Sunbury Press Orders Dept. at (855) 338-8359 or orders@sunburypress.com.

To request one of our authors for speaking engagements or book signings, please contact Sunbury Press Publicity Dept. at publicity@sunburypress.com.

FIRST SUNBURY PRESS EDITION: December 2025

Set in Adobe Garamond | Interior design by Crystal Devine | Cover by Lawrence Knorr | Edited by the authors.

Publisher's Cataloging-in-Publication Data
Names: Farrell, Joe, author | Farley, Joe, author | Knorr, Lawrence, author.
Title: Graves of our founders : Volume IV : their lives, contributions, and burial sites / Joe Farrell Lawrence Knorr Joe Farley.
Description: First trade paperback edition. | Mechanicsburg, PA : Sunbury Press, 2025.
Summary: Joe Farrell, Joe Farley, and Lawrence Knorr have traveled across the eastern USA to the graves of over 200 founding fathers (and mothers) responsible for the birth of the United States of America. Included in this fourth volume are biographies and grave information for 55 of these luminaries who made significant contributions to the Revolutionary cause.
Identifiers: ISBN 979-8-88819-390-7 (softcover).
Subjects: HISTORY / United States / Revolutionary Period (1775-1800) | BIOGRAPHY & AUTOBIOGRAPHY / Political.

Designed in the USA
0 1 1 2 3 5 8 13 21 34 55

For the Love of Books!

Contents

Introduction. 1

James Madison The Father of the Constitution 5
Dolley Madison The Elegant Hostess 21
James Monroe "The Last Cocked Hat". 28
Abraham Baldwin The Founder of the University of Georgia 35
John Banister The Master of Hatcher's Run. 40
Simon Boerum "Congressman from Brooklyn" 44
Richard Caswell Revolutionary Governor. 47
George Rogers Clark Conqueror of the Old Northwest 53
Tench Coxe Economist & Opportunisty 60
Stephen Crane "Bayoneted by Hessians". 64
John DeHart Mayor of Elizabethtown 68
Johann Robais, Baron de Kalb French Major General 71
William Duer "The Panic of 1792". 75
William Few The Farm Boy Who Signed the Constitution 80
Lyman Hall The Delegate to Congress Who Couldn't Vote 85
John Harvie Friend of Jefferson. 89
Patick Henry Revolutionary Orator. 93
Thomas Heyward Jr. The Last to Sign the Declaration 102
Michael Hillegas The First Treasurer. 108
Samuel Holten Physician Continental Congressman 113
Charles Humphreys A Patriot Who Followed His Conscience 117
James Iredell An Original Supreme 121
William Jackson Secretary of the Constitutional Convention 125
Jame Kinsey The Jurist from Jersey 131
Henry Knox "Miracle on the Dorchester Heights". 135
Francis Lewis "All That Glitters Is Not Gold". 141
William Livingston "First Governor of New Jersey". 147
Thomas Lynch South Carolina Son of Liberty 153

Joseph Plumb Martin Private Yankee Doodle 157
John Marshall The Great Chief Justice 163
James McHenry Secretary of War 170
Thomas McKean "First Elected President of the Confederation" 177
Samuel Meredith Silk Stockings Associator 183
Lewis Morris III "The Last Lord of Morrisania" 189
William Moultrie Hero of Sullivan's Island 195
Andrew Pickens The Wizard Owl 200
David Rittenhouse Scientist, Surveyor, and First Mint Director 205
Daniel Roberdeau Pennsylvania Associator 211
Betsy Ross American Seamstress 216
Nathaniel Scudder "The Only Congressman to Die in Battle" 220
Jonathan Bayard Smith Quaker Educator 224
Richard Dobbs Spaight The Dueling Signer 227
John Stark "Hero of Bennington" 232
William Alexander, Lord Stirling "The Bravest Man in America" 238
Edward Telfair Master of Sharon 246
Matthew Thornton First Speaker of the New Hampshire Assembly 250
George Walton The Orphaned Founder 256
Samuel Ward Colonial Governor and Continental Congressman 260
John Wentworth Jr. New Hampshire Scion 265
William Whipple Hero of Saratoga 269
John Williams North Carolina Speaker of the House 274
Hugh Williamson "The Ben Franklin of North Carolina" 277
Thomas Willing Banker and Financier 282
Paine Wingate Last Continental Congressman to Die 287
Oliver Wolcott Connecticut Yankee 290

Sources 294
Index 298

Introduction

Welcome to *Volume 4* of Graves of Our Founders. In 2017, we were on a field trip for the Keystone Tombstones series, of which there are five volumes, when we began to discuss doing a series on our founders. We agreed to do a four-volume series with each covering approximately fifty founders. We have now met that goal, and the series covers 212 founders. It was a real challenge to visit graves in more than 13 states.

The first question we had to answer was who to include. The standard we settled on resulted in the inclusion of signees of the Continental Association, the Declaration of Independence, the Articles of Confederation, or the Constitution. In addition, we included non-signers of the above documents who made significant contributions to the founding of the United States of America. Francis Marion, better known as the Swamp Fox, and Paul Revere are examples.

In 2019, we decided to do an extra volume on the founders from Pennsylvania (*Pennsylvania Patriots*) since there were so many, and Pennsylvania played such a central role. The book was well received and realizing that 2026 was the 250th birthday of the United States, we decided to do a volume containing the founders for each of the original states, in addition to two special volumes, one containing those who attended the Congress held in York in 1777and 1778 (*The Congress at York)* and one about the men who served as President of Congress (*Before George)* before the ratification of the Constitution. Accessing information about some of the lesser-known individuals who made contributions at times has been challenging. We hope our efforts will please our readers.

We all agree that our visits to the gravesites and the research on the founders have been rewarding and educational. However, in some cases, the visits have been sobering, shocking, and shameful. The well-known founders, such as Washington, Jefferson, Hamilton, and Madison, have been laid to rest in well-maintained graves accessible to the public. Unfortunately, this is not the rule. Too many of our nation's founders are buried in neglected places that have been left unattended, and thus are subject to decay. Some are inaccessible, and others cannot be located at all due to the development of the land and poor record-keeping. One of our goals in doing this series and including photographs of the graves is to bring this problem to light and hopefully stimulate action to address this issue before it is simply too late.

Considering the condition of many of these graves, we have established a website, www.adoptapatriot.com, where one can find information on all the people we have identified as founders. We continue to update this site as we come across new information. In addition, the website includes a Wall of Shame where we highlight those gravesites we have concluded are in the worst shape due to neglect or are in remote, difficult-to-reach locations or where the founder is under-memorialized, given their contribution to the nation. It is our sincere hope that many of those graves will be restored, renewed or relocated.

Here are some interesting statistics gleaned from our project:

- 212 included in the project
- 15 are lost (no body or grave location lost)
- 197 can be visited – and at least 20 are tough to get to
- Only 28 make our "Best Condition" list
- 121 are in average condition – worn tombstones in mostly suburban or rural settings
- 47 are in terrible locations or completely lost (15)
- 39 have limited or no access
- 76 have stones in badly worn or worse condition
- 30 have poor or no maintenance
- 70 are poorly memorialized
- *Over 1/3 of the Founders' graves are deficient in some way*
- We have put 46 graves on our Wall of Shame (mentioned above)

INTRODUCTION

Sadly, here is the list of 15 who are lost:

- Thomas Adams
- John Banister
- Edward Biddle
- Jonathan Dayton
- John DeHart
- John Hanson
- Daniel of St. Thomas Jenifer
- Edward Langworthy
- James Lovell
- Thomas Lynch
- Thomas Lynch, Jr.
- Thomas Paine
- Richard Smith
- John Walton
- John Williams

Here are the ones who are tough to get to:

- David Brearley
- Charles Carroll of Carollton
- Samuel Chase
- John Collins
- Francis Dana
- William Richardson Davie
- James Duane
- Titus Hosmer
- John Jay
- Henry Laurens
- Francis Lightfoot Lee
- Richard Henry Lee
- Henry Middleton
- Gouverneur Morris
- Lewis Morris
- William Paca
- Timothy Pickering
- Peyton Randolph
- Jonathan Bayard Smith
- John Sullivan

One thing we have learned about the founders in writing this series, and we are confident that most of them would agree with us, is that they were products of their times and not perfect nor infallible. They disagreed on many of the issues they faced, and none may have been as hotly debated as slavery. It is difficult to reconcile men who undertook a war against the most powerful army in the world, proclaiming that all men are created equal, while, at the same time, many of these same men held other men, women, and children in bondage. The contradiction is obvious and quite difficult to excuse. Nevertheless, we have attempted to tell each founder's story truthfully.

As our country celebrates the 250th anniversary of the Declaration of Independence, we view these volumes as timely reminders of the founders' sacrifices and contributions to create this nation. We should never forget those who put their lives and fortunes on the line and succeeded in establishing the greatest country the world has ever known. We are inspired by the words of Marcus Cicero:

POOR IS THE NATION THAT HAS NO HEROES
SHAMEFUL IS ONE THAT, HAVING THEM, FORGETS

James Madison
(1751–1836)

The Father of the Constitution

Buried at Madison Family Cemetery at Montpelier,
Montpelier Station, Orange County, Virginia.

U.S. Constitution • Congress • 4th United States President

This founder played a pivotal role in both the passage and ratification of the United States Constitution. He was a co-author of *The Federalist Papers*. He also played a pivotal role in the drafting of the first amendments to the Constitution, known as the Bill of Rights. With Thomas Jefferson, he organized the Democratic-Republican Party to oppose the Federalist Party. When Jefferson was elected president, he served as his Secretary of State. During his tenure, he convinced Jefferson to submit the Louisiana Purchase Treaty to the Senate for approval. In 1808, he was elected to succeed Jefferson as president. He led the country through the War of 1812 and was reelected that same year. Historians rank him as one of the most significant founding fathers. His name was James Madison.

Madison was born on March 16, 1751, at the Belle Grove Plantation in Virginia. His father was James Madison Sr., one of the largest landowners in the colony. The younger Madison was tutored by Donald Robertson, who was known for working with prominent families. In 1769, he enrolled at the College of New Jersey, now known as Princeton University.

James Madison

One of the main reasons Madison decided to study in New Jersey rather than at the College of William and Mary, like most college-bound Virginians, was due to his health. The Williamsburg climate was considered to harbor more infectious diseases. As detailed by Lynne Cheney in her work *James Madison: A Life Reconsidered*, Madison had suffered seizures during his childhood that are common in temporal lobe epilepsy. Cheney writes that based on the available evidence, this was the pattern "of Madison's ailment: fever-related episodes when he was a toddler, then sudden attacks later in life."

As related by Cheney, Madison did well enough on his Latin and Greek entrance exams to be able to skip his freshman year. During his sophomore year, he decided to complete his junior and senior studies concurrently. After he received permission to do so, he began what he described as "an indiscreet experiment of the minimum of sleep and the maximum of application which the constitution could bear." He earned his degree, but at a price. Dr. Witherspoon carried a letter to Madison's father, explaining that his son's efforts had led to a health crisis. Cheney maintains that it is reasonable to suppose that the crisis was described as "sudden attacks, somewhat resembling epilepsy." Madison returned to Virginia in a state of depression. Writing to a friend, he said, ". . . I think my sensations for many months past have intimated to me not to expect a long or healthy life." As it turns out, in this instance, Madison was mistaken, as he lived a long and fruitful life.

In 1773, 130 men disguised as Indians dumped thousands of pounds of tea into the Boston Harbor in what became known as the Boston Tea Party. While Madison agreed that Boston had been singled out for assaults by the British, he preferred what he called Philadelphia's more temperate approach. He wrote, "I wish Boston may conduct matters with as much discretion as they seem to do with boldness." He admired the conduct of those in Philadelphia and hoped to visit the city. He got his wish when his father decided to send his brother to a northern boarding school. Madison was probably in Philadelphia when the news arrived that the British had closed the Boston harbor. This action resulted in many Americans, including Madison, to harden their opinions due to these harsh tactics. He would make many more visits to Philadelphia in the years to come.

Madison's career in politics and government began in 1774 when he took a seat on the local Committee of Safety, a group that favored revolution. A year later, he became a colonel in the Orange County militia. Where he served under his father until he was elected as a delegate to the Fifth Virginia Convention, which led to the creation of Virginia's first Constitution. At the Virginia Constitutional Convention, he was instrumental in gaining the alteration of the Declaration of Rights, changing the word "tolerance" to "equal entitlement" in the practice of religion. He then became a member of the Virginia House of Delegates, where he formed a close friendship and strong alliance with Thomas Jefferson.

In 1779, Madison was elected to the Second Continental Congress. The historian J. C. A. Stagg described Madison as a legislative workhorse as he studied financial issues and coalition building. He was also a strong supporter of the American alliance with France and the country's westward expansion. After his term in Congress ended, he was elected to the Virginia House of Delegates in 1784. In this position, he, along with Jefferson, continued to support religious freedom. The two future presidents drafted the Virginia Statute for Religious Freedom. It passed in 1786 and resulted in the guarantee of freedom of religion, as well as the disestablishment of the Church of England.

During this period, Madison grew concerned about the weakness of the federal government established by the Articles of Confederation. He wrote, "A crisis had arrived which was to decide whether the American experiment was to be a blessing to the world, or to blast forever the hopes which the republican cause had inspired." In 1787, Madison was among the Virginians chosen to represent the state at the Constitutional Convention in Philadelphia.

Madison arrived in the City of Brotherly Love over a week before his fellow Virginia delegate, George Washington, made his much-anticipated entry. Washington's carriage was escorted by Philadelphia's City Troop and cheered by crowds as he made his way to the home of Robert Morris. Madison was more than pleased to see the hero of the Revolution because he knew that Washington's presence at the convention would be beneficial in securing the support of the people.

It took over a week for enough state delegations to arrive, allowing the convention to begin. The initial order of business was to elect a presiding officer, and Washington was the unanimous choice. In Madison's view, the gathering would "decide forever the fate of republican government." He was also determined to preserve a record of the proceedings for historical purposes. Therefore, he kept detailed notes on the remarks made by the delegates. In the evening, he would work long hours transcribing his notes, an arduous process that he would recall "almost killed him."

Clearly, Madison was very serious about the convention's success. Historian Clinton Rossiter, in his book *1787: The Grand Convention*, notes that Madison was one of the delegates who never missed a single session. Rossiter calls him the leading spirit and quotes Major Jackson, who called Madison the "most efficient member" in the conclave. The historian points to Madison's foresight in drafting the Virginia Plan and making it the agenda of the convention, his willingness to debate great issues and small with courteous and learned intensity, his dozens of suggestions of ways for his colleagues to extricate themselves from thickets, his membership on three of the four essential committees, even perhaps his doggedness in the major struggle for power—these are the solid credentials of the one Framer who stands, modestly and eternally, first among his splendid peers. Madison's performance at the convention has led many to call him the "Father of the Constitution."

On September 17, 1787, the delegates gathered to sign the finished product. Three delegates, George Mason, Edmund Randolph, and Elbridge Gerry, refused to sign the document. The Constitution was then sent to the states for ratification. Madison knew his work had only begun. Mason and Randolph were also from Virginia and were sure to oppose ratification at the state's ratifying convention. Their primary concern was that the Constitution did not include a Bill of Rights. Those who supported ratification were known as Federalists, and Madison was a member of this faction. Those opposed were known as Anti-Federalists.

The Anti-Federalists began a public campaign opposing ratification. In response, beginning in October 1787, two New York Federalists, Alexander Hamilton and John Jay, wrote a series of letters in support of ratification that appeared in New York newspapers. The letters or essays were published under the name Publius. When illness forced Jay to drop out of the effort, Hamilton approached Madison, who was in New York serving in Congress, to take his place. Madison agreed, and the trio produced 85 essays that became known as *The Federalist Papers*. The articles were published in book form and used by the Federalists in the state ratifying conventions. The work became highly regarded for its advocacy of representative democracy. The historian Clinton Rossiter wrote, "*The Federalist* is the most important work in political science that has ever been written, or is likely ever to be written, in the United States."

The Virginia Ratifying Convention convened on June 2, 1788, and Edmund Pendleton was elected to preside over it. By this time, Madison had convinced Edmund Randolph to support ratification, and the duo became the leaders of the Federalists. The Anti-Federalists, who would make most of the speeches during the convention, were led by Patrick Henry and George Mason. When the convention began, both sides acknowledged that the outcome was highly uncertain.

Henry, who was widely known for his speaking ability, argued that the delegates in Philadelphia should only have suggested amendments to the Articles of Confederation. He said that the proposed Constitution would put an end to Virginia's liberty and the state government. Randolph, who had altered his position since refusing to sign the Constitution, argued that the confederation of states had proven to be totally inadequate and that if the Constitution was not ratified, the Union could well be lost.

Mason took the position that a national government would burden Virginia with direct taxes and that a government that rules such a vast territory would destroy liberty. He said he wanted a clear distinction between the powers of the federal and state governments, including the judiciary because shared authority would result in "the destruction of one or the other." Madison took the position that the history of Confederations was proved inadequate in the long run. He said the proposed Constitution would provide the country with a Republic, with each branch of the government grounded in the people.

On June 27, George Wythe put forward a motion to ratify. The motion passed 89 to 79, although Virginians reserved the right to withdraw from the new government. The gathering also recommended amendments, including the addition of a Bill of Rights. Patrick Henry's opposition never wavered. He refused to serve in the new government, turning down offers to serve as Secretary of State and as a justice on the Supreme Court. Using his influence over the Virginia legislature, he successfully made Virginia the only state to send two Anti-Federalist senators to the First Congress.

After serving in the Congress of the Confederation, Madison returned to Virginia and made an unsuccessful attempt to run for the U.S. Senate in 1788. At this point, he feared that Patrick Henry and the Anti-Federalists would arrange for a second constitutional convention. Against this background, he ran for a seat in the House of Representatives. Again, he was opposed by Henry, who recruited James Monroe to run against him. In the midst of this challenging race, Madison pledged to support constitutional amendments that protect individual rights. This promise was pivotal in his victory as he was elected to the First Congress, receiving 57 percent of the vote.

While there was no doubt that Washington would be the first president, who would fill the second spot was a question. Prior to the electors being chosen, Madison sent a ciphered letter to Thomas Jefferson. He expressed his dissatisfaction with the two most prominent names being put forward. He described John Hancock as "weak, ambitious, a courtier of popularity given to low intrigue." When it came to John Adams, Madison was convinced that his feelings of self-importance would doom him. In the same missive, he claimed he had always been in favor of a Bill of Rights. He took this position despite the fact that at the Virginia Ratifying Convention, he declared that supporting such a position was "dangerous because an enumeration which is not complete is not safe" and "unnecessary because it was evident that the general government had no power but what was given it." He now favored a Bill of Rights because he had made a promise to deliver it to get elected and because he would be the one framing it.

Madison studied more than two hundred amendments that had been proposed at the state's ratifying conventions. He then introduced a Bill of Rights on June 8, 1789. His proposal faced virtually no opposition. He had successfully quashed the Anti-Federalist goal of a second convention and, at the same time, avoided including anything that would alienate supporters of the Constitution. The ten amendments were ratified on December 15, 1791.

The country wasn't long into the Washington administration before political factions began to emerge. Alexander Hamilton led one faction that championed northern financial concerns and strong ties with Great Britain. This group became the Federalist Party. Thomas Jefferson and Madison led the other faction, which supported Southern interests and close ties with France, forming the Democratic-Republican Party. The two groups battled over Secretary of the Treasury Hamilton's financial plan. Among other things in the plan was the establishment of a national bank. Madison argued that the Constitution did not give Congress the authority to create such an institution. His argument failed; Congress

James Madison's house

voted to create the First Bank of the United States, and Washington signed the law in February 1791.

Jefferson and Madison continued to oppose Hamilton by taking their positions to the people. They aided Philip Freneau in the founding of a Philadelphia newspaper, the *National Gazette*. In the fall of 1792, prior to the second presidential election, Madison wrote that the country had been divided into two distinct camps. On one side, some believed "that mankind are capable of governing themselves." He contended that the Federalists supported the creation of a class of aristocrats who would favor the wealthy. In the election that followed, both parties supported Washington, but the Democratic-Republicans made an unsuccessful effort to remove Adams as Vice President.

Jefferson and Hamilton had often clashed during Washington's first term. As told by Fawn Brodie in *Thomas Jefferson: An Intimate History*, Jefferson had concluded that his rival was impregnable. He decided to resign and return to Virginia. He submitted his resignation effective December 31, 1793. When Jefferson left office, Madison became the leader of the Democratic-Republican Party in Washington. When England and France went to war in 1793, the question was, who would the United States support? Madison favored France, while Hamilton favored England. When England began seizing American ships trading with French colonies, war with the mother country seemed imminent. Washington, looking to avoid a war he felt the young country was ill-prepared to fight, secured friendly relations with England through the Jay Treaty of 1794. Madison's strong opposition to the treaty led to a break with Washington, ending their friendship.

On September 15, 1794, Madison married. The bride was Dolley Payne Todd, a 26-year-old widow. The couple had been introduced by one of New York's senators Aaron Burr. The couple never had children, though Madison adopted Dolley's son from her previous marriage.

After serving two terms, Washington decided to retire. In the 1796 election, Madison convinced Jefferson to run for the highest office in the land. The Federalists were supporting Vice President John Adams. This became the first presidential election in which competing parties vied for the presidency. The campaign was bitter as the Federalists identified the Democratic-Republicans with the violence of the French Revolution.

Meanwhile Jefferson's party accused the Federalists of favoring a monarchy. The Jay Treaty was also attacked as being too favorable to England. The Federalists countered by calling Jefferson an atheist who was a coward during the American Revolution. Adams won a close election, garnering 71 electoral votes to Jefferson's 68. Based on the Electoral College rules in place at the time, Jefferson became the Vice President because he had received the second-highest total of votes. Madison had declined to run for reelection and returned to Virginia.

Madison may have been out of office, but he was still a prominent leader of the opposition party. Both Jefferson and Madison held the view that the Federalists had violated constitutional rights by passing the Alien and Sedition Acts. Madison firmly believed that the acts set a dangerous precedent by giving the government the authority to disregard the rights of people in the name of national security.

With his election to the Virginia legislature in 1799, Madison made his return to office. At this point, he was also planning Jefferson's 1800 run for president. In that controversial election, the Federalists were divided between those who supported Adams and those who supported Hamilton. When Jefferson and his running mate, Aaron Burr, received an equal number of electoral votes, the election was decided by the House of Representatives. Jefferson was elected president, and Burr was elected vice president.

Despite his lack of foreign policy experience, Madison was appointed Secretary of State, where he wielded considerable influence in Jefferson's cabinet. It was in this position that he began to rely on Dolley Madison to manage the social demands of being a high-ranking public figure in Washington. She would fulfill that role throughout his life.

With the rise of Napoleon, Democratic-Republican support for France cooled. Madison pursued a position of neutrality relative to the conflict between the French and the British. In 1802, Jefferson and Madison sent James Monroe to France to negotiate the purchase of New Orleans, primarily due to the control of access to the Mississippi River. Napoleon countered with an offer to sell the entire Louisiana territory. Monroe, along with American Minister to France Robert Livingston, negotiated the Louisiana Purchase despite the fact that such authorization from Jefferson was lacking. Jefferson was concerned about the constitutionality of the purchase. He favored a constitutional amendment authorizing Congress to obtain territories. Madison convinced him that such an amendment was not required. The administration then submitted the Louisiana Purchase Treaty to Congress for approval without an accompanying amendment. In Madison's view, treaties between the United States and other countries were already authorized by the Constitution. Both houses of Congress quickly accepted the treaty.

During the Napoleonic Wars, Madison played a pivotal role in managing trade relations with both France and Great Britain. He viewed England as a significant problem due to their use of impressment, where they forcibly conscripted American sailors into the British navy. He attempted to negotiate a treaty with England that would protect American trade rights and prohibit the practice of impressment. Failing in this endeavor, he supported the implementation of economic sanctions against the British, including the Embargo Act of 1807. This act prohibited all exports to foreign nations. It was unpopular and very difficult to enforce, particularly in New England. Early in 1809, Congress replaced the Embargo Act with the Non-Intercourse Act, which permitted trade with nations other than England and France. The impressment issue was one he would inherit when he succeeded Jefferson as president.

By 1808, when the presidential election to select Jefferson's successor took place, the Federalist Party had collapsed. As a result, Madison's main opposition came from within his party, particularly from Congressman John Randolph, who attacked Madison due to his association with the ongoing embargo. James Monroe and Vice President George Clinton challenged Madison for the Democratic-Republican nomination. Madison, with the strong backing of Jefferson, prevailed. He then easily defeated the Federalist candidate, Charles Cotesworth Pinckney, receiving 122 electoral votes to his opponent's 47.

As told by the historian Kevin R. C. Gutzman in *The Jeffersonians: The Visionary Presidencies of Jefferson, Madison and Monroe* Jefferson declined Madison's invitation to tide with him in his carriage to the inauguration. Jefferson explained the decision, saying, "I wished not to divide with him the honors of the day." Instead, Jefferson followed the carriage as a member of the crowd unattended on horseback. When he was directed to a seat near Madison, he also declined, saying, "This day I return to the people, and my proper seat is among them."

When Madison began his inaugural address, he appeared nervous, but he soon found his footing. He laid out a set of principles that would guide him. These included peace with nations that wanted it, neutrality toward belligerents, and diplomacy instead of war when practicable. Commitment to the Union and the Constitution, supporting the freedom of conscience and respect for individual rights, particularly the freedom of the press. He favored limitations on military spending during times of peace and a reliance on the militia. He wished to support agriculture, manufacturing, commerce, science and education. He said he would continue to convert the Indians from "savage" to "a civilized state." Gutzman concluded that Madison "would indeed hew to these principles as president, for good and for ill."

Jefferson, during his time as president, generally enjoyed unified support. Such was not the case with Madison. He would encounter political opposition from former allies, including Monroe. He had hoped to make Albert Gallatin his Secretary of State, but due to opposition, he kept him as Secretary of the Treasury. According to historians Ketcham and Rutland, his cabinet was chosen to promote political harmony but was unremarkable and incompetent. For example, he appointed Robert Smith as his Secretary of State, but due to Smith's incompetence, Madison found that he had to perform most of the duties of that office. Madison would replace Smith with Monroe in 1811.

In the early months of his presidency, Madison continued Jefferson's policies of low taxes and debt reduction. In 1811, he allowed the charter of the First Bank of the United States to lapse. Throughout his first term, he continued to struggle with both French and English attacks on American shipping. Hoping to pit those two countries against each other, he offered to trade with whichever country would cease their attacks. In 1810, Napoleon dictated a letter addressed to the American minister in Paris, offering to lift the Berlin and Milan decrees, which were the French justification for seizing American ships. This offer was conditioned on the British renouncing their blockades or on the United States, causing "their rights to be respected by the English." Madison accepted the offer, and as Cheney points out in her biography, critics at the time and since have noted this as a sign of Madison's gullibility. They questioned how Napoleon could be trusted. Madison wrote to Jefferson, saying, "We hope from the step the advantage of having but one contest on our hands at a time," adding, "The original sin against neutrals lies with Great Britain."

As told by Gutzman in his work on the period, a significant change occurred when Congress convened on November 4, 1811. It marked a generational shift in the American republic's leadership. Additions to the House of Representatives included Henry Clay of Kentucky and South Carolina's John C. Calhoun. These men were determined to confront England. In their time, Clay, Calhoun, and Daniel Webster were regarded by historians as more significant figures than all but a couple of presidents between James Monroe and Abraham Lincoln.

Madison delivered his State of the Union Address on November 5, 1811. He made it clear that, after years of patience with the two belligerents, he was at a breaking point. Madison's private secretary, Edward Coles, looking back on those days, told William Cabell Rives, a former

U. S. senator and Madison biographer, "It was congenial alike to the life and character of Mr. Madison that he should be reluctant to go to war." However, Britain's decision demanding substantial concessions from the United States had "closed the door to peace in Madison's opinion."

With Britain embroiled in the Napoleonic Wars, many Americans, including Madison, believed the United States could easily capture Canada and use it as a bargaining chip. On June 12, 1812, Madison asked Congress for a declaration of war, saying that the country could no longer tolerate England's "state of war against the United States." Madison asked Congress to quickly put the country on war footing by expanding both the army and the navy.

Madison believed the war would end quickly with an American victory. He ordered three invasions of Canada. First, there was to be an assault from Fort Detroit aimed at destroying British supply lines from Montreal. Madison had no standing army and relied on state militias; however, the governors of northeastern states refused to cooperate. Meanwhile, the British had trained soldiers and allied with American Indians led by Tecumseh. The British attacked Fort Detroit and killed two American officers. Major General William Hull, who, by reports, had been drinking heavily, then surrendered unconditionally. He was later court-martialed for cowardice, but Madison interceded and saved him from execution. Another defeat followed at Queenston Heights when the American commanding general had to deal with mutinous New England troops and was forced to retreat to Albany. At this point, Madison lacked the revenue to fund the war and had to rely on high-interest loans from banks in New York and Philadelphia.

The 1812 presidential election took place under the shadow of war. The British, to this point, had fought a defensive war, so there were no disruptions to the voting. Madison was renominated without opposition. However, a dissident group of Democratic-Republicans nominated New York's lieutenant governor, DeWitt Clinton, to oppose Madison. This group hoped to defeat the sitting president by forming a coalition of those opposed to the war, as well as those who felt Madison had been too slow to respond to the British and northerners who had grown tired and unhappy with Southern control of the White House. Madison won reelection by sweeping the south and carrying Pennsylvania. Clinton won the majority of the northeast and received 89 electoral votes to Madison's 128.

Dismayed by the dismal start to the war, Madison was quick to accept Russia's offer to arbitrate the conflict. He sent a delegation that included Albert Gallatin and future president John Quincy Adams to Europe to negotiate a peace treaty. During this period, despite the notion that "Britannia Rules the Waves," the United States experienced naval successes. This included a victory in the Battle of Lake Erie, where the United States severely damaged the British supply lines and their ability to reinforce military forces in the western theater of the war.

On land, the Americans were meeting with mixed success. General William Henry Harrison defeated the British and the Tecumseh Confederacy at the Battle of the Thames. The death of Tecumseh in the battle ended any chance of the establishment of a United Indian nation. In 1814, Major General Andrew Jackson secured a victory at the Battle of Horseshoe Bend. Despite these victories, the British continued to repel attempts to invade Canada. At the same time, the British succeeded in capturing Fort Niagara and burned the city of Buffalo.

In August of 1814, a British force landed at the Chesapeake Bay, where they defeated the Americans at the Battle of Bladensburg. Prior to the English capturing Washington, Madison fled into Virginia. The British burned a number of buildings, including the White House. The British next moved to Baltimore, where they were repelled and subsequently left the region in September. In the same month, American forces successfully defeated the British Invasion from Canada. The English people were growing weary of the war, and the country's leaders began looking for a way to end it.

The Treaty of Ghent ended the war on December 24, 1814. Prior to this news reaching Madison, General Jackson's troops won what may have been the most significant American victory at the Battle of New Orleans. With Napoleon's defeat at Waterloo marking the end of the Napoleonic Wars, the seizure of American ships by the French and the English also came to an end. Although the outcome of the War of 1812 was considered a standoff, the end of the conflict enhanced Madison's presidential reputation.

James Madison (1751–1836)

Grave of James Madison

Early in Madison's second term, the country entered what is known as the "Era of Good Feelings." The Federalist Party continued to decline in both influence and popularity. The opposition party held the Hartford Convention, which began on December 15, 1814, and ran until January 5, 1815. As related by Cheney, many Republicans viewed the convention as a step on the road to secession. Vice President Elbridge Gerry advised Madison to issue a "spirited manifesto" in response. The soon-to-be Governor of Virginia, Wilson Cary Nicholas, urged Madison to send in troops. The results of the convention became known, and while there was no insistence on immediate secession, the convention insisted that the United States government "consent to some arrangement whereby the (New England" states may separately or in concert be empowered to assume upon themselves the defense of their territory" - and allow the states to pay for this by withholding federal tax money. The Federalists had overplayed their hand, as the convention proved to be a burden the party had to carry at a time when Americans had moved toward unity in celebration of what many viewed as a successful "second war of independence" against England.

Madison also contributed to the fall of the Federalists by supporting programs he had previously opposed. He proposed the re-establishment of a national bank and called for a tariff on imported goods. He was successful on both counts, causing strict constructionists such as John Randolph to complain that Madison now "out Hamiltons Alexander Hamilton."

In the 1816 election, both Jefferson and Madison supported James Monroe. Monroe easily defeated the Federalist candidate Rufus King of New York. Madison left office as a very popular president. The former Federalist president John Adams wrote that Madison had "acquired more glory, and established more union, than all of his three predecessors, Washington, Adams and Jefferson, put together."

On June 28, 1836, Madison passed away in his home. He was buried in the family cemetery, but since he had not designed a tombstone, his grave was unmarked. Madison's legacy is a great one. The historian J. C. A. Stagg wrote, "In some ways because he was on the winning side of every important issue facing the young nation from 1776 to 1816 - Madison was the most successful and possibly the most influential of all the Founding Fathers."

Dolley Madison
(1768–1849)

The Elegant Hostess

Buried at Madison Family Cemetery at Montpelier, Montpelier Station, Orange County, Virginia.

Spearhead of Bipartisan Cooperation

She was the wife of the fourth President of the United States. In this role, she was instrumental in defining the role of the President's spouse, later known as the First Lady. She came to the White House with some experience, having served as an unofficial hostess for the widowed Thomas Jefferson during his presidency. Until her husband became President, social gatherings at the White House were typically attended by members of only one political party at a time, as mixing the two parties sometimes resulted in physical altercations and the occasional duel. She demonstrated that members of each party could gather and socialize in a peaceful, bipartisan manner. Her name was Dolley Madison.

Dolley was born as Dolley Payne on May 20, 1768, at Paige's Tavern in Person County, North Carolina. Her parents, John Payne Jr. and Mary Cole, who were married in 1761, hailed from two prominent Virginia families. The couple were Quakers, and in 1769, they decided to return to Virginia. Some historians have speculated that the reason for the move may have been due to local opposition to their religion, a failure in farming, or a combination of both. Eventually, the family, she had three sisters

Dolley Madison

and four brothers, moved back to Cedar Creek, North Carolina, where she experienced a strict Quaker upbringing and education. The historian Richard N. Côté wrote that it was a situation she was "chafing" under.

Dolley's father, John Payne, being a pacifist, did not participate in the American Revolutionary War. By 1783, he had emancipated all his slaves. That same year, he moved the family to Philadelphia. Here, Dolley grew into womanhood, and one of her biographers writes that she was described "as one of the fairest of the fair."

As recounted by Lynne Cheney in her work, *James Madison: A Life Reconsidered*, Payne attempted to support his family by manufacturing laundry starch. The business failed in 1789, which was seen as a weakness by the Quakers, and he was expelled from the Quaker meetings. Devastated and overwhelmed by the turn of events, he took to his bed. Dolley fulfilled her father's dying wish by marrying a promising twenty-seven-year-old Quaker attorney, John Todd. The newly married couple, together with Dolley's sister Anna, moved into a brick house at Fourth and Walnut Streets. Meanwhile, Dolley's mother began to take in borders, one of whom was Aaron Burr.

Dolley and Todd had two sons: John Payne, born in 1792, and William Temple, who entered the world on July 4, 1793. In August of that year, a yellow fever epidemic broke out in Philadelphia. More than 5,000 people died in four months. Dolley lost her husband, her son William and both her father-in-law and mother-in-law.

Dolley's husband had left her money in his will. Now, she was without financial support, and her brother-in-law, who was the executor of the will, was withholding the funds. With the assistance of Aaron Burr, she filed a suit to get what she was owed. In a will written at the time, Burr was also named the guardian of Dolley's surviving son.

James Madison had known Burr since they had both been students at Princeton. So, it was not unusual when he approached Burr to be introduced to the widow Todd. Dolley wrote to a friend, "Aaron Burr says that the great little Madison has asked him to bring him to see me this evening." Congressman Madison was immediately smitten after the meeting. Soon, he confided in Dolley about his feelings through her friend, Catherine Cole. "Now for Madison," Cole wrote on June 1, 1794, "He told me I might say what I pleased to you about him. To begin, he thinks so much of you in the day that he has lost his tongue; at night, he dreams of you and starts in his sleep calling on you to relieve his flame, for he burns to such an excess that he will be shortly consumed, and he hopes that your heart will be callous to every other swain but himself."

Dolley had several other suitors, including a prominent Philadelphia attorney. Madison, however, had quite a bit going for him. He had already reached a level of fame and respect that few in the young nation could match. Not to mention the fact that even greater successes might well be in his future. As told by Cheney, Dolley realized that she would be expelled from meetings if she married outside the Quaker faith but notes she may well have looked to that event with relief.

In August 1794, Dolley wrote to Madison a letter accepting his marriage proposal. On the morning of her wedding, she wrote a letter to a friend saying Madison was "the man whom of all others I most admire." The couple exchanged vows on September 15, 1794. It was a union that would endure for forty-two years until the death of James Madison.

The couple lived in Philadelphia for the next three years. In 1797, rejecting the advice of Jefferson, who urged him to remain in office, Madison decided not to run for reelection. He moved his family back to Montpelier. John Adams wrote to his wife Abigail on Madison's retirement, saying, "It is marvelous how political plants grow in the shade." While Madison had no plans to reenter the political fray, he certainly supported the ambitions of his friend Jefferson. If Jefferson succeeded in gaining the presidency, there was little doubt he would call on Madison to assist him in some capacity. In that event, Madison would, as Adams had said, benefit from time spent out of the political glare.

The Madisons lived in Virginia until 1800, when Jefferson was elected President and picked Madison to serve as his Secretary of State. They moved to Washington into a large house on F Street because, in Dolley's view, space was needed for entertainment, which she believed would be important in the new capital.

They weren't long in Washington before the Madison's began to entertain and in a markedly different way than that of President Jefferson. The President hosted small dinner parties, where the guests were generally all men. In those instances when women were included, he would invite Dolley and her sister Anna to act as hostesses. At first, his dinners were bipartisan, but this ended quickly because he disliked political debates at the table. Soon, he invited only members of one party, and even then, he discouraged discussions of political issues. The Madison's invited both men and women, members of both parties and were fine with political issues being the topic of conversation. As related by Cheney, the Federalist John Quincy Adams wrote in his diary of a party at the Madisons', "There was a company of about seventy persons of both sexes," and he noted that he "had considerable conversation with Mr. Madison on the subjects now most important to the public." People enjoyed the Madisons' parties in large part because of Dolley's considerable and seemingly artless charm. As for the Secretary of State, he dropped his public persona and was warm, friendly and witty. Republicans grew fonder of him, and Federalists soon found it more difficult to demonize him.

Dolley Madison (1768–1849)

After serving two terms, Jefferson, following Washington's lead, announced he would not seek another term. In the 1808 election, it was evident that the Republican nominee would be the next President. Madison had Jefferson's backing and another key advantage with the congressional caucus in naming the Republican nominee. Dolley was skilled at dealing with members of Congress. She repeatedly invited them to her home, where they were welcome to spend hours at a time. In her Madison biography, Cheney notes that Senator Samuel Mitchell, in a letter to his wife, described the edge that Dolley's social gatherings gave Madison over his rival, Vice President George Clinton. "The former gives dinners and makes generous displays to the members. The latter lives smug at his lodgings and keeps aloof from such captivating exhibitions. The secretary of state has a wife to aid his pretensions. The vice president has no female support on his side. And in those two respects, Mr. M is going greatly ahead of him.

Another potential challenger to Madison was James Monroe. Dolley, according to John Quincy Adams, "spoke very slightly of Mr. Monroe." It was easy to understand this when one considers that Monroe was supposed to be her husband's friend, and it was likely that, for the second time, he was being encouraged to run against him. In 1788, Patrick Henry had convinced Monroe to run against Madison, and now Congressman John Randolph of Roanoke was doing the same.

As the election approached, rumors circulated regarding Dolley's morals. Senator Mitchell wrote his wife, "Your friend Mrs. Madison is shockingly and unfeelingly traduced in the Virginia papers." It was clear that one of those encouraging rumors was John Randolph. While Monroe never presented himself as a candidate, he also failed to shut the door on the possibility, saying he would serve if elected. Ultimately, Madison was nominated and subsequently elected as the county's fourth president. He would be reelected in 1812 and serve as the chief executive from 1809 to 1817. Dolley became the official White House hostess, where she was known for her social graces, which contributed to her husband's popularity. She was the only First Lady given an honorary seat on the floor of Congress and the first American to respond to a telegraph message.

In June 1812, during the presidential election campaign, the United States declared war against Great Britain. In 1814, a British force attacked

Grave of Dolley Madison

Washington, D.C., following the defeat of inexperienced American militia forces in the Battle of Bladensburg. As the English force approached and the White House staff prepared to flee, Dolley had her servant, Paul Jennings, save the Stuart painting of George Washington. On August 23, she wrote her sister saying, "Our kind friend Mr. Carroll has come to hasten my departure and in a very bad humor with me, because I insist on waiting until the large picture of General Washington is secured, and it requires to be unscrewed from the wall. The process was found to be too tedious for these perilous moments. I have ordered the frame to be broken and the canvas taken out . . . It is done, and the precious portrait placed in the hands of two gentlemen from New York for safekeeping." At the time, Dolley was credited with removing the painting and portrayed as a national heroine. As it turns out, in an 1865 memoir written by Jennings, he stated that Dolley had ordered him to save the painting and that Jean Pierre Sioussat and a gardener removed it.

Dolley fled Washington in her carriage along with numerous other families. She went to Georgetown and crossed the Potomac into Virginia the following day. The British entered the city and burned the White House and other buildings. When the Madison's returned to the capital, they found the White House to be uninhabitable, so the couple moved into Octagon House.

When Madison left office in 1817, he and Dolley returned to the Montpelier in Virginia. Madison died there at the age of 85 on June 28, 1836. Dolley stayed at the plantation for a year, and her sister Anna and her son John Payne Todd moved in with her. In the fall of 1837, she returned to Washington, leaving Todd to run the plantation. As a result of his alcoholism, he failed. Dolley was forced to sell Montpelier, the remaining slaves, and the furnishings to pay outstanding debts.

Dolley died in Washington in 1849 at the age of 81. She was originally laid to rest in Washington's Congressional Cemetery but was later re-interned at Montpelier next to her husband.

James Monroe
(1758 – 1831)

"The Last Cocked Hat"

Buried at Hollywood Cemetery,
Richmond, Virginia.

President • Secretary of State • Secretary of War

James Monroe played many roles in the founding of the United States. He was a very busy man who fought bravely in the Continental Army in the Revolutionary War at many key battles and was almost killed at the Battle of Trenton. He was a lawyer and served in the Virginia Legislature, Continental Congress, and United States Senate. He served as Minister to France for George Washington and then Minister to Great Britain for Thomas Jefferson. In between those assignments, he was elected Governor of Virginia and helped secure the Louisiana Purchase. Under President Madison, he served as Secretary of State and Secretary of War and for a while, he was both. Finally, he was elected as our fifth President and served two terms, after which he was elected as a delegate to the Virginia Constitutional Convention and served as the presiding officer until his failing health caused him to withdraw.

James Monroe was born on April 28, 1758, in his parents' house in Westmoreland County, Virginia. A roadside plaque marks the spot and is listed on the National Registry of Historic Places. He was the second of five children born to Spence and Elizabeth Jones Monroe. Spence was

James Monroe (1758 – 1831)

James Monroe

a prosperous planter of Scottish descent and was involved in protests against the Stamp Act. Little is known about Elizabeth except she was the daughter of a wealthy Welsh immigrant. The family owned 600 acres in Virginia.

At the age of eleven, he enrolled at Campbelltown Academy and took advanced courses in Latin and Math at the College of William and Mary. He became lifetime friends with a classmate and future Chief Justice of the Supreme Court, John Marshall.

By 1774, he had lost both parents and was looked after by his uncle Joseph Jones. Jones was a member of the Virginia House of Burgesses and close friends with George Washington, Thomas Jefferson and James Madison. In 1774, Jones took Monroe to Williamsburg and enrolled him at William and Mary. A year and a half later, the War for Independence erupted, and Monroe dropped out of college and joined the Continental

Army. As he was literate, healthy and a good shot, after months of training, he was ordered to serve in the New York and New Jersey campaigns, and his regiment played an important role in the Army's retreat. In late December 1776, Monroe was with George Washington as he planned and executed the famous attack on Hessian troops at Trenton, New Jersey. Monroe was sent ahead to secure a crossroad leading into Trenton. A local man, Dr. John Riker, when he discovered that the detachment was American, insisted he be allowed to go along, saying he "may be able to help some poor fellow. Monroe finally agreed, and Dr. Riker rode along into the battle. The attack was successful, but Monroe was seriously wounded and nearly died. A bullet grazed the left side of Monroe's chest, then hit his shoulder and injured an artery that bled profusely. His life was saved by Dr. Riker, who stopped the bleeding by sticking his index finger into the wound and applying pressure. Surgeons later attempted to remove the bullet but could not find it. He recovered in eleven weeks but carried the bullet in his shoulder for the rest of his life. George Washington cited Monroe for his bravery and promoted him to Captain. He was eighteen years old.

After recovering, Monroe asked to be returned to the front and was at the Battle of Brandywine, where he formed a close friendship with the Marquis de Lafayette. He went on to serve in the Philadelphia campaign and spent the winter of 1777–78 at Valley Forge, sharing a hut with John Marshall. In late 1777, he was promoted to Major. After serving as a scout at the Battle of Monmouth, he resigned from the Army and began to study law at William and Mary under Thomas Jefferson, who was then Governor of Virginia. Through Thomas Jefferson, Monroe formed a friendship with James Madison. He was elected to the Virginia assembly in 1782 and to the Continental Congress in 1783 at the age of twenty-five. While in New York serving in Congress, he met Elizabeth Kortright, and they married at Trinity Church in Manhattan on February 16, 1786. She was seventeen, and he was twenty-seven. The couple would have three children.

In the fall of that year, Monroe resigned from Congress, moved to Fredericksburg, Virginia, and became an attorney for the state. The next year, he was elected again to the Virginia House of Delegates and in 1788, he became a delegate to the Virginia Ratifying Convention. The Ratifying Convention ratified the Constitution, but Monroe voted against it. He opposed the Electoral College and wanted the direct election of Senators and a strong Bill of Rights. After the Constitution was ratified, Monroe challenged James Madison for a seat in the House of Representatives. Monroe lost by 300 votes, and the two became close friends. In a twist of fate, when Senator William Grayson died in 1790 while serving in the Senate, John Walker was appointed to serve from March 31 to November 9, when Monroe was elected to replace him.

While in the Senate, Monroe was on a committee to investigate charges of financial malfeasance against Alexander Hamilton. When interviewing Hamilton, he revealed that the transactions in question were hush money to keep Hamilton's affair with James Reynolds' wife secret. Word got to the press, and Hamilton blamed Monroe for the leak. It almost led to a duel, but ironically none other than Aaron Burr stepped in and defused the tension. It was the nation's first political sex scandal.

In 1794 Washington appointed Monroe as his Minister to France. Monroe's tenure in France was far from easy. France was an unstable place, and Monroe had to be careful. His mission was to uphold Washington's policy of neutrality between France and Britain. He had early success, but the Jay Treaty with Britain caused relations with France to deteriorate. Monroe was blamed, and with Hamilton's urging, Monroe was recalled in November 1796. He returned to Virginia to practice law and tend to his plantations. He was elected governor in 1799 and worked vigorously in support of Thomas Jefferson for President in 1800. He served as governor until 1802 and then was appointed as a special envoy to help negotiate the Louisiana Purchase.

Monroe then served as the United States Minister to Britain from 1803 to 1807. During this time, Jefferson offered him the position of First Governor of Louisiana Territory, but Monroe turned it down and remained Minister to Britain. His main assignment was to negotiate an end to the impressment of US sailors. Jefferson sent William Pinkney to London to assist Monroe. The two negotiated a treaty with Britain that contained no provision against impressment. Jefferson was upset that they disregarded their instructions and refused to submit the treaty to the Senate for ratification. This caused a rift in Monroe's relationship with Jefferson and James Madison, the Secretary of State.

Monroe returned home in 1807 and ran for President against James Madison in the 1808 election. Madison won big, and afterward, the two reconciled. In 1810, Monroe returned to the Virginia House of Delegates and, in 1811, was again elected Governor, though he did not serve for long. That April, Madison named him Secretary of State. The Senate unanimously confirmed him 30–0. He was unable to make progress with Britain on attacking American merchant ships and impressment of US sailors to serve on British war ships against France. Thus, Madison asked Congress to declare War on Britain, and Congress did so on June 18, 1812.

The War went badly, and in August 1814, British troops and warships appeared at the mouth of the Potomac. Monroe personally scouted the Chesapeake Bay and, on August 21, sent the President a warning so that he and his wife could flee. The British burned the Capitol and the White House on August 24. Madison removed John Armstrong as Secretary of War and appointed Monroe on September 27. No successor was appointed at State, and thus Monroe held both posts from October 1814 to February 28, 1815. The Treaty of Ghent ended the war in February 1815. Monroe resigned as Secretary of War in March and returned to State, his popularity soaring. In 1816, Monroe was elected President, defeating Rufus King, the Federalist candidate. He was the last founder to serve as President. He received 183 electoral votes to 34 for King. He was reelected in 1820, receiving all electoral votes but one. He had a calm, peaceful, prosperous administration, which has been called the Era of Good Feelings.

He ignored old party lines in making appointments and appointed a geographically balanced cabinet including John Quincy Adams as Secretary of State. The main events of his administration were the acquisition of Florida from Spain via the Adams-Oni Treaty, the Missouri Compromise, which temporarily settled the slavery issue in the territories, recognition of former Spanish colonies in Central and South America (Argentina, Peru, Columbia, Chile and Mexico), and the Monroe Doctrine in which Monroe warns European nations that the US would not tolerate further colonization or puppet monarchs in the Western Hemisphere.

James Monroe (1758–1831)

James Monroe's crypt

Throughout his tenure, Monroe was the last president to wear a powdered wig tied in a queue, a tricorn hat, and knee-breeches as was customary in the late 1700s, earning him the nickname "The Last Cocked Hat." At the end of his second term, Monroe retired to his home, an estate called Oak Hill in northern Virginia, now included in the grounds of the University of Virginia. He began working on an autobiography but died before it could be completed. It was published in 1959 and is still available. He was plagued by money problems in retirement and sold his Highland Plantation, which is now owned by the College of William and Mary and is open to the public as a historic site.

In 1829, Monroe was elected as a delegate to the Virginia Constitutional Convention and elected by the convention to be the presiding officer. He withdrew after two months due to health concerns. He moved to New York in 1830 to live with his daughter Maria. His wife had died a year before. He died there in 1831 at the age of 73 on July 4, thus becoming the third president on Independence Day. Thomas Jefferson and John Adams both died on Independence Day, five years before him. He was originally buried in the New York City Marble Cemetery. In 1858, the centennial year of his birth, his remains were reinterred at the Presidents Circle in Hollywood Cemetery in Richmond, Virginia. The James Monroe Tomb is a United States National Historic Landmark. After Liberia was created in 1821 as a haven for freed slaves, its capital city was named Monrovia in his honor. He had supported the repatriation of black people to Africa.

James Monroe was the last president not photographed in his lifetime. His successor, John Quincy Adams, was the first.

Abraham Baldwin
(1754–1807)

The Founder of the University of Georgia

Buried at Rock Creek Cemetery,
Washington, D.C.

U.S. Constitution

Abraham Baldwin, a native of Connecticut, was a minister, lawyer, signer of the U.S. Constitution, congressman, senator, and founder of the University of Georgia.

Abraham Baldwin was born November 22, 1754, in North Guilford, Connecticut, the son and one of five children of Michael Baldwin, a blacksmith, and his wife, Lucy (née Dudley) Baldwin. Lucy died in childbirth with the fifth child when Abraham was four. Michael was a single parent for ten years until he married Theodora Wolcott, with whom he had seven additional children, including Henry Baldwin, who became a supreme court justice.

Michael worked hard to support his large family and borrowed money to provide secondary education for young Abraham. Baldwin attended Guilford Grammar School and then Yale College in 1768 when he was 14. He was a member of the secret Linonian Society, graduating in 1772. Baldwin studied theology in preparation to become a Congregationalist minister. In 1775, he was given a license to preach and was also hired as a teacher at Yale. During the early years of the Revolution, he served as

Abraham Baldwin

a tutor until 1779. In 1777, he enlisted as a chaplain in the Continental Army, serving with the Second Connecticut Brigade through 1783.

After the war, Yale president Ezra Stiles offered Baldwin the opportunity to be a professor of divinity, but he declined, instead pursuing law studies. He was encouraged by his former commanding officer General Nathanael Greene to follow him to Georgia, where Greene had a plantation. Baldwin did so and was admitted to the Georgia bar in 1783. Baldwin first practiced in Fairfield before moving to Augusta, Georgia. There, in 1785, he was elected to the Georgia House of Representatives where, at the urging of another transplanted New Englander, Lyman Hall, he focused on establishing an education system in the state. On May 5, 1785, Baldwin was also elected to the Continental Congress and regularly attended, except 1786.

Abraham Baldwin (1754–1807)

The first college established through Baldwin's legislative efforts in the Georgia House was Franklin College, now the University of Georgia. Baldwin served as its first president from 1786 to 1801 while the institution was being formed. Wrote biographer Henry Clay White,

> [Baldwin] came to Georgia seeking neither land nor fortune. He came as a missionary in the cause of education. Happily, we may well believe, his mission, for the moment, proved ill-timed. It was not abandoned but deferred, and, in the political service to which, he, perforce, was turned, he developed a genius which was of the inestimable benefit to his State and Country.

In 1787, Baldwin was appointed as a delegate to the Confederation Congress and then to the Constitutional Convention, along with William Few, William Pierce, George Walton, William Houston, and Nathaniel Pendleton. Baldwin was the most distinguished of the delegates. In September 1787 signed the U.S. Constitution. The Georgia Historical Society retains Baldwin's draft copy with his signature and handwritten notes.

Under the new government, Baldwin was elected to the U.S. House of Representatives in 1788, serving in the First Congress through the Fifth Congress from 1789 to 1799. He was then appointed by the Georgia legislature to the U.S. Senate and was re-elected in 1805 to a second six-year term. During his time in the Senate, from 1801 to 1803, he was the president pro tempore.

Back in Georgia, Franklin College finally had its first students in 1801. At that point, Baldwin resigned as president, and fellow Yale graduate Josiah Meigs took his place. The college buildings had been modeled after their alma mater, and the bulldog was adopted as the mascot, also borrowed from Yale.

On March 4, 1807, while serving as a U.S. senator from Georgia, Baldwin died. His remains were first in Rock Creek Cemetery, Washington, D.C., beside his colleague, Senator James Jackson. They were then transferred to Kalorama, another area within D.C., and finally again to Rock Creek, just down the slope from the famous Saint Gaudens' figure.

GRAVES of our FOUNDERS

Wrote historian Ralph D. Smith in 1877,

> It is a remarkable circumstance, and an instance of assiduity almost without parallel that, during his long congressional life, he was never known to be absent a single hour during the session of congress [sic], on account of disposition or any other cause, until the week preceding his death. He was a man of great industry and talents, and his distinguished patriotism, learning, and public services shed an honor on his active state as well as that of his adoption.

The grave of Abraham Baldwin

Abraham Baldwin (1754–1807)

The *Georgia Historical Quarterly* concluded in 1919,

> During the violent agitation of parties which have disturbed the repose of public men in this country for the last ten years, [Baldwin] has always been moderate but firm; relaxing nothing in his republican principles but retaining all possible charity for his former friends who may have abandoned theirs. He has lived without reproach and has probably died without an enemy.

Abraham Baldwin has been honored in many ways. Baldwin counties in Georgia and Alabama are named after him. His name also adorns Abraham Baldwin Agricultural College in Tifton, Georgia, and Abraham Baldwin Middle School in Guilford, Connecticut. There are Baldwin streets in Madison, Wisconsin, and Athens, Georgia. A statue of Baldwin was erected on the campus of the University of Georgia, and the U.S. Postal Service issued a stamp in his honor as part of the Great Americans series.

John Banister
(1734–1788)

The Master of Hatcher's Run

Buried at Hatcher's Run Estate,
Dinwiddie County, Virginia.

Articles of Confederation

Colonel John Banister was an attorney and plantation owner from Petersburg, Virginia. He served in the Virginia House of Burgesses and as an officer in the Virginia Militia. He was elected to the Second Continental Congress, where he signed the Articles of Confederation.

Banister, born December 26, 1734, at the family's estate, Hatcher's Run, near Petersburg, Dinwiddie County, Virginia, was the son of Captain John Banister, a ship's captain, and his wife, Martha Wilmette (née Munford) Banister. Banister's grandfather, John Baptist Banister (1654–1692), was one of the first university-trained naturalists in North America, referred to as "the first Virginia botanist of any note."

Young Banister traveled on his father's ship, crossing the Atlantic to England, where he attended Wakefield, a private school south of Leeds. He then studied law at the Temple Inn in London, admitted on September 27, 1753. Upon graduation, Banister was admitted to the Virginia bar and opened a law practice in Petersburg. He also managed his plantation.

Banister married Elizabeth Munford in 1755. He was first elected to the Virginia House of Burgesses in 1765 and served until 1769. During

John Banister (1734–1788)

John Banister

this time, he and Elizabeth built a suburban villa in Petersburg called Battersea. It was in the five-part Palladian style and completed in 1768. John Banister Jr., known as Jack, was born to this couple, though the exact year is not recorded. Likewise, a daughter, Maria Ann, was born, though the date is lost. She later married the physician George Wilson from Petersburg. Unfortunately, Elizabeth died in 1770.

Banister next married Elizabeth "Patsy" Bland, the daughter of Theodorick Bland of Cawsons, a descendant of one of Virginia's first families, and a son of Continental Congressman Richard Bland. She was also the sister of Colonel Theodorick Bland, who later became a Continental Congressman and member of the First Congress. The couple gave birth to son Robert Bannister in 1771, but he lived only until 1794.

Banister returned to the House of Burgesses in 1772 until 1775, when his wife died that year.

Home of John Banister

As tensions rose with England, Banister was a member of the Virginia Convention, which declared Virginia independent in 1776. He was elected to the new Virginia House of Delegates in 1776 and served until 1778.

On November 19, 1777, Banister was elected to the Second Continental Congress, which met in York, Pennsylvania. There, he was one of the framers of the Articles of Confederation, which he signed on July 8, 1778.

Banister next joined the Virginia Militia as a cavalry officer in 1778 at the major, rising to the rank of lieutenant colonel by 1781. During this time, Banister became good friends with Thomas Jefferson.

In 1779, Banister married Agan Blair of Williamsburg, Virginia, the daughter of John Blair Sr., a nephew of James Blair, the founder of William and Mary College, and the father of John Blair Jr., who signed the Constitution. John Blair Sr. was a longtime member of the House of Burgesses and acting governor. The couple had sons Burrell Banister (1779–1837) and Theodorick Blair Banister (1780–1829) early in their marriage.

During the weeks before the Battle of Yorktown in 1781, Lieutenant Colonel Banister, highly regarded by George Washington, aided in supplying and repelling the British army from Virginia. In so doing, he lost most of his personal property to the British led by General William Phillips, who often stayed at Battersea and confiscated his valuables.

John Banister (1734–1788)

Sign pointing the way to John Banister's estate, Battersea.

After the war, Banister returned to the House of Delegates from 1781 until 1784. By 1782, he appears to have recovered his assets, as Dinwiddie County records note: three free males, 46 adult slaves, 42 underage slaves, 28 horses, 126 cattle, and one chariot. He and Agan had another son, John Monro Banister (1784–1832). Also, in 1784, son "Jack" accompanied Thomas Jefferson to France.

In 1785, Banister was appointed the first mayor of Petersburg and was noted for his knowledge of current affairs and his writing accomplishments.

Banister died on September 30, 1788, at Hatcher's Run, three months short of his 54th birthday. He was buried in the family plot there. His eldest son, "Jack" Banister, died eleven weeks later, owing Thomas Jefferson 3173 livres following his time in Europe. This great debt may have greatly impacted the Banisters, leading to small or no inheritances for the minor children, Burrell and Monro.

Daughter Maria Ann Wilson died in October 1792. Ann Blair Banister died on December 23, 1813.

Simon Boerum
(1724 – 1775)

"Congressman from Brooklyn"

Buried at Green-Wood Cemetery,
Brooklyn, New York.

Continental Association

Simon Boerum was a New York assemblyman and clerk in Kings County who was appointed to the First Continental Congress, where he signed the Continental Association. Boerum, a strong Patriot, did so when New York was reluctant to participate in the cause. Unfortunately, he passed away before he had an opportunity to sign the Declaration of Independence.

Boerum, born February 29, 1724, in New Lots (now Brooklyn), New York, was one of six children of William Boerum and his wife, Rachel (née Bloom) Boerum. The family was of Dutch origin, the grandfather, Jacob Willemse Van Boerum, having arrived from Holland in the 1680s and establishing holdings on the west end of Long Island. Boerum was baptized at the Flatbush Church and attended the Dutch school there.

Boerum first worked on the family farm and at their mill. In 1748, he bought a home and garden nearby and married Maria Schenk on April 30. The two lived here for the rest of their lives. Today, the site is in downtown Brooklyn near the corner of Fulton and Hoyt Streets.

Simon Boerum (1724–1775)

An early view of Brooklyn before the Revolution

In 1750, at age 26, colonial Governor George Clinton appointed Boerum a clerk in Kings County, New York, and a clerk of the New York Board of Supervisors.

Boerum and Maria had one son, John Boerum, born 1759.

In 1761, Boerum entered politics and was elected to a seat in the New York colonial Assembly.

Wife Maria died in 1771 and was interred at the Old First Reformed Church Cemetery in Brooklyn.

In 1774, widower Boerum supported the Patriot cause and was elected to the First Continental Congress in Philadelphia, representing Kings County. The colony of New York did not initially send an official delegation. That October, he joined in signing the Continental Association and the Declaration of Rights and Resolves on behalf of New York. Previously, he had opposed the Galloway Plan to attempt a reconciliation with England by creating an American parliament.

Boerum was reelected to the Continental Congress in 1775, and on April 20, 1775, served as a deputy to the Provincial Convention in New York City, attempting to contravene the British government and Loyalist assembly.

Unfortunately, Boerum fell ill and had to leave the Continental Congress in Philadelphia, returning to Brooklyn. He died suddenly on July 11, 1775, at age 51. He was initially interred with his wife at the Old First Reformed Church Cemetery in Brooklyn, but in 1848, they were exhumed and reinterred at Green-Wood Cemetery.

Boerum has been mostly forgotten in the history books, but his family name remains associated with the Brooklyn neighborhood, Boerum Hill, bordered by Schermerhorn Street on the north, Fourth Avenue on the east, either Smith or Court Streets on the west, and Warren or Wykoff Streets on the south.

A portion of the neighborhood is known as Boerum Park, located from Warren Street to Baltic Street, between Hoyt and Smith Streets.

The grave of Simon Boerum.

Richard Caswell
(1729–1789)

Revolutionary Governor

Buried at Caswell Memorial Cemetery,
Kinston, North Carolina.

Military • Continental Association

This founder served as the first and fifth governor of the state of North Carolina. During the American Revolution, he served as a senior officer in the militia in the Southern theater. As a delegate to the First Continental Congress, he signed the 1774 Continental Association. John Adams referred to him as a model man and a true patriot. His name was Richard Caswell.

Caswell was born on August 3rd, 1729, in Harford County (present-day Baltimore), Maryland, at the seaport of Joppa. His father, Richard Caswell Sr., had migrated from London to Maryland in 1712. A descendant of English gentry, he found success as a planter and merchant. He also served as a county court justice, legislator, and militia captain. He and his wife, Christian Dallam Caswell, raised their children at the family plantation, Mulberry Point.

As told by Joe A. Mobley in his work, *North Carolina Governor Richard Caswell: Founding Father and Revolutionary Hero*, in 1743, Caswell's father began experiencing health problems. Additionally, Joppa declined as a seaport, which had an adverse impact on the family finances. Caswell

Richard Caswell

Jr. and his brother, William, moved to North Carolina to find work and buy land, establishing a place where the rest of the family could join them. The pair, carrying a letter of recommendation from Maryland's governor, arrived in New Bern, North Carolina, in 1745. The rest of the family soon joined them.

In New Bern, William became the deputy clerk of the Johnston County Court, while the 17-year-old Caswell became an apprentice to North Carolina's surveyor general. He would eventually become the deputy surveyor general, and he also acquired a small plantation. Caswell's family joined him there, and when his father died in 1755, he was buried on the property.

In 1754, Caswell was elected to the Colonial Assembly, where he would continue to serve until the American Revolution. By this time, he had married Mary Mackilwean, and the couple had three children, although their only son alone survived to adulthood, and Caswell's wife passed away due to complications from childbirth. Caswell would marry again in 1758 when he wed Sarah Herritage, who was the daughter of

Richard Caswell (1729–1789)

William Herritage, who was mentoring Caswell in the study of law. This second marriage would produce eight children, seven of whom survived to adulthood. In 1759, Caswell was admitted to the bar and began serving as the deputy attorney general while continuing to work in the Colonial Assembly.

As a member of the Assembly, Caswell was an active and influential figure, making numerous important contributions. He introduced bills aimed at increasing trade and commerce. He supported public welfare reforms, including providing a speedier release for those in debtor's prison. He championed both public education and court reform. Among his proposals was establishing a free school in every county using funds the colony had received for service during the French and Indian War.

On May 16th, 1771, Caswell commanded the right wing of the colonial governors' forces at the Battle of Alamance during the Regulator Insurrection in North Carolina. The conflict took place from 1766 to 1771, during which citizens took up arms against what they viewed as corrupt colonial officials. They were motivated by economic concerns, wanting a system that provided better economic conditions for more than just the colonial officials and plantation owners. On the day of the battle, Governor Tyson's militia numbered approximately 1,000 men. They faced a force twice that size. The Regulators were not a standing army but hoped that a show of force would result in the governor giving in to their demands. Tyson ordered the Regulators to disperse and waited an hour with no results. He then opened fire with cannons and muskets. When the smoke cleared, the Regulators had lost 100 killed and 200 wounded. Tyson's forces lost 9 men. Tyson followed the battle by conducting a terror campaign where he burned homes, hanged Regulators, and forced others to take loyalty oaths.

In 1774, Caswell was elected along with William Hooper and Joseph Hewes to represent North Carolina at the First Continental Congress. As told by Mobley in his Caswell biography, North Carolina's Governor Josiah Martin, who opposed the gathering, was initially pleased that Caswell had been elected. The governor wrote to the Earl of Dartmouth that "Richard Caswell has been appointed a delegate to the Continental Congress, but he disapproves of these measures in his heart, I am persuaded, and undertakes this office purely for the sake of maintaining his popularity on which he depends for continuance in the Treasureship which he has ever shown the best disposition to employ for the advantage of the government." Within one year that Governor's opinion changed dramatically saying of Caswell "he now shows himself to be the most active tool of sedition."

Caswell took his seat in Congress on September 17th. The evening before, he and his son, William, attended a banquet held to honor members of Congress. During the course of the celebration, 32 toasts were offered. Some of these noted loyalty to the mother country and the hope for reconciliation. Others declared an opposition to tyranny and support for Boston. Before Congress adjourned, it approved the Continental Association, which prohibited all trade with England. In addition, it authorized the formation of Committees of Safety to enforce the boycott, as well as the establishment of militias. Caswell affixed his signature to the measure.

Caswell, Hooper, and Hewes returned to Philadelphia to represent North Carolina in the Second Continental Congress. Some historians have noted that Caswell received no significant committee assignments and question whether this contributed to his decision to leave Congress on June 28th. According to Mobley, his actual motivation to leave Philadelphia was to "undertake the task of organizing North Carolina's Third Provincial Congress. That body approved the actions of the Continental Congress and raised two regiments for the new Continental Army. The Provincial Congress also elected Caswell, Hooper, and Hewes to serve in the Continental Congress for another year. Caswell was also appointed treasurer of the Southern District of North Carolina. Maintaining that he could not do both jobs, he resigned from Congress.

Caswell was the president of the North Carolina Provincial Congress, which, in 1776, drafted the first Constitution of North Carolina. That Congress elected him acting governor. He would be reelected and serve three terms, which was the maximum permitted by the new constitution. During his tenure, he oversaw issues related to the revolution, including raising troops, acquiring arms, and securing provisions. When he stepped down in 1780, he took over command of the militia and state troops.

Richard Caswell (1729–1789)

Grave of Richard Caswell

Inscription on top of headstone of Caswell's grave

In 1780, at the Battle of Camden Court House, the troops under his command fled after the Virginia militia broke, leaving him exposed to a British attack. The battle was a major victory for the English. After this defeat, Caswell returned to his home with an unnamed illness. Meanwhile, the North Carolina General Assembly appointed William Smallwood of Maryland to command the North Carolina militia without informing Caswell, and as a result, he resigned from his position. In 1781, Smallwood returned to Maryland, and Caswell was again appointed Major General of the Militia. He would serve in this position until the end of the American Revolution.

After the Revolution, Caswell served as state comptroller in 1782. He was a member and later served as President of the North Carolina State Senate from 1782 to 1784. He was once again elected governor in 1785. In 1787, he was appointed to be a delegate to the Constitutional Convention, but he did not attend. His final political position was as speaker of the North Carolina House of Commons. He passed away on November 10th, 1789, and was laid to rest in the Caswell Memorial Cemetery.

George Rogers Clark
(1752–1818)

Conqueror of the Old Northwest

Buried at Cave Hill Cemetery,
Louisville, Kentucky.

Major General

George Rogers Clark was a Virginia military officer and surveyor who led Patriot forces to victory in what became the Northwest Territory, now most of the Midwestern United States. He led the Virginia militia in Kentucky County (later the state) and won victories at Kaskaskia and Vincennes during the campaign in Illinois. Ultimately, the British ceded the Northwest Territory to the United States at the Treaty of Paris in 1783. Clark was dubbed "Conqueror of the Old Northwest" and "Washington of the West." His younger brother was William Clark of the Lewis and Clark Expedition following the Louisiana Purchase.

Clark was born on November 19, 1752, in Albemarle County, Virginia, near Charlottesville. He was the son of John Clark and his wife, Ann (née Rogers) Clark. Clark was the second of ten children. Five of the six sons were officers during the American Revolution, except for the youngest son, the aforementioned William.

When Clark was very young, in 1756, following the start of the French and Indian War, the family moved east to Caroline County, Virginia, to a 400-acre farm, which later grew to a 2000-acre plantation.

George Rogers Clark

As a lad, his grandfather managed his education. Clark preferred being outdoors and did not take to the classroom. He was tutored at home and attended Donald Robertson's school, where James Madison and John Taylor of Caroline also attended. Clark was then apprenticed to a surveyor and began exploring the land.

At age 19, in 1771, Clark surveyed western Virginia for the first time. The following year, he traveled into the Kentucky region via the Ohio River at Fort Pitt and stayed for two years, surveying the Kanawha River region and learning the natural history and Native tribes of the region.

Meanwhile, following the Treaty of Fort Stanwix in 1768, settlers began entering the area. Unfortunately, not all the tribes with claims to the region were involved in the treaty, and by 1774, hostilities had broken out. Clark was appointed as a captain in the Virginia militia in what became known as Lord Dunmore's War, won by the colonists.

George Rogers Clark (1752–1818)

Following the victory, Clark began surveying the Kentucky territory and assisted in organizing Kentucky as a county of Virginia after North Carolinian Richard Henderson purchased the same land from the Cherokee in an illegal treaty. Clark and Gabriel Jones were sent to Williamsburg to petition the Virginia General Assembly to include Kentucky within Virginia. Governor Patrick Henry agreed, and Clark was given five hundred pounds of gunpowder to help defend the settlements. Now 24 at the outset of the American Revolution, Clark outranked older settlers such as Daniel Boone, Benjamin Logan, and James Harrod.

In 1777, without support from the Continental Army, Clark was commissioned as a lieutenant colonel in the Illinois Regiment of the Virginia militia as the leader of a secret expedition to attack British forts north of the Ohio River, specifically the villages of Kaskaskia, Cahokia, and Vincennes. Clark raised troops in Pennsylvania, Virginia, and North Carolina, and headed to Redstone, on the Monongahela River, south of Fort Pitt, in what is now Fayette County, Pennsylvania.

On May 12, 1778, the troop left Redstone and headed down the Monongahela on boats, heading for Fort Henry and Fort Randolph at the mouth of the Kanawha River. They reached the Falls of the Ohio (modern-day Louisville, Kentucky) on June 12 and camped and trained on Corn Island for twelve days.

On June 24, Clark and his brigade floated down the Ohio River to the Mississippi River, where they took Fort Kaskaskia on July 4, 1778, without firing a shot. Captain Joseph Bowman and his men captured Cahokia the next day, also without a shot. Fort Sackville, also known as Vincennes, along the Wabash River, was taken in August, but the British took it back in December. Rather than wait for an attack on Kaskaskia, Clark led a winter march to retake Fort Sackville at Vincennes.

Clark and 170 men left Kaskaskia on February 6, 1779, and trekked overland through melting snow, ice, and freezing rain, arriving at Vincennes on February 23. They laid siege to Fort Sackville and executed five captured Natives with hatchets in view of the fort. Two days later, the British surrendered and Lieutenant Governor Henry Hamilton was captured. News of the victory traveled to General Washington and was mentioned in the discussions with France regarding potential support.

Virginia followed by claiming the Old Northwest region, calling it Illinois County. The victory was the highlight of Clark's career.

In 1780, Clark could not motivate the Kentucky soldiers to head north to attack Fort Detroit, so he continued to defend the Ohio River Valley from the Falls of the Ohio. In June, a mixed British-Indian force attacked from Fort Detroit, capturing two settlements and hundreds of prisoners. In August, Clark led a successful retaliatory strike at the Shawnee village of Peckuwe, near present-day Springfield, Ohio.

During 1781, Governor Thomas Jefferson made Clark a brigadier general responsible for the militia in Kentucky and Illinois counties. Clark prepared to attack Fort Detroit, but the regulars sent by General Washington to assist were defeated in August before they could meet up.

In August 1782, the British and their Native allies again attacked the Kentucky militia, defeating them at the Battle of Blue Licks. Clark was not present and was roundly criticized. Three months later, he led a retaliatory expedition, destroying Native villages along the Great Miami River.

When the Treaty of Paris was signed on September 3, 1783, Britain ceded the Old Northwest Territory to the United States. This doubled the size of the original thirteen colonies, and Clark's victory at Vincennes was romanticized. George Mason dubbed Clark the "Conqueror of the Northwest."

Clark has a reputation as an Indian hater. He proposed raising a force of two thousand soldiers to clean out the Ohio Valley of Natives. He warned them that if they attacked, they "should know that the next thing would be the Tomahawk" with "Your Women & Children given to the Dogs to eat." The expedition was never approved.

Meanwhile, settlers continued to move to the Illinois country and Kentucky. On December 17, 1783, Clark was made the Principal Surveyor of Bounty Lands, and for the next five years, he assisted war veterans with their land grants. However, the relations with the Natives did not improve.

Despite the Treaties of Fort McIntosh (1785) and Fort Finney (1786), which Clark helped negotiate, the Natives continued to attack settlers, killing upwards of 1500 of them. Clark raised an expedition of 1200 drafted men to attack the Natives along the Wabash River, but some of the troops mutinied due to a supply shortage, and Clark turned the brigade around. Afterward, James Wilkinson accused Clark of drunkenness, and Clark's actions were condemned by the Virginia Council. This ended his military career.

In 1787, Clark left Kentucky and moved to Indiana Territory, near present-day Clarksville. He tried to recover expenses owed to him by Virginia, but they refused, claiming his purchases were "fraudulent." Clark struggled with debt. Virginia then followed with "Clark's Grant" of 150,000 acres of land in Indiana, which encompassed what is now Clark County, Indiana, and portions of adjoining counties. However, Clark was unable to develop the land for lack of funds.

In the early twentieth century, Clark's account books were found in Richmond, and they were determined to be complete, sound, and accurate. Thus, he seemed exonerated from "fraudulent" purchases, but this was not official, and a century too late to help Clark.

Desperate to raise some funds, Clark next signed up with the ambassador from France, amid its revolution, to lead an expedition against the Spanish in the southern Mississippi River region. On February 2, 1793, Ambassador Edmond-Charles Genêt appointed Clark "Major General in the Armies of France and Commander-in-chief of the French Revolutionary Legion on the Mississippi River." Clark then began to organize a campaign to take St. Louis, New Madrid, Natchez, and New Orleans. He spent thousands of dollars of his own funds to gather supplies. Clark was also romantically interested in Teresa de Leyba, the sister of Fernando de Leyba, the lieutenant governor of Spanish Louisiana, but this relationship fell apart, and Clark never married everyone.

One year, later, before the expedition could be launched, President Washington forbade it and threatened to send General Anthony Wayne to enforce the ban. The French backed off and canceled the commissions granted to Americans. Clark's efforts to be reimbursed for the supplies went unanswered. Clark's reputation now sunk even lower.

Now in an even deeper hole, Clark's creditors began coming after him with more intensity. Quickly, he transferred ownership of his lands to family and friends to avoid losing them altogether. In the end, after the creditors claimed most of what remained, Clark was left with a small plot at Clarksville.

In 1803, Clark built a small cabin overlooking the Falls of the Ohio. He also purchased a small gristmill nearby operated by two slaves. Over the years, Clark entertained the likes of John Pope, James Audubon, William Clark, Meriweather Lewis, Allan Bowie Magruder, and John P. Campbell. Sadly, his alcoholism continued to plague him as did his anger toward Virginia, the perceived cause of his financial difficulties.

In 1805, Clark was named to the board of directors of the Indiana Canal Company, which planned to build a canal around the Falls of the Ohio. The company collapsed the following year when board members Vice President Aaron Burr and Governor of the Louisianna Territory, James Wilkinson, were arrested for treason. Over $1.2 million in investments went unaccounted for and never found.

Clark stayed here until 1809 when his health began to fail after suffering a severe stroke. Then he fell into a lit fireplace and burned his right leg so severely it had to be amputated. Now immobile, he moved to his sister Lucy Croghan's home at Locust Grove. She was the wife of Major William Croghan.

Finally, in 1812, Virginia granted Clark a pension of $400 per year and granted him a ceremonial sword in recognition of the Revolutionary War services.

On February 13, 1818, Clark suffered another stroke and was buried at Locust Grove Cemetery. In 1869, his remains and those of his family were moved to Cave Hill Cemetery, at Louisville, Kentucky. Said Judge John Rowan at the funeral, "The mighty oak of the forest has fallen . . ."

Finally, several years after his death, the government of Virginia began reimbursing Clark's estate, with an initial sum of $30,000. Payments continued to the estate for nearly one hundred years, until 1913.

Clark is remembered in many ways. In 1928, a memorial to him was erected at Vincennes, Indiana. Numerous other statues have been installed throughout the country and Clark's name adorns numerous schools, counties, towns, and streets.

George Rogers Clark (1752–1818)

Clark graves

Tench Coxe
(1755 – 1824)

Economist & Opportunist

Buried at Christ Church Burial Ground,
Philadelphia, Pennsylvania.

Continental Congress • Revenue Commissioner

Tench Coxe was an American political economist and served in several political offices including as a delegate for Pennsylvania to the Continental Congress. Coxe proved to be one of the nation's more controversial founders. He is remembered more for his work on behalf of commercial and trade issues than for his political work. He is best known as an economic writer who preached a brand of mercantilism that elevated manufacturing to a prominent role. He never achieved the position or acceptance he so desired and never understood that those from whom he sought rewards doubted his loyalty, consistency, and objectivity. He was called "Mr. Facing Bothways" by many of his contemporaries.

Tench Coxe was born in Philadelphia, Pennsylvania on May 22, 1755, into a family that continually held a leading role in public affairs. He was named for his maternal grandfather Tench Francis, a leading attorney in Pennsylvania, who served as the Attorney General of Pennsylvania in 1741. His parents were William Coxe and Mary Coxe and were landowners.

Young Tench received his education in the Philadelphia schools and entered the Philadelphia College and Academy (now the University of

Tench Coxe (1755–1824)

Tench Coxe

Pennsylvania) in 1771 at the age of 16. By the end of 1772, he had left school and become a merchant in Philadelphia, opening his own trading house. He thought of studying law, but his father urged him to join his commercial concern. In 1776, amid the revolution, he joined Coxe, Furman, and Coxe as a partner. He was more interested in business than politics.

At one point in 1776, he enlisted in the 4th Pennsylvania Regiment but quickly decided he did not want to fight and resigned his commission. When his name became associated with Loyalists who were siding with the British against the American cause, Coxe panicked and fled to New York City, then under British control. When the British raided Pennsylvania and seized control of Philadelphia, forcing the Continental Congress to flee, Coxe marched alongside the British troops into the city on September 26, 1777. The British held Philadelphia for a time while Continental forces tried several attempts to force them out including battles at Brandywine and Germantown. During this time, Coxe was able to go about his business, making a tidy profit from the increased British business.

When the British were forced to flee from Philadelphia in 1778, Coxe remained. Some Patriots accused him of having Loyalist sympathies and having served in the British Army. For some reason, no harm came to him. His trading successes during the period of British occupation lent considerable support to the charges, yet nothing came of the allegations.

When the revolution ended, Coxe formed the international merchant firm of Coxe and Frazier and began to take an interest in politics. In 1778 his first wife Catherine McCall died suddenly, and in 1782 Coxe married his first cousin Rebecca Coxe, with whom he had ten children. By this time he was an extremely wealthy man. One of his many civic activities was serving as secretary of the Pennsylvania Society for Promoting the Abolition of Slavery, of which Benjamin Franklin was president. In 1786, Coxe represented Pennsylvania by serving as the secretary for the Annapolis Convention, the effort to revise the ineffective Articles of Confederation, which set the stage for the Constitutional Convention the next year.

In the summer of 1787, while the Constitutional Convention met in Philadelphia, Coxe presented a paper urging industrial development to the Society for Political Enquiries at Ben Franklin's house. He became a Whig and published three articles in the *Philadelphia Independent Gazetteer* that fall. The articles examined the new U.S. Constitution and compared it favorably to the British Constitution.

In 1788 Coxe served as one of Pennsylvania's last delegates to the Constitutional Convention. According to historian Edmund Cody Burnett, Coxe attended the Congress for a single day, January 10, 1789. On March 3, the Continental Congress was dissolved, and the following day the new U.S. Congress came into being.

Coxe next became a Federalist and was appointed as the Assistant Secretary of the Treasury by Alexander Hamilton. As the Assistant Secretary, Coxe gathered research that Hamilton used to promote manufacturing. They co-authored the famous "Report on Manufactures" in 1791. In 1792, Hamilton made Coxe the Commissioner of the Revenue in charge of the collection of all tax revenues. He served in that role until removed by President John Adams.

Tench Coxe (1755–1824)

The grave of Tench Coxe

Coxe then turned Democratic-Republican, and President Thomas Jefferson appointed him Purveyor of Public Supplies. In that role, he was responsible for procuring arms for the standing army and the militias. He served in that capacity from 1803 to 1812.

Coxe retired from public service in 1818 after having served three years as Clerk of The Quarter Sessions in Philadelphia. He spent his remaining years as a writer. He championed tariffs to protect the nations growing industries and the second amendment right to bear arms. It should be noted that firearms were among the many commodities dealt in for many years by the firm of Coxe and Frazier.

Tench Coxe died on July 17, 1824, in Philadelphia. He is buried in Christ Church Burial Ground.

Stephen Crane
(1709 – 1780)

"Bayoneted by Hessians"

Buried at First Presbyterian Church,
Elizabeth, New Jersey.

Continental Association

Stephen Crane was a New Jersey sheriff, judge, and politician who was also a member of the First Continental Congress, where he signed the Continental Association. Crane worked for many years to unite East and West New Jersey into one state. He was wantonly killed by Hessian soldiers on their way to battle in 1780. While his contributions to the American Revolution are mostly forgotten, many of his descendants were noteworthy, including his namesake, a great-great-grandson who wrote *The Red Badge of Courage*.

Crane, born circa 1709 in Elizabethtown, New Jersey, was one of five sons of Daniel Crane and his wife, Hannah Susannah (née Miller) Crane. He married Phoebe, maiden name lost to history, and the couple had seven children.

In 1743, the town elders selected Crane to travel to England with Matthias Hatfield to present a petition to King George II regarding colonial matters, likely about the festering divisions between East and West New Jersey. Several years later, he was elected to the town committee in 1750. He also served as the high sheriff and a judge of the Court of

Stephen Crane (1709–1780)

Stephen Crane

Common Pleas. From 1766 to 1773, Crane was a member of the New Jersey General Assembly, including a stint as speaker in 1771.

Next, Crane was elected the mayor of Elizabethtown. As hostilities increased with England, Crane served on the New Jersey Committee of Correspondence and Inquiry in 1774 and 1775. In June 1774, he was president of the convention that nominated delegates to the Continental Congress. He himself was nominated, and from 1774 to 1776, Crane was elected to the Continental Congress, where he signed the Continental Association.

Following his wife's passing, he declined to continue in Congress and remained in New Jersey to deal with the East/West divisions. He continued to serve in the New Jersey legislature and other local positions. In the meantime, Elizabethtown was at the center of Hessian and British troop movements to and from Staten Island. In 1779, Crane's ferry building, a parsonage, and other structures were burned by Hessians led by Baron von Knyphausen.

On June 23, 1780, while on their way to the Battle of Springfield, Hessian soldiers passing through Elizabethtown bayonetted Crane, mortally wounding him. According to a bronze marker erected in 1913 by the Daughters of the American Revolution:

> Here the British turned into Galloping Hill Road from Elizabethtown to Connecticut Farms and Springfield at the time of the battles June 7 and 23, 1780. Washington afterwards said of the New Jersey militia "They flew to arms universally, and acted with a spirit equal to anything I have seen during the war." A son of Gen. William Crane is said to have been bayoneted to death by British soldiers near this spot.

Author Stephen Crane, the great-great-grandson of the patriot.

Why was Crane, a seventy-year-old man bayonetted by soldiers? Crane was not in the military, but he was known to have been one of the organizers of the rebellion. Perhaps Crane was taunting the troops, angry at the burning of his ferry building the prior year. It should be noted Crane was the grandfather of General William Crane and not the son.

Stephen Crane died from his bayonet wounds on July 1 and was buried at the First Presbyterian Church in Elizabeth next to his wife and father. His gravestone reads, "Sacred to the Memory of Stephen Cane Esq. who departed this Life July Year A.D. 1780 In the 71 Year of his Age."

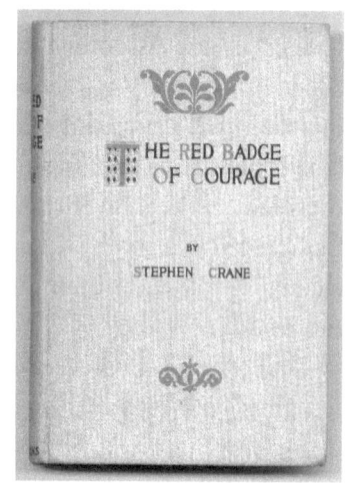

Crane's famous novel.

He was the only civilian member of the Continental Congress killed by the enemy.

Stephen Crane (1709–1780)

Among Crane's many descendants:

- Grandson William Crane (1778–1830) served as mayor of Essex County, New Jersey, and fought in the War of 1812 with Richard Montgomery at the Battle of Quebec, eventually losing a leg from his injuries. He rose to brigadier general of the New Jersey militia following the war.
- Grandson Ichabod Crane (1787–1857) served in the US Marine Corps and fought in the War of 1812, rising to the rank of colonel. He served aboard the USS *United States*.
- Grandson Joseph Halsey Crane (1782–1851) served as an Anti-Jacksonian member of the US House of Representatives from Ohio (1829–37).
- Great-grandson Charles Henry Crane (1825–1883) was a brigadier general and served as Surgeon General of the United States (1882–83).
- Great-grandson Jonathan Townley Crane (1819–1880), author and clergyman who was the father of author Stephen Crane.
- Great-great-grandson and namesake Stephen Crane (1871–1900) became famous through his numerous written works, including *Maggie: A Girl of the Streets* (1883), and *The Red Badge of Courage* (1895). He died at age 28 from tuberculosis.
- Painter Bruce Crane (1857–1937).

The grave of Stephen Crane.

John DeHart
(1727–1795)

Mayor of Elizabethtown

Buried at St. John's Episcopal Churchyard,
Elizabeth, New Jersey.

Continental Association

John DeHart was a delegate from New Jersey to the Continental Congresses in 1774 and 1775. He was one of the signers of the Continental Association and a member of the committee that prepared the draft for the New Jersey State Constitution in June 1776. He was elected Chief Justice of the State Supreme Court in 1776 and later elected Mayor of Elizabethtown in 1789.

John DeHart was born in Elizabethtown (now Elizabeth) in Union County, New Jersey, on July 25, 1727. His parents were Jacob and Abigail DeHart. He was one of four children, having a brother and two sisters. His brother, Captain Jacob DeHart, was in the British military and died in Haiti in 1758—perhaps during the Seven Years War.

He completed preparatory studies and then took up the study of law. In 1756, he married Sarah Dagworthy. Record keeping being imprecise in those days it is uncertain how many children the couple had. Various sources have them with three, eight, and twelve. DeHart was admitted to the New Jersey Colonial Bar in 1770 and opened a law practice.

On July 21, 1774, he was named as a delegate to the first Continental Congress along with James Kinsey, William Livingston, Stephen Crane,

John DeHart (1727–1795)

John DeHart

and Robert Smith. The Congress opened on September 5, 1774. DeHart was in favor of reconciliation with Britain, although he supported the first Petition to the King and the non-importation agreement. The Petition to the King was a letter to King George III in October by Congress calling for the repeal of the Intolerable Acts. It contained a statement of loyalty to the Crown and became known as the Olive Branch Petition. The King rejected the Petition, although he never gave a formal reply. The non-importation agreement was part of the Continental Association, which DeHart signed along with 53 of the 56 members of the first Congress.

In 1775, DeHart was returned to the Second Continental Congress. As differences with Great Britain became more pronounced, Congress took a harder line, and DeHart became more alienated from his peers. Finally, on November 13, 1775, he wrote his resignation to the New Jersey Assembly. The Assembly accepted it on November 22. The following June 22, 1776, New Jersey appointed an entirely new delegation to the Continental Congress and authorized them to vote for independence. They were Abraham Clark, John Hart (not to be confused with John DeHart), Francis Hopkinson, Richard Stockton, and John Witherspoon.

After his service in the Continental Congress ended, DeHart came home to New Jersey and helped prepare the draft bill that eventually became the New Jersey State Constitution when enacted in June 1776. Later that year, he was appointed as Chief Justice of the new New Jersey Supreme Court but also practiced law. Governor William Livingston replaced him in February 1777 for failing to attend court sessions.

While the status of his children are uncertain, DeHart had three nephews who fought in the Revolution—sons of his brother Dr. Mattias DeHart.

In 1789, he was elected as the Mayor of Elizabethtown and served until his death. He died at his home in Elizabeth on June 1, 1795, at the age of 67. He is buried in St. John's Episcopal Churchyard in Elizabeth. On our attempt to visit his grave and the burial place of a more prominent founder, Jonathan Dayton, who is also buried there, we found an overgrown, neglected, inaccessible cemetery. Attempts to reach anyone there were unsuccessful. Numerous subsequent phone messages went unanswered.

The grave of John DeHart.

Johann Robais, Baron de Kalb
(1721–1780)

French Major General

Buried at Bethesda Presbyterian Churchyard,
Camden, South Carolina.

Military

Born in what is now Germany, Major General Johann de Kalb served with honor in the Continental Army during the American Revolutionary War. After arriving in America with the Marquis de Lafayette, de Kalb played a key role in shaping the early U.S. Army—training and leading Soldiers, instilling discipline, and strengthening the force during its formative years. He led troops through the harsh winter at Valley Forge and later commanded forces in the Southern Campaign. At the Battle of Camden in 1780, de Kalb was mortally wounded while leading troops from Maryland and Delaware in fierce combat. His final words reflected the heart of a true patriot: "I die the death I always prayed for—the death of a soldier fighting for the rights of man."

De Kalb was born in Hüttendorf, a German village near Erlangen, Principality of Bayreuth, on June 29, 1721, the son of Johann Kalb and Margarethe Seitz. He went to school at Kriegenbronn and left home when he was sixteen. He received his first military training in 1743 as a Lieutenant in a German regiment of the French infantry. He served with distinction in the War of the Austrian Succession and in the Seven Years' War. He was promoted to Lt. Colonel and made Assistant Quartermaster

Johan de Kalb

General in the Army of the Upper Rhine. In 1763, he was awarded the Order of Military Merit and elevated to the nobility with the title of Baron.

In 1764, de Kalb resigned from the Army, got married, and started farming near Versailles. His wife was Anna Elizabeth Emilie Van Robais, a French heiress. The couple had three children.

In 1768, he was sent to the colonies as a secret agent to determine the sentiment of the colonists towards the British. He traveled extensively throughout the colonies, clandestinely observing the temperament of the colonists. He was arrested on suspicion of spying but was released for lack of evidence. When he returned to Paris, his report to the French government told of the dissatisfaction of the colonies with British rule.

In July 1777, de Kalb returned to America with his protégé, the Marquis de Lafayette, and joined the Continental Army. He had previously met with Benjamin Franklin and an American diplomat named

Silas Deane in Paris to discuss joining the Continental Army, and Deane, citing the Continental Army's need for experienced officers, promised de Kalb a major general's commission. He was disappointed and angry to learn that he would not be made a Major General and arranged for his return to France. He was, however, appointed to the rank on September 5, 1777, due to Lafayette's influence.

De Kalb was with George Washington's army during the winter at Valley Forge, the Monmouth Campaign, and the operations around New York City.

In the fall of 1779, the British commander Sir Henry Clinton decided to focus on the Southern colonies. Clinton's first target was Charleston. Major General Benjamin Lincoln and 5,000 Americans defended Charleston. Clinton opened the siege in April 1780. Washington, hoping to reinforce Lincoln's garrison, sent de Kalb to South Carolina. De Kalb and his men were unable to reach Lincoln in time. Lincoln surrendered to Clinton on May 12, 1780.

In response to the fall of Charleston, Congress appointed Major General Horatio Gates to lead the American Army in the South. Gates decided to strike the British, now led by Lord Charles Cornwallis, at one of the British outposts at Camden, South Carolina. On August 16, the two armies clashed. It quickly went badly for the Americans. The Virginia and North Carolina militias broke ranks and fled before a vicious bayonet charge. The American panic got even worse when Cornwallis ordered a cavalry unit to move in on the rear of the American forces. De Kalb attempted to rally his troops during the confusion, but de Kalb's horse was shot from under him, causing him to tumble to the ground. Before he could get up, he was shot three times and bayonetted repeatedly by British soldiers.

It is reported that Cornwallis supervised the dressing of de Kalb's wounds by his own surgeons. It was then that de Kalb issued his last words as previously reported. He died three days later, August 19, 1780, at the age of fifty-nine. He was buried near the hospital where he died. In 1825, he was disinterred and reburied beneath a monument in the yard of the Bethesda Presbyterian Church on East DeKalb Street in Camden. His original headstone is now part of the foundation of the steps of the Kershaw County Chamber of Commerce.

Death of de Kalb at Camden.

Upon visiting de Kalb's grave several years after his death, George Washington is reported to have said: "So there lies the brave de Kalb. The generous stranger, who came from a distant land to fight our battles and to water with his blood the tree of liberty. Would to God he had lived to share its fruits."

Grave of Johann de Kalb

William Duer
(1743–1799)

"The Panic of 1792"

Buried at Grace Episcopal Churchyard,
Queens, New York.

Articles of Confederation

William Duer was a British-born financier and land speculator from New York City who was elected to the Continental Congress, where he signed the Articles of Confederation on behalf of New York. During the debates concerning the U.S. Constitution, he wrote under the pen name "Philo Publius," backing the Federalist perspective. Near the end of his life, he was caught up in the 1792 financial panic and died in debtors' prison.

Duer, born March 18, 1743, in Devon, Devonshire, England, was the son of John Duer, a wealthy plantation owner, and his wife, Frances (née Frye) Duer, the daughter of Sir Frederick Frye of Antigua. John Duer owned a villa in Devon and plantations in the Caribbean on the islands of Antigua and Dominica, which generated significant income. The couple met in Antigua and were married there.

Duer was taught by private tutors before attending the prestigious boarding school, Eton, in the northwest of London. Though underage in 1762, Duer entered the British army as an ensign, accompanying Robert Clive as his aide-de-camp as he returned to India to be the governor-general of the British East-India Company. Duer did not adjust to the climate and returned to England.

William Duer

The British government contracted Duer to build masts and rigging for the British Navy in 1764. He traveled to New York to purchase supplies and noted the potential of the American colonies. Philip Schuyler, one of the wealthiest men in New York, urged Duer to invest in the timber lands near Saratoga on the Hudson, which he did. This area became known as Fort Miller and served as Duer's first residence in New York. He set up sawmills, warehouses, and a store.

Upon his father's death in 1767, Duer inherited his father's estates in the Caribbean. He now supplied lumber from New York to the islands and the British Navy and traded extensively with Schuyler. By the early 1770s, Duer had moved to Fort Miller permanently. In 1773, he made his final trip to England to settle his affairs, sold his properties, and returned to New York.

As an English gentleman with Caribbean plantations, Duer quickly became an influential citizen in New York. He held local positions of influence including jurist of the Charlotte County court and serving on the road commission.

In 1775, Duer was a delegate to the New York Provincial Congress and was appointed as a colonel and deputy adjutant general of the New York militia. In June 1776, he was a delegate to the New York convention to create a new state constitution. He was then elected as a state senator, serving from September 9, 1777, to June 30, 1778.

On March 29, 1777, the New York Provincial Congress elected Duer to the Continental Congress, serving until November 16, 1778. During his tenure, he was worried about the financing of the army and weary of the disagreements in Congress. However, he impressed John Adams, Robert Morris, and others with his participation on the finance committee and the "Board of War." He signed the Articles of Confederation in November 1777.

After leaving Congress, Duer returned to his business pursuits in partnership with John Holker, a French commercial agent. Robert Morris arranged contracts to supply the American army, benefitting Duer.

In 1779, Duer married Lady Catherine Alexander, a daughter of Major General William Alexander "Lord Stirling" and Sarah (née Livingston) Alexander. The wedding was at Stirling's elegant country home, "The Buildings," near Basking Ridge, New Jersey. The marriage connected Duer to the powerful Alexander and Livingston families of New York and New Jersey. The couple had eight children:

- William Alexander Duer (1780–1858) was a justice of the New York State Supreme Court and, for many years, the President of Columbia University. He married Hannah Maria Denning (1782–1862), daughter of U.S. Representative William Denning.
- John Duer (1782–1858) was a noted lawyer and jurist of New York. He married Anna Bedford Bunner (1783–1864), sister of U.S. Representative Rudolph Bunner.
- Frances Duer (1786–1869) was married to Beverley Robinson (1779–1857), grandson of merchant Beverley Robinson.
- Sarah Henrietta Duer (b. 1787) married John Witherspoon Smith, son and grandson of Princeton Presidents Samuel Stanhope Smith and John Witherspoon.

- Catherine Alexander Duer (1788–1882).
- Maria Theodora Duer (1789–1837) married Beverly Chew (1773–1851) in 1810.
- Henrietta Elizabeth Duer (1790–1839) married Morris Robinson (1784–1849), brother of Beverley Robinson and founder of the Mutual Life Insurance Company of New York.
- Alexander Duer (1793–1819) married Ann Maria Westcott (1808–1897), daughter of Colonel and New York State Senator David M. Westcott, in 1815.

Duer moved to New York City in 1783 and helped establish the Bank of New York in 1784. In 1786, he was elected to the New York Assembly. As the Constitution was signed and ratified, Duer was well connected to Robert Morris and Alexander Hamilton, Philip Schuyler's son-in-law. Duer entered into the debates about the merits of the Constitution, siding with Hamilton (who used the pen name "Publius") in three articles signed "Philo Publius" (aka Friend of Hamilton). In 1789, Hamilton became the first Secretary of the Treasury, and Duer was the first Assistant Secretary.

Duer then embarked on a scheme to speculate with government bonds involving the Bank of the United States and the Bank of New York. The goal was to buy up American debt at a discount, but the markets fluctuated wildly in early 1792, bankrupting Duer personally and resulting in the loss of significant funds to the federal government in what was known as The Panic of 1792. Secretary Hamilton, apparently not involved, requested the resignation of Duer, who refused. On March 23, 1792, Duer was arrested and thrown in debtor's prison. Historians still debate whether Duer's actions were deliberate or due to incompetence. Certainly, there was poor oversight.

While imprisoned, Duer managed to provide resources to his family via his lands in Vermont and Maine, not subject to confiscation. The end of his life was confusing, as there were contrary reports about his death. On April 17, 1799, *The Times* of Alexandria, Virginia, reported that the proceedings of the case of *United States vs. William Duer* in the District Court of the United States in Washington, D.C., was halted due to the "death of the Defendant." Other newspapers reported he was still alive. Another Alexandria paper reported Duer's death, having died in debtors' prison, on April 18, 1799. Reported the *Connecticut Gazette* of

New London, "Died, in [a] New-York prison, Col. WILLIAM DUER, aged 54, of speculating memory."

Duer was initially interred at St. Thomas Church in Floral Park, New York, in the Duer family vault. He was later exhumed and moved to Grace Episcopal Churchyard in Queens, New York.

Mrs. Duer remarried William Nelson on September 15, 1801.

Duer's noteworthy descendants include:

- Denning Duer, a grandson.
- William Duer (1805–1879), who served in the U.S. Congress representing New York, a grandson.
- James Gore King Duer, a great-grandson.
- Alice Duer Miller (1874–1942), the feminist poet and writer, a great-great-granddaughter.

The grave of William Duer.

William Few
(1748–1828)

The Farm Boy Who Signed the Constitution

Buried at Saint Paul's Episcopal Cemetery,
Augusta, Georgia.

Military • Confederation Congress • US Constitution

Founders like the subject of this chapter were, pun intended, few and far between. This founder was born into a poor farming family. His parents made a modest living raising tobacco. His educational opportunities were limited, but he made the most of what he learned from them. He had a family member hanged by loyalists. He overcame hardships and rose to become a political power. He demonstrated his ability to both lead and organize during the Revolutionary War. He represented Georgia at the 1787 Constitutional Convention, where he proudly added his signature to the document that the gathering produced. He would serve as one of the first United States senators from Georgia. His name was William Few.

Few was born on June 8, 1748, in Baltimore County, Maryland. His father was a Quaker and his mother a Catholic. They supported the family by farming, but in the 1750s, a series of droughts pushed them and many of their neighbors to near ruin. These people abandoned their holdings and moved to the southern frontier of North Carolina.

While prosperous farmers were able to provide for the education of their children, such was not the case with Few. As described by Denise

William Few (1748–1828)

Illustration of William Few

Kiernan and Joseph D'Agnese in their work *Signing Their Rights Away*, Few himself recalled an experience at a country school as being filled with "terror and anxiety" because of a teacher he absolutely hated. After the family moved, his second and last year of schooling was more enjoyable and provided Few with a love of reading and learning that would serve as a tremendous influence on his life.

When Few was sixteen, his family moved to Hillsborough. There, the Few's became involved with a group called the Regulators, a movement that resulted from the political and economic restrictions frontier farmers faced. These restrictions were imposed by merchants and local politicians. Many of their politicians and local sheriffs were corrupt and sought to exploit the farmers and the working class whenever possible. The protests by the Regulators grew and resulted in a confrontation on May 16, 1771, known as the Battle of Alamance, when 1,000 militia troops led by the Royal Governor William Tryon crushed the uprising. Few's brother James was captured and hanged. The family farm was destroyed, and Few's father, now being pressured by creditors, fled to Georgia. Few, his passion for American freedom fueled by the incident, stayed behind to settle his family's financial affairs and sell their property.

While in Hillsborough, Few also joined the militia and formed a volunteer company. He attended meetings to gain a deeper understanding of the conflict between the colonies and the mother country. As the American Revolution grew closer, Few wrote, "I felt the spirit of an American, and without much investigation of the justice of her cause, I resolved to defend it."

After handling his family's affairs, Few joined them near Augusta, Georgia. He joined the militia there and rose to the rank of lieutenant colonel. In 1777, his political life began when he was elected to the convention that would establish the Georgia constitution. He served in the state's first legislature and on the governor's advisory council.

In 1778, Few was called to active duty as Georgia prepared for a possible invasion by British and Loyalist troops stationed in Florida. While they did temporarily hold off the opposition, the trip was far from a success. Many Americans fell ill in the swamps. Only half of the American troops survived. By year's end, a sudden invasion by the British captured Savannah. By 1779, Few was second in command of a regiment that eventually forced the English to abandon Augusta. Few emerged from the southern fighting with a reputation as a skilled administrator and logistics expert. He was also recognized as a bold commander who could pick the time and place to engage small enemy parties. He also demonstrated that he possessed the physical strength to endure the hardships that came with fighting a guerrilla war.

In 1780, he was elected to serve in the Continental Congress. He would be in Congress for less than a year. When General Nathanael Greene drove the British out of Georgia, he returned there to assist in reassembling the state's government. He served in the state legislature and practiced law. He was a self-taught lawyer who later wrote that he had "never spent one hour in the office of an attorney to prepare for the business, nor did I know anything of the practice."

In 1786, Few once again represented Georgia in the Continental Congress. Congress was now meeting in New York City, so when, in

William Few (1748–1828)

1787, his state sent him as one of its representatives to the Constitutional Convention in Philadelphia, this resulted in a number of commutes between the two cities. He was one of the very few representatives at the convention in Philadelphia who came from what would be considered a working-class family farm background. He still managed to make an impression. As told in the aforementioned work, *Signing Their Rights Away*, Georgia delegate William Pierce wrote, "Mr. Few possesses a strong natural Genius, and from application has acquired some knowledge of legal matters; he practices at the bar of Georgia, and speaks tolerably well in the legislature. He has twice served as a Member of Congress, fulfilling his duties with fidelity to his state and honor to himself. In his work *1787: The Grand Convention*, historian Clinton Rossiter wrote that although he never spoke at the convention, Few made his presence felt by voting the right way at critical moments. Few would sign and then work to ratify the Constitution.

A few then served as one of Georgia's first U.S. senators. Here he became a supporter of Thomas Jefferson and an opponent of Alexander Hamilton. He strongly opposed the creation of the First Bank of the United States. He hoped to retire from public service in 1793 but was convinced by friends to serve another term in the state legislature. In 1796, he was appointed as a federal judge for the Georgia circuit. He earned a reputation as a fair jurist. He was a proud supporter of formal education, having been largely denied it himself, and was a founding trustee of the University of Georgia.

His wife, a native New Yorker, convinced him to move to the city in 1799. Here, he made a living in banking, where he served as the president

Grave of William Few

of the City Bank of New York. He was also elected to serve in the New York State Assembly. He also served as inspector of the state prisons, as a state commissioner of loans and as a city alderman.

When he finally retired at the age of sixty-eight, his wealth was estimated to exceed $100,000, which would amount to more than $2.5 million today. This was quite an accomplishment considering his humble beginnings. He died at the home of his daughter at the age of eighty. He was originally buried in New York, but his remains were later moved to St. Paul's Church in Augusta, Georgia.

Lyman Hall
(1724–1790)

The Delegate to Congress Who Couldn't Vote

Buried at Courthouse Grounds,
Augusta, Georgia.

Continental Congress • Declaration of Independence

This founder was born in the north but represented a southern colony in the Continental Congress. He was a clergyman and a physician. He was a fierce proponent of American independence. As such, he took pleasure in affixing his signature to the Declaration of Independence. Actor Jonathan Moore portrayed him in the 1972 movie *1776*. His name was Lyman Hall.

Hall was born on April 12, 1724, in Wallingford, Connecticut. His father was a minister named John Hall. His mother, Mary, was the daughter of the Reverend Samuel Street. He graduated from Yale in 1747 with the intention of becoming a minister, too. He began his ministry in 1749, but things did not go smoothly. He was serving in the pulpit of Stratfield Parish, and he found himself at odds with his congregation. In 1751, he was dismissed based on charges involving his moral character. According to one biographer, these allegations "Were supported by proof and also by his own confession." He continued to preach for two more years, filling in when a pulpit was vacant. At that point, he decided to change his career to medicine, and he apprenticed with a physician.

Illustration of Lyman Hall

In 1752, Hall married Abigail Burr. His bride passed away roughly a year later. In 1757, he married Mary Osborne, with whom he had one son. The Hall family then decided to move south. First to South Carolina and then to St. John's Parish along the Georgia coast. Here, Hall became involved in founding Sunbury, which later developed into a seaport hub. As told by Denise Kiernan and Joseph D'Agnese in their work *Signing Their Lives Away*, the swampy, malarial messes that needed to be drained in the area produced enough disease-carrying mosquitoes to keep Dr. Hall quite busy. He became one of the leading citizens in Sunbury and soon set up a plantation, Hall's Knoll, near the town.

Like Hall, many of Sunbury's residents were transplanted northerners. These people had ties to both friends and families in the north, and as a result, Sunbury became a supporter of the patriot cause. Georgia was one of the most remote colonies, and the majority felt that the relationship with England was not a threat. In fact, Georgia was the only colony that did not send any representatives to the First Continental Congress. Georgia also rejected the Congress recommendation for the Continental Association, which called for an embargo on trade with the mother country.

Hall and most of the people in St. John's Parish grew frustrated with the leadership in Georgia. Wanting representation in Congress, the

Parish, under Hall's leadership, contacted South Carolina with the goal of becoming part of that colony. South Carolina refused the offer.

In March of 1775, St. John's withdrew from the Georgia legislative body and held their own convention. They voted to send their own delegate to the Second Continental Congress, sending Hall as their representative. Arriving in Philadelphia that May, representing a single Georgia county, Congress was confused as to what Hall's place should be. Wanting Georgia to be represented in some manner, Hall was admitted as a nonvoting member. In July, after the battles at Lexington

The Signers' Monument in Augusta, Georgia, honors three patriots.

and Concord, the mood in Georgia changed. The colony acknowledged Hall's place in Congress and sent four other delegates to join him.

The Georgia delegates received no specific instructions. They were simply advised to do what they believed necessary for the common good. When the time came, Georgia voted for independence, and Hall was one of three Georgia representatives who signed their names on the Declaration of Independence.

In 1778, the British had turned their attention to the southern states. In January of 1779, Sunbury was burned, and the British destroyed Hall's plantation. Hall and his family fled north, back to Connecticut. He returned to Georgia when the English evacuated in 1782. He once again practiced medicine as he worked to repair his damaged finances.

In January of 1783, Hall was elected governor of the state. In this position, he worked on improving the economy, made treaties with the Cherokee Indians and advocated the chartering of a state university. His efforts resulted in the establishment of the University of Georgia. Upon leaving the governor's office, he resumed his medical practice.

In 1790, Hall moved to Burke County, where he purchased another plantation. Within a year of the move, he passed away on October 19 at the age of sixty-six. He was initially laid to rest on his plantation but later his remains were moved to Augusta. He is now buried beneath a monument honoring Georgia's signers of the Declaration.

Grave of Lyman Hall

John Harvie
(1742–1807)

Friend of Jefferson

Buried at Hollywood Cemetery,
Richmond, Virginia.

Articles of Confederation

John Harvie was an attorney and builder from Virginia, the son of Thomas Jefferson's guardian, John Harvie Sr. He served in the Virginia House of Delegates and operated a prison camp during the Revolution. He was elected to the Second Continental Congress, where he signed the Articles of Confederation. Later, he was the mayor of Richmond and was a lifelong friend of Jefferson.

Harvie, born in 1742 at the family's 2500-acre estate, Belmont Plantation, in Albemarle County, Virginia, was the son of Scottish immigrant John Harvie Sr., a planter, and his wife, Martha (née Gaines) Harvie. When Thomas Jefferson's father, Peter Jefferson, died in 1757 during Thomas's fourteenth year, neighbor John Harvie Sr. became his legal guardian. Young Harvie and Jefferson, only a year apart, became like brothers and were close for the rest of their lives.

Harvie studied law and was admitted to the Virginia bar. In 1767, he inherited Belmont Plantation when his father died and continued to live there. His mother moved to Georgia with his eight siblings, leaving the 25-year-old to run the estate. Harvie then married Margaret Morton

John Harvie

Jones, the daughter of Gabriel Jones, a longtime member of the House of Burgesses, and Margaret Strother Morton Jones. The couple had seven children: Lewis, John, Edwin, Jacquelin, Gabriella, Emily, and Julia.

Prior to the American Revolution, Harvie grew his business interests. He was also one of the first lawyers to practice at the Albermarle bar. In 1774, following what was later called Dunmore's War, he helped negotiate a peace treaty with the Shawnee following the Battle of Point Pleasant, which occurred in what is now West Virginia.

When Governor Dunmore abolished the House of Burgesses, Harvie was elected to Virginia's new assembly, the Virginia House of Delegates. He attended in 1775 and 1776 and was elected to the Second Continental Congress on behalf of Virginia. He was also a colonel in the Virginia militia in 1776 and helped to organize and purchase supplies.

While in the Continental Congress at York, Pennsylvania, Harvie worked on the Articles of Confederation. He also served on the Board of War for the Congress and inspected the camp at Valley Forge in the Winter of 1777/78. Congress was very concerned about the conditions there. Harvie said to Washington, "My dear General, if you had given some explanation, all these rumors [denigrating Washington] would have been silenced a long time ago."

Harvie signed the Articles on July 9, 1778, and promptly resigned from the Congress afterward. He also procured from Richard Anderson a 240-acre property west of Charlottesville called The Barracks. There, he established a prison camp that held 6000 Hessians and British soldiers by January 1779. The camp had brick buildings to house the troops as well as animals, poultry, gardens, and other outbuildings. Some of the prisoners deserted and headed into the hills. There, they married Native American women. When the camp closed in November 1780, the remaining soldiers were moved north.

In 1780, Harvie was appointed the registrar of Virginia's Land Office and moved to Richmond. He oversaw transactions in the Northwest Territory, western Virginia, Ohio, and Kentucky.

Harvie was elected the mayor of Richmond, Virginia, from 1785 to 1786. His holdings included the magnificent Belmont plantation, as well as the estates at Pen Park and The Barracks. In 1789, he was a presidential elector.

In 1798, Harvie added Judge Bushrod Washington's Belvidere estate in Richmond. Some compared it to Mount Vernon and said it was "an extremely handsome house, and of decidedly superior architecture, being beautifully proportioned."

Harvie died from injuries sustained following the fall from the roof of a building he was inspecting that was under construction. He passed on February 6, 1807, and was buried at Belvidere, which later became part of Hollywood Cemetery in Richmond.

Harvie is remembered by a street in Richmond. Jacquelin Street was named after his son, General Jacquelin Harvie. In 1982, Harvie descendant James Beverly Harvie Jr. placed a plaque near his ancestor's grave, which reads: "Within, and without, these walls rest members of the family of Col. John Harvie, 1742–1807. A guardian of Thomas Jefferson, and signers of the Articles of Confederation and the Bill of Rights. Here, too, lie his son, Jacquelin, and Mary, his wife, daughter of Chief Justice John Marshall. This area, part of the Harvie lands, became Hollywood Cemetery in 1847."

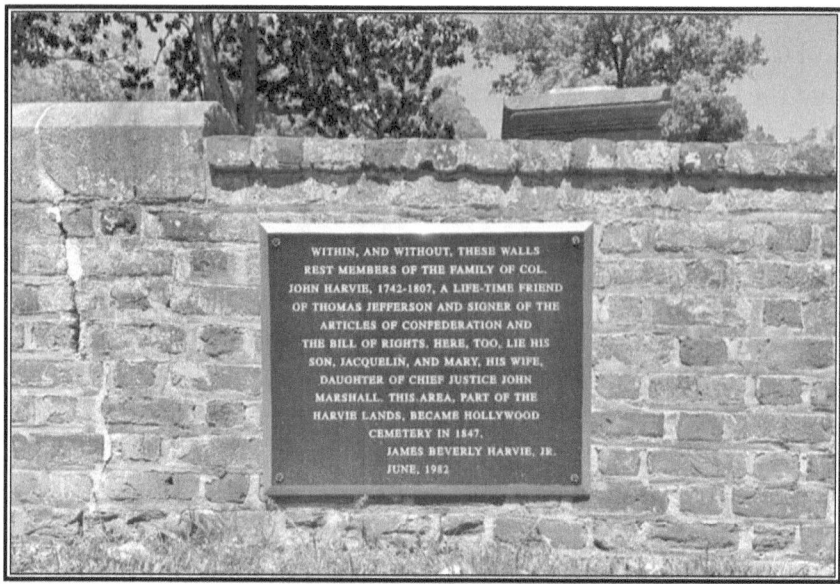

The Harvie family crypt is within these walls.

Patrick Henry
(1736 – 1799)

Revolutionary Orator

Buried at Henry Cemetery,
Aspen, Virginia.

Continental Congress • Continental Association

This founder joined the American Revolutionary cause early. He served in the Virginia House of Burgesses, where he became known for his inflammatory orations against the Stamp Act of 1765. He represented Virginia in the First Continental Congress, where he helped draft the Petition to the King. As a member of the body, he signed the Continental Association. After the Revolution, he served as the first and post-colonial Governor of Virginia. He feared a strong federal government, and he declined an appointment to serve as a delegate to the 1787 Constitutional Convention. He was a fierce opponent of the ratification of the Constitution that convention produced. American school children have long learned of him through a speech he delivered on March 23, 1775, to the Virginia House of Delegates, where he said, "Is life so dear or peace so sweet, as to be purchased at the price of chains and slavery? Forbid it, Almighty God! I know not what course others may take, but as for me, give me liberty or give me death." His name was Patrick Henry.

Henry was born in Hanover County, Virginia, on May 29, 1736. His father was John Henry, who was born in Scotland but made his way to

Patrick Henry

Virginia when he was in his mid-twenties. He found work as a surveyor's assistant while acquiring land of his own. After twenty years, he owned more than 23,000 acres. His mother was Sarah Winston Syme, who was a widow from a prominent family. Henry attended a local school for a few years, but his formal education came mostly from his father. Jon Kukla, in this biography, *Patrick Henry Champion of Liberty,* notes that Henry's boyhood friends remember that he was "remarkably fond of hunting, fishing, and playing on the violin."

During Henry's childhood years a religious movement known as the Great Awakening occurred. Religion played a key role in his life as both his father and the uncle he was named after were devout Anglicans. His exposure to ministers preaching helped shape what would become the technique he would use as an adult in delivering speeches. He concluded that oratory should aim at the heart and not rely solely on reason.

At the age of fifteen, Henry went to work as a clerk in a local store. Having gained this experience, he and his brother William went into business by themselves, opening their own store. In a short time, the business failed.

In 1754, Henry married Sarah Shelton. As a wedding gift, the bride's father gave the couple a 300-acre farm and six slaves. Henry attempted to work the land with the slaves, but this was a period of drought in Virginia. Then the main house burned down, and Henry had had enough. He moved to the Hanover Tavern, which his father-in-law owned. Henry worked at the tavern, acting as a host and entertaining guests playing the fiddle.

In 1760, Henry decided to study law. He was self-taught and he convinced a panel of Virginia attorneys that he was capable and was admitted to the bar. He opened a law practice that proved successful as he worked in the courts of Hanover and surrounding counties.

The case that cemented Henry's reputation as an attorney was the Parson's Cause. Droughts in Virginia had led to increased prices for tobacco. The Virginia House of Burgesses passed the Two Penny Act, which allowed tobacco debts to be paid at the rate of two pence per pound. The payees included the Anglican clergy. Several ministers appealed to the Board of Trade in London. The Board overruled the Virginia House. The clergymen filed suits for back pay, but only one of them, the Reverend James Maury, was successful, and a jury was appointed to assess and fix damages. After evidence was presented proving the facts at issue, Henry took the floor and gave a one-hour speech. He argued that the veto of the Two Penny Act by the English government and the King, who Henry called a "tyrant," had forfeited his right to his subjects' obedience. He also criticized the clergy for challenging a law aimed at bringing economic relief to the community. The opposing counsel then accused Henry of treason, but he continued his presentation, urging the jury to assess damages at one farthing. The jury deliberated for a short time before fixing the damages at one penny. The local community viewed Henry as a hero, and after the conclusion of the case, Henry became even busier, adding 164 clients for which he would provide legal representation. More importantly, as pointed out by Henry's biographer, Jon Kukla, Henry would transfer the lessons of the Parsons Cause in his arguments against the British government's passage of the Stamp Act.

On March 22, 1765, the British Parliament passed the Stamp Act. The act imposed a tax on all paper documents in the colonies and was the first internal tax levied by the British government on the American colonists. Henry was sworn-in to the Virginian legislature on May 20, 1765. Colonial resistance to Parliament's action was growing and Henry wasted no time in becoming one of the leaders opposing the Stamp Act. On May 29, he introduced the Virginia Stamp Act Resolves. The resolution maintained that the colonists enjoyed the same rights as the populous of the mother country. That taxes can only be enacted by the people's elected representatives. Finally, it stated that only the Virginia General Assembly had the right to tax.

The Resolves were printed in various newspapers around the colonies. In addition, Governor Francis Fauquier sent a report to the Board of Trade. He reported that "Very indecent language was used by Mr. Henry." The governor was successful in keeping the resolutions out of the *Virginia Gazette*. By August, the Resolves reached London. The *London Gazette* reported that "Mr. Henry has lately blazed out in the Assembly where he compared George III to a Tarquin, a Caesar, a Charles the First, threatening him with a Brutus, or an Oliver Cromwell." The Resolves established Henry as one of the first revolutionaries in the colonies.

Opposition to the Stamp Act grew steadily, and by early 1766, many of the stamp distributors had resigned their commissions as crowds of people threatened harm to them personally and to their property. Colonial resistance made it impossible for the British to enforce the act, and later, in 1766, Parliament repealed it. At the same time, they passed the Declaratory Act, which maintained that Parliament had the authority to pass laws governing the colonies.

In the years following the repeal of the Stamp Act, tensions between the English government and the American colonies continued to rise. In 1770, after the Boston Massacre, Henry and other Virginians established an intercolonial Committee of Correspondence. Parliament's passage of the Coercive Acts following the Boston Tea Party and the subsequent closing of the Boston Harbor resulted in uniting the colonies in their resistance.

Patrick Henry (1736–1799)

The First Continental Congress convened on September 5, 1774, in Philadelphia. Henry attended as one of Virginia's representatives. Henry's oratorical skills were impressive, but as Kukla points out in his biography, "the delegates placed greater weight on his ideas. He served on several important committees, and on the second day of the Congress he showed his ability as a speaker when he argued that old governments and colonial boundaries were no more. "The distinctions between Virginians, Pennsylvanians, New Yorkers, and New Englanders are no more. I am not a Virginian but an American." The meeting's main accomplishment was the adoption of the Continental Association, patterned after the Virginia Association. This pact established the nonimportation of British goods that would begin on December 1, 1774, unless Parliament rescinded the Intolerable Acts. It was also decided that a second Congress would meet the following year if the American grievances were not addressed. News of the Association reached King George III, who declared the colonies were "in a state of rebellion." Similarly, Lord Dartmouth, the secretary of state for American affairs, stated, "Everyone who signed it was guilty of treason." Having been accused of treason for more than a decade, Henry was probably unfazed. When Congress adjourned, Henry returned to Virginia. He never again served in a continental or national office.

In January 1775, Peyton Randolph called the Second Virginia Convention whose main purpose was to select delegates to the Second Continental Congress scheduled to be held in May. The convention lasted from March 20 to the 27th. On the convention's fourth day, Henry put forth three resolutions. The resolutions called for the establishment of a well-regulated militia. The third resolution stated, "Resolved therefore that this colony be immediately put into a posture of defense, that a committee be appointed to prepare a plan for embodying, arming, and disciplining such a number of men as may be sufficient for that purpose." This resolution sparked a spirited debate.

The opposition to the proposal argued that it was a "prophesy of war," and it would be seen as Virginia appearing to invite armed conflict. As told by Kukla, when Henry took the floor to respond those in attendance described him starting calmly praising the patriotism of the opposition while noting that his opinions were "the very opposite to theirs." Henry asked how best Americans could resist British oppression. He ridiculed those who favored petitioning the King, saying previous petitions had been disregarded: "And we have been spurned with contempt from the foot of the throne." When he paused, some members murmured, "Peace! Peace! Henry answered, "Gentlemen May cry Peace, Peace, but there is no peace." He noted that "Our brethren are already in the field." He slipped into the posture of a helpless slave so effectively that onlookers perceived manacles "almost visible" on his wrists. Henry asked, "Is life so dear or peace so sweet as to be purchased at the price of chains and slavery?" Raising his eyes and hands toward heaven, he continued, "Forbid it, Almighty God! I know not what course others may take, but as for me . . . give me liberty, or give me death!" The resolutions passed by a close vote of 65 to 60.

In May of 1776, Henry was once again a delegate this time to the Fifth Virginia Convention. Here, he introduced a motion declaring Virginia independent and urging the Continental Congress to declare all the colonies free of the rule of England. When he took the floor to speak, Edmund Randolph said he "appeared in an element for which he was born." The motion passed unanimously. The convention then passed a constitution creating Virginia's government and Henry was elected as the first post-independence Governor.

It was ironic that Henry was elected governor since he had opposed the limited power given to the executive office under the new Virginia constitution. Indeed, he was little more than a figurehead as the real power to govern resided in the House of Delegates. He corresponded regularly with Washington relative to the Revolutionary War effort. He worked at recruiting troops for Washington, but again, these efforts were hampered by, among other factors, the weakness of his office. In December of 1776, the news that the British had occupied Philadelphia reached Virginia, and the General Assembly responded by granting Henry temporary emergency powers. This may have resulted in a rift with Thomas Jefferson, which never healed as he felt Henry was trying to set himself up as a dictator.

Henry would serve until 1779. In 1778, he sent an appeal to Congress saying that naval aid was needed to protect Chesapeake Bay.

Congress did not act, and in May of 1779, British ships entered the bay and captured Suffolk and Portsmouth, where troops destroyed valuable supplies. Soon after, Henry left office. Thomas Jefferson succeeded him.

By this time, Henry had been married twice. First to Sarah Shelton in 1754. The couple had six children before she passed away in 1775. In 1777, he married Dorothea Dandridge. This coupling would produce eleven children, two of whom died very young. After serving as governor, Henry and his family moved to Leatherwood Plantation in Henry County which had recently been created and named for him.

At Leatherwood, Henry served on the county court. He turned down the opportunity to be elected to Congress. He did serve for a short time in the Virginia House of Delegates where he opposed a plan to impose certain taxes. Health problems forced him to leave Richmond and return home. In 1781, as the Revolutionary War moved south and the British occupied Richmond, Henry was active in recruiting soldiers to defend the state. By this time, the state government had moved to Charlottesville and was nearly captured when the British invaded that city; however, the lawmakers were successful in escaping to Staunton. Jefferson fled to a farm he owned in Bedford County, which resulted in Henry and other legislators calling for an inquiry into his conduct. This further deepened the animosity between Jefferson and Henry.

With the American victory at Yorktown, the Revolutionary War ended. Henry continued to represent his county as a delegate through 1784, when, once again, he was elected governor, serving from 1784 through 1786. The Virginian legislature passed a law to acquire new arms for the militia and Henry was active in attempting to acquire these arms from France. He also sought to improve Virginia's development, supporting the construction of canals. His efforts met with mixed results. It was Patrick Henry, acting in his capacity as governor, who signed Virginia's circular letter in February 1786 inviting the other twelve states to send delegates to attend the Annapolis Convention. The main accomplishment of this gathering was to call for a subsequent convention to meet in Philadelphia in 1787 the nation's Constitutional Convention.

Upon his return to Mount Vernon, after presiding over the Constitutional Convention, George Washington wasted no time in sending Henry a copy of the proposed Constitution. As explained by Kukla in his Henry biography, the document was accompanied by a letter in which Washington acknowledged that the proposal wasn't perfect but that he believed "it is the best that could be obtained at this time." Washington was probably disappointed by Henry's reply when he stated, "I have to lament that I cannot bring my Mind to accord with the proposed Constitution," adding, "The Concern I feel on this Account is really greater than I am able to express."

It is somewhat ironic that the man who years earlier declared himself to be an American and not a Virginian now opposed a measure designed to make the nation more than a confederation of states. Over time Henry had lost faith and trust in the northern states. Among other things, he blamed Congress for not supplying the troops necessary to protect Virginians who were settling in the Ohio River Valley. At the Virginia Ratifying Convention, he took the position that the Constitution gave the power to govern to too few, and he noted that it lacked a Bill of Rights and failed to protect individual liberty. On June 25, 1788, Virginia voted in favor of ratification.

Henry returned to the House of Delegates where he was successful in defeating James Madison, a strong supporter of the Constitution, in his effort to become a Senator from Virginia. He also served as one of Virginia's presidential electors, casting his vote for George Washington and John Adams.

Henry removed himself from the political stage until 1799, when Washington convinced him to return after the controversial Kentucky and Virginia Resolutions had passed. These acts were a response to the Alien and Sedition Acts of 1798, and they favored state action against the unconstitutional acts of the federal government and took the position that secession might be necessary. At this point, Henry argued that if a people are oppressed, they should overthrow the government, but he cautioned that it should not occur if there are other means to address the issue and find a remedy. He also warned that "you can never exchange the present government but for a monarchy." Henry once again won the election to the House of Delegates but passed away at his plantation on June 6, 1799, before the assembly convened. He was 63 years of age.

Patrick Henry (1736–1799)

Henry sealed a small envelope before his passing, inside of which was a message saying that whether America's independence would be a blessing, or a curse would depend on the use of the people of the blessings God has bestowed on us. He urged proactive virtue in thyself and encourage it in others. He was laid to rest at Henry Cemetery in Aspen, Virginia.

Grave of Patrick Henry

Thomas Heyward Jr.
(1746–1809)

The Last to Sign the Declaration

Buried at Heyward Family Cemetery,
Old House, South Carolina.

Declaration of Independence • Articles of Confederation • Military

Thomas Heyward Jr. was a wealthy planter from South Carolina who, as a Continental Congressman, signed the Declaration of Independence and the Articles of Confederation. He also fought in the South Carolina militia during the Siege of Charleston.

Heyward was born on July 28, 1746, at the family estate "Old House," near Beaufort, Jasper County, South Carolina, the son of Daniel Heyward and his wife, Mary (née Miles) Heyward. Oddly, the family already had a son named Thomas when Heyward was born, and they liked the name so much that they had another and appended "Junior" to it. The Heyward ancestors were among the first to settle in what was then Carolina in 1670 and became wealthy planters.

In his early years, Heyward was educated at home. Then he decided to study law and traveled to London to attend the Middle Temple, starting on January 10, 1765. He achieved the bar on May 25, 1770.

The following year, now twenty-five, Heyward returned to South Carolina and was admitted to the bar there. He then followed in his father's footsteps as a planter and attorney. Next, the young scion found

Thomas Heyward Jr. (1746–1809)

Thomas Heyward Jr.

himself elected to the South Carolina Commons House of Assembly in 1772, where he served for several years.

When tensions rose with England, Heyward was a delegate to the South Carolina provincial convention to determine the course of action in the colony. During this time, Heyward married Elizabeth Matthews of Charleston, the sister of John Mathews, a future governor of South Carolina. The couple had two sons.

When the new General Assembly was formed, Heyward was elected to it and appointed to the Council of Safety, serving in 1775 and 1776. On February 16, 1776, the General Assembly elected Heyward to a seat in the Continental Congress. He attended sessions from April 24, 1776, to September 4, 1776. During this time, he signed the Declaration of Independence and was likely the last to do so.

Heyward then returned to South Carolina and served in the General Assembly again. He was reelected to the Continental Congress and served from December 24, 1776, until October 31, 1777. During this time, he escaped with the Congress to York, Pennsylvania, and signed the Articles of Confederation.

Again, Heyward headed home to South Carolina, alternating between his plantation "White Hall" and his home in Charleston. In 1778, Heyward became a judge. At one trial, Heyward presided over a treason trial for several traitors. They were convicted and executed within sight of the British.

When the British besieged Charleston, Heyward took up arms, fighting with General William Moultrie. He was badly wounded and unable to escape when the British took the city. On August 27, 1780, he was captured, and all 130 of his slaves were taken as booty, and then White Hall was burned. For this loss, he was later described by the press as a "martyr of the revolution."

Heyward and 28 others were taken to a ship in Charleston harbor. On September 4, they were moved to St. Augustine, Florida, where they remained until they were exchanged eleven months later. To pass the time in prison, Heyward rewrote the British song "God Save the King" and to reflect an American version, changing the title to "God Save the Thirteen States."

During his captivity, his wife and children lived in Philadelphia. Unfortunately, while awaiting his release, she died in childbirth in 1782. She was buried in the St. Peter's Episcopal Churchyard in Philadelphia. Although they had six children, only Daniel survived to adulthood.

Following his release, Heyward was elected to the American Philosophical Society in 1784. The following year, he was one of the founders of the South Carolina Agricultural Society and was its first president.

In 1786, he married Elizabeth Savage, with whom he had three children. During these intervening years, he worked as a judge. In 1790, he was a delegate to the convention to draft a state constitution.

Thomas Heyward, Sr., Heyward's older brother, died in October 1795, after a painful illness that he handled with "Christian fortitude." Three years later, Heyward retired as a judge, and citing the pain from his war injuries, withdrew from public life soon after.

Heyward died on April 17, 1809, at the rebuild White Hall, in St. Luke's Parish (now Jasper County), South Carolina. He was buried at

Thomas Heyward Jr. (1746–1809)

Memorial of Thomas Heyward Jr.

the Heyward Family Cemetery at "Old House," the site of the former White Hall. A marker near his tomb reads, "Tomb of Thomas Heyward, Jr. 1746–1809. Member of South Carolina Provincial Congress and Council of Safety and of Continental Congress. Signer of Declaration of Independence and Articles of Confederation and captain of militia at Battle of Port Royal and Siege of Charleston. Prisoner of war 1780–81. Circuit Court Judge 1778–89."

In 1835, several newspapers heralded Heyward:

He was at that a very young man, not more than twenty-five or thirty . . . he was, perhaps, the wealthiest planter in the Southern country. His estate consisted entirely of land and negroes [*sic*], a species of property very easily got hold of by the goods, he heard of the Declaration of Independence. To him, it appeared to be an act of great indiscretion, and altogether premature. The total conquest of the country, with a confiscation of all of the property belonging to the rebels, was to be, he feared, the sad result of this effort to throw off the yoke of the mother country . . . Thomas Heyward was one of the few Signers of the Declaration of Independence who

Grave of Thomas Heyward Jr.

returned home, and took up arms in defense of that Independence which they had declared . . . in fighting for his country, Thomas Heyward was severely wounded. He had the honor of sealing with his blood the written appeal which he had signed with his hand.

All white Heyward descendants alive today trace their lineage to the three children, Thomas, William, and Elizabeth, descended from the second wife. Thomas E. Miller (1849–1938) was the grandson of Heyward and a slave woman. Miller was one of five African American congressmen from the South in the 1890s.

Descendant DuBose Heyward's (1885–1940) novel *Porgy*, published in 1927, was used by George Gershwin to create *Porgy and Bess* in 1935, which critiqued racism.

It is estimated that Heyward's younger brother Nathaniel was the largest slaveholder in the United States with over 2,000 slaves working over 35,000 acres.

Michael Hillegas
(1729 – 1804)

The First Treasurer

Buried at Christ Church Burial Ground,
Philadelphia, Pennsylvania.

1st Treasurer of U.S.A.

Michael Hillegas, of Huguenot descent, though not an elected member of the Continental Congress, served as the first treasurer of the United States along with George Clymer. They worked together to create a stable financial foundation for the young nation. He later served as the sole Treasurer of the United States and Treasurer for the state of Pennsylvania.

Born in Philadelphia, Pennsylvania on April 22, 1729, Michael Hillegas was the son of George Michael Hillegas (1696-1749) and his wife Margaret (née Schiebenstock). The elder Hillegas was originally from Alsace but moved to the Palatinate to escape religious persecution. A merchant by trade, he emigrated to Pennsylvania, settling in Philadelphia, where he became a naturalized citizen and leader in the German community. The elder Hillegas amassed real estate functioning as a potter, innkeeper, and storekeeper. He passed away in 1749 and is buried at Christ Church. His wife passed in 1770 and is buried next to him.

Michael Hillegas was well-educated thanks to his father's social standing. He followed in his father's footsteps as a businessman. According to *The Magazine of History* (1907), "Mr. Hillegas was rated among the wealthiest citizens of Philadelphia in pre-Revolutionary times. He was

Michael Hillegas (1729–1804)

Michael Hillegas

the owner of the largest sugar refinery in the city, was interested in the manufacture of iron, was a merchant whose services were sought by the State and city governments, and prominent in the best society of the city." On May 10, 1753, he married Henrietta Boude at Christ Church. The couple had ten children.

Before age 35, in 1762, Hillegas was appointed as one of the commissioners to recommend a site for a fort to defend Philadelphia. This later became Fort Mifflin. In 1763 or 1765 (sources vary), he was elected to a seat in the Pennsylvania Provincial Assembly which he held until 1775.

Throughout his experience with the Pennsylvania Assembly, he became adept at accounting and learned how to manage government spending. As the royal government began to collapse in 1774, Hillegas was named to the Committees of Observation and Safety to oversee the embargos demanded by the Continental Association. In 1775, he was appointed as a member of the Pennsylvania Council of Safety led by Benjamin Franklin, and, on June 30 of that year, was named its Treasurer.

Hillegas was well-known to those in the colonies who were planning the Revolution. John Adams wrote in his diary on October 28, 1775:

The Congress and the Assembly of this Province [Pennsylvania] were invited to make an excursion, upon [the] Delaware River, in the new row gallies built by the Committee of Safety of this Colony. About ten in the morning, we all embarked. The names of the gallies are the *Washington*, the *Effingham*, the *Franklin*, the *Dickinson*, the *Otter*, the *Bull Dog*, and one more whose name I have forgotten. We passed down the river, by Gloucester, where the *vaisseaux de frise* are. These are frames of timber, to be filled with stones, and sunk in three rows in the channel. I went in the *Bull Dog*, Captain Alexander, commander, Mr. Hillegas, Mr. Owen Biddle, and Mr. [David] Rittenhouse, and Captain Faulkner were with me. Hillegas is one of our continental treasurers; is a great musician; talks perpetually of the forte and piano, of Handel, etc., and songs and tunes. He plays upon the fiddle.

On July 29, 1775, the Continental Congress voted Michael Hillegas and George Clymer as co-treasurers of the United Colonies. Their initial task was to manage the distribution and circulation of over three million dollars in continental currency.

On May 30, 1776, Hillegas was named the Treasurer for the Province of Pennsylvania, a position he held even after Pennsylvania declared its statehood.

During the summer of 1776, Clymer signed the Declaration of Independence. Because Hillegas was an editor of the document, he did not sign, though he was present. The following month, upon Clymer's resignation as Treasurer, Hillegas became the sole Treasurer of the United States, a position he held until 1789.

In the *Dictionary of American Biography*, historian John Frederick wrote, "During the Revolution, he [Hillegas] contributed a large part of his fortune, by gift or loan, to the support of the army, and in 1781 he was one of the first subscribers to the Bank of North America. By direction of the Pennsylvania General Assembly he compiled and published, in 1782, Volume I of [the] Journals of the House of Representatives of the Commonwealth of Pennsylvania, covering the period between

November 28, 1776, and October 2, 1781. This task stimulated his interest in the preservation of historical material. In a letter of August 20, 1781, to the governor of New Hampshire, he suggested 'the propriety of each legislature in the Union adopting measures similar to those taken by this state for the above purpose.'" Hillegas was also one of the founders of the Bank of Pennsylvania in 1780.

As the new constitution was being ratified, Hillegas lobbied George Washington to continue in his duties. In a letter to Washington on September 5, 1789, Hillegas wrote:

> From Michael Hillegas
> New York Septr 5. 1789
>
> Sir.
> As the time for making appointments under the Treasury Law draws near, I beg leave to Request Your Excellency's remembrance of the present Treasurer, who has the honor to be with the greatest Respect Your Excellency's most Obedt humble Servt
>
> M. Hillegas

On September 11, 1789, under the new United States Constitution, Alexander Hamilton was sworn in as the first Secretary of the Treasury, and Michael Hillegas resigned from his position.

His national duties behind him, Hillegas retired to Philadelphia affairs where he continued to function as an alderman and an early member of the American Philosophical Society until his death in 1804. He was laid to rest at Christ Church Burial Ground in Philadelphia, a few yards from Benjamin Franklin.

Relatives of Hillegas later petitioned to have his portrait appear on the ten-dollar gold certificate. These notes bearing his likeness were issued from 1907 to 1922.

Said an unnamed historian in *The Magazine of History* (1907):

> That Michael Hillegas' fame should have been obscured so long is explainable only on the ground that he was of German-French

descent, and that the principal historians of the day were Quakers who preferred to have it appear that the followers of William Penn were the principal actors in the history of Philadelphia. That this is the explanation is indicated by the president of a Quaker college who recently wrote a history of Pennsylvania, and who explained his omission of all reference to Mr. Hillegas by saying it was an "oversight," adding that he found Mr. Hillegas' name "hundreds of times" in his investigations. Another reason may be that while the descendants of Robert Morris and Samuel Meredith, other claimants to the title of first treasurer, have been busy inducting States to erect monuments to their forebears, there have been no such active descendants of Mr. Hillegas, there being no lineal stock bearing his name.

The grave of Micahel Hillegas

Samuel Holten
(1738 – 1816)

Physician Continental Congressman

Buried at Holton Cemetery,
Danvers, Massachusetts.

Continental Congress • Articles of Confederation • U.S. Congress

Samuel Holten was a physician from Salem Village (now Danvers), Massachusetts, who became a long-serving Continental Congressman who signed the Articles of Confederation. He also served in several state positions, including nearly twenty years as a local judge. He was briefly a member of the US House of Representatives in the early republic.

Holten was born on June 9, 1738, in Salem Village, Massachusetts, the son of Samuel Holten, Sr., and Hannah (née Gardner) Holten, who was a member of the famous Gardner family of the colony. Holten was descended from his great-grandfather, Joseph Houlton, from Bedfordshire, England, who came to the colonies with his wife, Sarah Ingersoll, of the Connecticut Ingersolls.

Holten attended local grammar schools and then studied medicine under Dr. Jonathan Prince. Upon his certification as a physician, Holten opened a practice in Gloucester, Massachusetts. In 1758, he married Mary Warner with whom he had two daughters.

The young doctor and his family soon returned to Salem Village, where he continued his practice and became very popular. In 1768, he was appointed to the General Court.

Judge Samuel Holten

As tensions began to mount with England, Holten was elected to the Massachusetts Provincial Congress from 1774 to 1775. He was next a member of the Massachusetts Committee of Safety.

Holten was appointed to the Continental Congress on February 10, 1778, to replace John Adams, who had been sent to France. He arrived in York, Pennsylvania, in time to sign the Articles of Confederation on behalf of Massachusetts on March 10, 1778. He was then reelected on October 15, 1778, serving with Samuel Adams, John Hancock, Elbridge Gerry, Francis Dana, James Lovell, and Timothy Edwards through 1779.

In the 1840s, historian Mellen Chamberlain had the opportunity to make notes from Dr. Holten's diary used during the Continental Congress. Some of the entries follow:

> 1778, June 23. Attended in Congress, and the chief of the day was taken up in disputes on the articles of confederation [sic].
>
> 1778, July 11. This day was the first time that I took any part in the debates in Congress. We have accounts of the arrival of a French Fleet in the Delaware. 12 Ships of the line & 4 Frigates.
>
> 1778, July 14. I let the Hon. Samuel Adams Esqr. have 400.00, of which he is to pay to James Otis (a minor) being my part of what the delegates of our state have agreed to advance to sd [said] minr. & Mr. Adams is to write to his friends & procure the money, & account with me for the same.

1778, Oct. 7. Met a committee on this evening on General [Benedict] Arnold's accounts.

1778, Oct. 15. A manifesto or Proclamation from Commr. of the British king appeared in the papers of the day, offering a Gen. Pardon, but I believe there is but few people here want their pardon.

1778, Dec. 14. Monday. There was a grand ball at the City Tavern this evening, given by a number of French gentlemen of distinction. I had a card sent me, but declined attending. I think it is not a proper time to attend balls when the country is in such great distress.

Holten was again appointed to the Continental Congress on November 18, 1779, continuing his service until he resigned on July 29, 1780, when he began two years of service in the Massachusetts Senate and the Massachusetts Governor's Council, a role he held off and on for fourteen years. He was again appointed to the Continental Congress on October 4, 1780, but did not attend any sessions in 1781.

On October 4, 1782, Holten was again appointed to the Continental Congress. He served through November 1, 1783. The following year, in addition to his state senate seat, he returned for another term, serving through October 1785. On August 17, 1785, Holten was elected the president pro tempore of the Continental Congress, when President Richard Henry Lee was unable to preside. Holten ran the Congress until the new president, John Hancock was able to attend. During this time, he, Elbridge Gerry, and Rufus King blocked the call for a convention to reform the Articles of Confederation, believing not enough time had passed to judge the effectiveness of it.

In 1786, Holton continued in his state senate seat and was again elected to the Continental Congress, serving until August 9, 1787. Holten changed his mind about the Articles and participated in the Constitutional Convention in Philadelphia in 1787. However, he did not approve of its final form, with a strong central government and lacking a Bill of Rights. He opposed ratification of the Constitution. Meanwhile, he also served in the state House of Representatives and was in attendance at the Massachusetts ratifying convention in 1788. There, he allied himself with the anti-Federalists and opposed ratification. Unfortunately, Holten became ill at this time and was unable to have the desired impact.

As the Federalists took control of the Federal Government, Holten seemed finished with national politics. He sat in the state Senate in 1789 and 1790 and on the Governor's Council. He twice failed to be elected to the US House of Representatives in 1788 and 1790. He also lost a bid to be appointed to the US Senate in 1790.

In 1792, Holten finally won his seat in the US House of Representatives, serving in the Third Congress, from 1793 to 1795, representing Massachusetts' First District.

Following his single term, Holten returned to Danvers and served as a judge on the Essex County Probate Court for nearly twenty years, from 1796 to 1815.

In his 77th year, with his health failing, Holten resigned his judgeship in 1815. He died soon after on January 2, 1816. He was buried in the Holten Family Cemetery in Danvers, Massachusetts. His large tombstone reads:

> Erected to the Memory of the Hon. Samuel Holten, Who Died Jan. 2, 1716, aged 78 years. He Sustained Various Offices of Trust, Under the State Government, and That of the Union, With Ability and Integrity, to the Almost Unanimous Acceptance of His Constituents.

The Judge Samuel Holten House remains a historic site in Danvers, Massachusetts.

The grave of Samuel Holten

Charles Humphreys
(1717 – 1786)

A Patriot Who Followed His Conscience

Buried at Old Haverford Friends Meeting House Cemetery, Havertown, Pennsylvania.

Continental Association

This founder was one of the older members of the Continental Congress. A miller by trade he did not begin his political career until he was 50 years of age. As a member of Congress, he signed the Continental Association. He voted against the Declaration of Independence and refused to sign the document. The decision to vote against independence led to his resignation from Congress soon after independence was declared. Though he did not take part in the Revolution, his sympathies were with the Americans, and he criticized what he saw as oppression by the British government. His name was Charles Humphreys.

Humphreys was born at his family estate which was located about seven miles northwest of Philadelphia in the village of Haverford on September 19, 1714. His father was a Welsh immigrant who arrived in the colonies in 1682 and went into business as a miller, one who mills grains like wheat, for example. Charles Humphreys attended local schools, but there is no evidence that he received any advanced schooling. After completing his preparatory studies, he took up his father's profession.

Charles Humphreys

Based on information in *The Pennsylvania Magazine Of History And Biography*, Humphreys "was held in high regard for his talents, his integrity in private and public life, his hospitality and courteous and dignified manners." Perhaps based on this sterling reputation in 1764 the British government appointed him to a seat in the Pennsylvania Provincial Congress. Humphreys would serve in that body for a full decade. Though the organization served as little more than a rubber stamp for decisions made by the British Parliament, as a result of his efforts his status as a local statesman continued to flourish.

In 1774 Humphreys was elected to the Continental Congress. That same year in response to the British Parliament passing the Coercive Acts restructuring the administration of the colonies and specifically punishing Massachusetts for the Boston Tea Party, Congress adopted the Continental Association. The Association was a system designed to implement a trade boycott aimed at the banning the importing and consumption of any goods from England, Ireland and the British West Indies. The Association avoided blaming the king for the problems instead pointing the finger at Parliament and lower British officials for a "ruinous system of colony administration." Humphreys was among the delegates that signed the Continental Association.

There is little doubt that the toughest question Humphreys wrestled with as a member of Congress was that of American independence. Based on his religious beliefs, Humphreys, a Quaker, opposed going to war. But, he was well aware, as pointed out in 1923 by the lawyer and scholar Hampton L. Carson in the *Philadelphia Inquirer,* that the charter of William Penn included a provision that allowed the Crown to tax the colonists without their consent. In the end, his religious beliefs, more than anything else, led him to vote against American independence and refuse to sign the document authored by Jefferson once it was passed. Humphreys, much like John Dickinson, was a patriot who did not believe that separation from the mother country was the right course to pursue.

After the Declaration was adopted, Humphreys left Congress. Little is known about his later life. Mr. Carson mentioned earlier wrote that Humphreys contributed his share to the patriot cause. The Humphreys family continued to work for the country after the Revolution. For example, his nephew Joshua Humphreys was a shipbuilder and naval architect who was responsible for the construction of the original six frigates

The grave of Charles Humphreys

of the United States Navy. These ships included the USS *Constellation* and the USS *Constitution*.

Charles Humphreys died on March 11, 1786, at his estate near Philadelphia. He was laid to rest in the Old Haverford Friends Meeting House Cemetery. After his death, a newspaper said of him, "From a very early period of his life distinguished by integrity and sound understanding, his country fixed on him to fill those public stations with which she rewards the upright and the just. In the General Assembly - in Congress, he was known to be liberal and impartial. In private life open, hospitable, and generous - and in death, serene and unruffled - so that we may safely say he died sincerely lamented by friends, and much respected even by his enemies."

James Iredell
(1751–1799)

An Original Supreme

Buried at Hayes Plantation Cemetery, aka Johnston Family Cemetery, Edenton, North Carolina.

First Supreme Court

James Iredell, of North Carolina, was an English-born lawyer and political essayist who was appointed to the first US Supreme Court by President George Washington. He was a leading Federalist in the state and the father of a governor of North Carolina, James Iredell Jr.

Iredell was born on October 5, 1751, in Lewes, England, the son of Francis Iredell, a merchant in Bristol, and his wife, Margaret (née McCulloch) Iredell, of Dublin, Ireland. Iredell was the oldest of five surviving children. Circa 1768, due to his father's business failure, young James, at age 17, sailed to America to become the Comptroller of Customs for King George III in the village of Edenton, North Carolina. The position had been arranged by relatives. This also provided the funds and opportunity to study law under Samuel Johnston, who later became a governor of North Carolina and a US Senator.

In 1771, Iredell was admitted to the North Carolina bar. Two years later, in 1773, he married Samuel Johnston's sister, Hannah. After twelve childless years, the couple ultimately had four children. In 1774, Iredell was made the tariff collector for the port.

James Iredell

Despite working for the crown, in 1774, Iredell wrote *To the Inhabitants of Great Britain*, challenging parliamentary supremacy over the colonies. At age 23, Iredell became the most influential political essayist in North Carolina. He followed this with *Principles of an American Whig*, laying out many of the themes that later appeared in the Declaration of Independence.

During the American Revolution, Iredell served North Carolina by helping to organize the court system as a member of the commission that drafted the initial court bill. He was elected a judge of the superior court in 1778, serving only to make one circuit to settle old lawsuits. He then filled numerous roles over the years, including the state's second attorney general from 1779 to 1781. He resigned soon after the surrender at Yorktown to return to his family to "repair the sufferings [his] poor circumstances had received in the public service."

In 1787, Iredell was appointed by the state assembly to lead a commission to compile and revise North Carolina's laws. This was later published in 1791 as *Iredell's Revisal*. As the new U.S. Constitution was being debated, Iredell was the first to support it in North Carolina. He responded in 1788, under the pseudonym "Marcus," to George Mason's eleven objections with what were later called *Iredell's Answers*. This preceded the more famous *Federalist Papers*. Ultimately, the Constitution did not pass in North Carolina, despite his efforts. Only after the Bill of Rights was passed did North Carolina affirm in 1789. Regardless, Iredell was lauded as the intellectual leader of the Federalists' victory.

As a reward for his efforts to ratify the Constitution, George Washington appointed Iredell to the first U.S. Supreme Court on February 8, 1790, as an associate justice. He was confirmed by the Senate two days later and sworn into office on May 12.

Grave of James Iredell

During his nearly decade on the bench, Iredell was an ardent Federalist, vigorously supporting the administrations of Washington and Adams. However, the court only met twice a year and made its first decision in 1791. Iredell was involved in two noteworthy decisions:

- *Chisholm v. Georgia* (1793): Concerning interstate lawsuits. Iredell's dissent led to the 11th Amendment.
- *Calder v. Bull* (1798): Concerning ex post facto laws.

During his tenure, Iredell also "rode the circuit" as did all the Supreme Court justices twice a year. Over the years, this travel proved very taxing. Iredell died at age 48 on October 20, 1799. He was buried in the Johnston family cemetery in Edenton, North Carolina.

Iredell County, North Carolina, and the SS *James Iredell*, a ship from World War II, were named in his honor. The James Iredell House in Edenton is on the National Register of Historic Places.

Iredell and his wife appeared as characters in the historical novel by Natalie Wexler titled *A More Obedient Wife: A Novel of the Early Supreme Court*.

William Jackson
(1759 – 1828)

Secretary of the Constitutional Convention

Buried at Christ Church Burial Ground,
Philadelphia, Pennsylvania.

U.S. Constitution • Military

William Jackson was an officer in the Continental Army who served with distinction during the American Revolution. He leveraged his connections, especially with George Washington, to become the secretary of the United States Constitutional Convention where he was the 40th person to affix his signature. Jackson also served President George Washington as one of his secretaries during his administration.

William Jackson was born March 9, 1759, in the county of Cumberland, England, located in the northern part of the country near Scotland. He was just a boy when his parents passed away. Now an orphan, neighbors arranged for his emigration to Charleston, South Carolina soon after. There he was raised by a family friend, Owen Roberts, who was a prominent merchant and militia commander. Roberts, a veteran of the French and Indian War, involved the young man in many of the militia's activities.

When the Revolutionary War began in 1775, Roberts was an ardent patriot and brought his teenaged charge along with him. By May of 1776, just seventeen years of age, Jackson was commissioned as a

William Jackson

second lieutenant in the 1st South Carolina Regiment led by Colonel Christopher Gadsden.

The following month, in June 1776, Jackson saw his first action defending against British General Clinton's assault on Fort Sullivan, since renamed Fort Moultrie, at the entrance to Charleston harbor. He then spent most of the next year garrisoned in Charleston until, under Major General Robert Howe, he was part of the failed attempt to take St. Augustine, Florida, from the British. While many were struck down by disease, Jackson survived and returned to South Carolina in 1778.

After his return, Congress replaced Howe with Major General Benjamin Lincoln. Charles Cotesworth Pinckney convinced Lincoln he, a northerner from Massachusetts, could use a local aide to assist him with his southern troops. Jackson was tapped for the position and promoted to major. Jackson then served with Lincoln in the skirmishes that followed the loss of Savannah, including the battle of Stono Ferry in June

1779, where his guardian Owen Roberts was killed, and the American counteroffensive at Savannah in conjunction with comte d'Estaing's French forces. Jackson experienced defeat in both instances, and the allies retreated from Savannah, blaming each other for the failure.

Worse yet, in 1780, General Clinton turned his focus from Savannah to Charleston and was this time successful. Lincoln was forced to surrender after a lengthy siege of forty-two days. Jackson and 5,000 rebels were captured and taken prisoner. Jackson was taken to Philadelphia on parole and held there by the British until he, Lincoln, and others were exchanged.

Jackson was next assigned as secretary to South Carolinian Lieutenant Colonel John Laurens, the son of Henry Laurens, who was George Washington's aide thanks to Lincoln's recommendation. In 1781 this put Jackson on John Barry's boat with Laurens on the mission to France to negotiate for war supplies. Jackson's mastery of French was highly valued. For six weeks they dealt with Minister of Foreign Affairs comte de Vergennes at Versaille to no avail. Finally, direct contact was made with the King of France and Washington's request handed to him. The King then loaned the requested funds, most of which was spent on supplies.

Laurens returned to America with three ships full of materiel while Jackson went to Holland where John Adams had contracted for a fourth ship. This, however, never came to pass. Either Adams was deceived, or the ship was sunk. Despite being chased by the British navy, Laurens arrived in Boston in September. Jackson finally returned in February 1782.

Next, Jackson served as the assistant secretary of war under Benjamin Lincoln and helped settle the Pennsylvania Mutiny of 1783. Hundreds of Pennsylvania soldiers demanded to be paid for their services during the Revolution and took over Congress in Philadelphia. Eventually, the revolt was put down, but Congress moved to New Jersey and then New York for a time.

In October 1783, with the demobilization of the Continental Army complete, Jackson resigned his office and his commission to become Robert Morris's agent in England for several months. His prospects had changed since Owen Roberts was killed in 1779 and he needed to earn a living. When he returned in 1784, Jackson studied law in Philadelphia with William Lewis.

Before concluding his law studies, getting wind of the upcoming Constitutional Convention in Philadelphia, Jackson wrote to Washington to apply for the post as secretary. On May 25, 1787, Alexander Hamilton nominated Jackson. He won out over Benjamin Franklin's grandson, William Temple Franklin, who had been his grandfather's secretary during the negotiations of the Treaty of Paris.

As convention secretary, Jackson was sworn to secrecy regarding the proceedings, kept the official minutes, and destroyed all records except for the official journal after the final draft of the Constitution was signed. There had been a debate about the destruction of the journals which contained many proposals and counterproposals not adopted. Said Rufus King of Massachusetts, "If suffered to be made public a bad use would be made of them." Two suggestions were made regarding them: destroy them or deposit them into the custody of the president, George Washington, "until Congress, if ever formed under the Constitution" would give him further instructions. It was decided to do the latter, and the records remained with Washington until December 1796 when he gave them to the Department of State. Congress prohibited publication of the journals until 1818 when John Quincy Adams, the Secretary of State, discovered the decaying state of the papers.

While not a voting member of the Constitutional Convention, Jackson signed the document "Attest William Jackson Secretary" and thus became the fortieth signer of the U.S. Constitution, his signature authenticating the others.

Days after the signing, on September 20, 1787, Jackson was sent to the Congress assembled in New York City with a copy of the Constitution and read it aloud.

Jackson was admitted to the Pennsylvania Bar in 1788 but had to wait two years to practice before the Pennsylvania Supreme Court, as was customary. In the meantime, he applied to be the secretary to the United States Senate but did not get the position; however, George Washington brought him on as his secretary while he was president.

Jackson resigned in 1791 to start his law practice, despite being offered the post of Adjutant General of the Army, and worked with Henry Knox, the Secretary of War, and William Bingham who were selling off

William Jackson (1759–1828)

The grave of William Jackson

a large land grant in Maine they had acquired. Jackson went to England and France to sell the land on commission.

Jackson returned to the United States in the summer of 1795 and married Elizabeth Willing, the sister of Mrs. Bingham, that November. The ladies were the daughters of Thomas Willing, the Philadelphia financier. George and Martha Washington, Robert and Mary Morris, Alexander Hamilton, and Benjamin Lincoln were among those who attended the wedding.

The Jacksons produced four children. A son William married Martha James but had no children. There were also three daughters: Mary (married Rigal), Ann (married Willing), and Caroline.

In January 1796, during his final months in office, Washington appointed Jackson Collector for the Port of Philadelphia responsible for collecting customs tariffs.

Due to his Federalist associations, Jackson was dismissed by President Thomas Jefferson in 1801 despite the fact Jefferson had been a guest at Jackson's nuptials. Jackson then started the *Political and Commerical Register*, a Federalist newspaper based in Philadelphia. Jackson was the editor until 1815.

Jackson also returned to the law, and in one of his last significant cases, he represented Continental Army veterans who were petitioning for pensions. Jackson had succeeded Henry Knox as secretary-general of the Society of the Cincinnati in 1799, a post he held until his death.

In 1824, Jackson welcomed his old friend and ally General Lafayette to Philadelphia during his tour of America.

Jackson passed away at the age of 69 on December 18, 1828, in Philadelphia. He was buried at Christ Church Burial Ground in Philadelphia near his father-in-law. His wife lived another 30 years, passing on August 5, 1858.

James Kinsey
(1731–1802)

The Jurist from Jersey

Buried at Friends Burying Ground,
Burlington, New Jersey.

Continental Congress • Continental Association

This founder was born in Pennsylvania, but he made a name for himself in neighboring New Jersey. A lawyer, after being admitted to the bar he practiced his craft in both of the aforementioned states. He served as a member of the New Jersey General Assembly. He represented that state as a member of the Continental Congress from July 23, 1774, until November 22, 1775. In Congress, he was one of the signers of the Continental Association. In 1789, he was appointed chief justice of the New Jersey Supreme Court, and he served in that position until he died in 1802. His name was James Kinsey.

Kinsey was born in Philadelphia on March 22, 1731. His father, John Kinsey, was a prominent Philadelphia attorney. In 1919, James Issac Sharpless wrote, "After William Penn, no colonial Quaker had the absolute confidence of Friends in church affairs, and at the same time the strong leadership in the state to the extent possessed by John Kinsey. During the last decade of his life, he was the clerk of the yearly meeting and its most responsible and influential member. He was also the chief justice of the Supreme Court of the Province, Speaker of the Assembly and the undoubted leader of its party in political management.

James Kinsey

Kinsey's Education was centered in Philadelphia local schools. He then studied law and was admitted to the New Jersey colonial bar in 1753. While he practiced law in both Pennsylvania and New Jersey, he resided in Burlington County which was located in the latter named colony. He began his political career in 1772 when he was elected to the Colonial General Assembly. He also served as a member of the Committee of Correspondence for Burlington County.

In July of 1774, the New Jersey General Assembly elected Kinsey to represent the colony at a meeting set to convene that September in Philadelphia, a gathering that became known as the First Continental Congress. That Congress brought together representatives of 12 of the 13 colonies. The meeting was brought about by the British decision to blockade Boston Harbor and Parliament's passage of the Intolerable Acts as a response to the Boston Tea Party. The Congress agreed on a Declaration of Resolves that included the Continental Association. Kinsey added his signature to the Continental Association.

The Association, which was passed on October 20, 1774, is considered to be a major accomplishment of the initial Congress. It called for a

James Kinsey (1731–1802)

trade boycott against British merchants. Congress believed that economic sanctions on British imports and exports would pressure Parliament to deal with colonial grievances and the repeal of the very unpopular Intolerable Acts.

The General Assemblies of each colony, with the exception of New York, approved the de+idioms made by the Congress. The boycott was implemented, but any hope that it would be successful in changing British behavior ended with the outbreak of hostilities in April of 1775.

Prior to adjourning, the First Congress voted to meet again the following year if their grievances had not been addressed. This gathering became the Second Continental Congress, and this time every colony sent representatives. Once again, Kinsey was among the New Jersey delegates. The Second Congress convened in Philadelphia on May 10, 1775. Kinsey, a Quaker, opposed war and was not in favor of independence. Perhaps because he saw the direction the Congress was heading with regard to independence, Kinsey resigned in November of 1775. His resignation was accepted.

Returning to New Jersey, Kinsey served on the state's Supreme Court until his death in January 1802. After his death, *The New York Evening Post* printed the following:

Kinsey's is among the many unmarked graves at the Burlington Friends Cemetery.

The valuable and eminent qualities of this worthy gentleman are too well and generally known to us and in need of an obituary eulogium, independence of mind, ever disdaining to stoop even in the appearance of dissimulation; manly rectitude of principle and unspoiled integrity, directing a vigorous and enlightened understanding; honorable and social pursuits were the strongly marked textures of his public character.

Kinsey was laid to rest in the Friends Burying Ground located in Burlington, New Jersey.

Henry Knox
(1750–1806)

"Miracle on the Dorchester Heights"

Buried at Thomaston Village Cemetery,
Thomaston, Maine.

Major General • **Secretary of War**

Henry Knox was a Boston bookseller who became a senior general of the Continental Army during the Revolutionary War. When our fledgling country needed a miracle, he delivered one. In 1775, as the siege of Boston wore on, George Washington placed Knox in command of an expedition to retrieve artillery and supplies recently captured at Fort Ticonderoga on Lake Champlain in New York. Facing barely navigable roads and dangerously inclement weather, Knox made the three-hundred-mile trek north, arriving on December 5, 1775. After recovering the 120,000-pound lot of guns, mortars, and cannons from Ticonderoga, Knox transported the convoy by boat down Lake George and then led a caravan of sleds and oxen to continue the journey overland from the lake's southern end to Boston. He arrived in Boston with the guns on January 27, 1776, just in time to deploy them on Dorchester Heights. The appearance of Knox's guns on the high ground compelled the British Army and Navy to withdraw on March 17, 1776.

Henry Knox's parents, William and Mary, were Scots immigrants who came to Boston in 1729. He was the seventh of ten children. Henry's father was a shipmaster and abandoned the family and died in the West

Major General Henry Knox

Indies in 1762. Henry had been attending the famous Boston Latin School but quit after his father died and apprenticed to a bookbinder to help his family. He had access to many books and read voraciously. He educated himself in many subjects, particularly military strategy and weaponry. He also got involved in Boston's street gangs and became known as one of the toughest fighters in his neighborhood.

Knox's life changed as tensions between the American colonies and Britain escalated. He became an ardent supporter of the Patriot cause, participating in the political protests that culminated in the American Revolution. He was present at the Boston Massacre in 1770 and played an active role in the Sons of Liberty, a secret organization advocating for colonial rights.

In 1772, Knox founded the Boston Grenadier Corps, a local militia unit. In 1773, an accident with a gun cost him two fingers on his left hand. For the rest of his life, Knox would keep his hand wrapped in a handkerchief whenever he was in public.

Henry Knox (1750–1806)

In 1774, Knox began courting Lucy Flucker, the daughter of one of Boston's most prominent Loyalist families. She was a frequent visitor to his bookstore which he opened in 1771 and was very popular. John Adams was one notable patron. In June of that year, the couple wed despite opposition from her father. Lucy's brother served in the British army. After the war broke out at Lexington and Concord, the couple fled Boston. Her family disowned her after she chose to side with her husband. Their commitment to each other and the American cause would endure throughout the war and beyond.

After they left Boston, Knox volunteered for the Continental Army. His abandoned bookstore was looted, and all its stock was destroyed or stolen. He served under General Artemas Ward and built fortifications around the city. He directed cannon fire at the Battle of Bunker Hill. When George Washington arrived, he was impressed by the work Knox had done. With John Adams' help in the Continental Congress, Knox received a commission as the colonel of the artillery regiment.

As the siege of Boston wore on, Knox suggested that an expedition be sent to capture the cannons and supplies at the recently captured Fort Ticonderoga, New York. Washington agreed to put Knox in charge of the expedition. It became known as The Noble Train of Artillery, as described in the opening paragraph. It was a complete success; not one gun was lost. This pivotal maneuver forced the British to evacuate Boston in March making a significant early victory for the Continental Army. Historian Victor Brooks called the maneuver "one of the most stupendous feats of logistics" of the entire war. Knox's effort is commemorated by a series of plaques marking the Henry Knox Trail in New York and Massachusetts.

After Boston, Washington took his forces to defend New York, and Knox joined the army there. The British forces numbered about 30,000, while American forces numbered about 18,000. The outnumbered Americans were forced to retreat all the way to Pennsylvania on December 8, 1776.

On the evening of December 25, Washington made his famous trip back across the Delaware River, directed by Knox, to surprise the Hessian forces at Trenton, capturing 1000 men and much-needed supplies, greatly boosting sagging American spirits. Knox was promoted to brigadier

Knox's brigade moving cannons from Ticonderoga to the Dorchester Heights

general for this accomplishment and given command of an artillery corps expanded to five regiments. He then participated in the Battles of Princeton, Brandywine, Germantown, and Monmouth. In 1780, Knox sat on the court-martial of Major John André, the British officer who had conspired with American Brigadier General Benedict Arnold to gain British control of West Point. Knox further contributed to the Patriot cause by placing the artillery for Washington during the victorious siege of Yorktown and establishing an artillery school.

Since Cornwallis' surrender on October 19, 1781, Knox had been serving as commander of West Point. The following March, Knox became the army's youngest major general.

With peace at hand, the Confederation Congress began to order the demobilization of the army in April 1783. The next month, in May, Knox founded the Society of the Cincinnati, a fraternal society of Revolutionary War officers that survives to this day. He served as its first Secretary General. After the Treaty of Paris formally ended the war that September, Knox oversaw the withdrawal of British troops from New York. When the last British troops left New York City in November 1783, Knox rode at the head of forces that took over the city and attended Washington's farewell address to his officers at Fraunces Tavern. As Washington completed his speech, Knox was the first officer to come up and embrace Washington with a hug and tears. With Washington's resignation, Knox held the post of senior officer in the army.

In March 1785 the Confederation Congress appointed Knox the nation's second United States Secretary of War. He served in that position until Washington was elected President and appointed him as Secretary of War under the new constitution in 1789. As Secretary, he supported plans for a national militia, supervised the initial steps of forming a regular navy and managed conflicts with many groups of native peoples.

Knox's grave

In January 1795, Knox was forced to resign due to rumors that he had profited from contracts for frigates to fight pirates. Washington accepted his resignation with regret. Knox and his family settled on an estate at Thomaston, Massachusetts (now Maine), which he called Montpelier. During this period, Knox reportedly gained a lot of weight, approaching nearly 300 pounds. On October 22, 1806, he swallowed a chicken bone that lodged in his throat and caused an infection. He died three days later, on October 25, at age 56. He was buried on his estate with full military honors. Numerous towns, cities and military installations bear his name, most notably Fort Knox, Kentucky.

Francis Lewis
(1713–1802)

"All That Glitters Is Not Gold"

Buried at Trinity Church Cemetery,
New York, New York.

Declaration of Independence • Articles of Confederation

Francis Lewis was a Welsh-born merchant from New York City who was elected to the Continental Congress, where he signed the Declaration of Independence and the Articles of Confederation.

Lewis was born March 21, 1713, in the village of Llandaff, Glamorganshire, Wales, slightly northwest of the capital, Cardiff. He was the only child of Reverend Francis Lewis, an Anglican clergyman, and his wife, Amy (née Pettingal) Lewis, the daughter of an Anglican clergyman. Lewis was orphaned at age five and went to live with relatives, including a maternal aunt. He grew up in both Wales and Scotland and learned the Gaelic and Welsh languages. The Pettingal family, especially an uncle who was the dean at St. Paul's Cathedral, saw to his education at the prestigious Westminster School in London.

Upon graduation, Lewis became an apprentice at a mercantile business in London. When he turned 21, he inherited properties left by his father. He sold them and used the proceeds to start his own business in partnership with Edward Annesley. He acquired merchandise and sailed for New York City, arriving in 1734 or 1735. He left some of the goods

Francis Lewis

with his partner in New York and took the rest to Philadelphia. There, he lived for two years before returning to New York.

Back in New York, Lewis was involved in the trans-Atlantic trade, making trips to several northern European ports, Saint Petersburg, Scotland, and Africa. Twice, he survived shipwrecks off the Irish coast. Circa 1743, Lewis broke up his business partnership with Annesley but married his sister, Elizabeth Annesley, on June 15, 1745. The couple had seven children, three of whom survived to adulthood:

- Ann Lewis (1748–1802) married Captain George Robertson (1742–1791) of the Royal Navy.
- Francis Lewis Jr. (1749–1814) served as churchwarden of St George's Parish in Flushing, New York, from 1791 to 1794. He married Elizabeth Ludlow (d. 1831), daughter of Gabriel Ludlow, Esq.
- Morgan Lewis (1754–1844) married Gertrude Livingston, the daughter of Judge Robert Livingston of Clermont. He was a governor and attorney general of New York.

Francis Lewis (1713–1802)

In 1756, at the outbreak of the French and Indian War, Lewis supplied uniforms to the British. He was at Fort Oswego that August, delivering uniforms, when General Montcalm's forces and Indian allies attacked. Lewis was standing next to Colonel James Mercer, the fort's commander, when a cannonball killed him. The fort was surrendered to Montcalm, who permitted the natives to select thirty prisoners to keep or kill. Lewis was among them. While being tortured by his Indian captors, Lewis spoke in Welsh. The natives recognized similarities in the language and stopped and spoke with him. The chief then took Lewis to Montreal where he requested to return to his family. However, he was instead sent to France as a prisoner, where he remained until the end of the war.

In 1763, Lewis was exchanged and returned to New York. There, the British granted him 5,000 acres for his service. He re-established his mercantile business and quickly accumulated a large fortune, permitting him to retire at age 52 in 1765. The *Encyclopedia of American Wealth* estimated that his holdings ranked him fifth among all the signers of the Declaration.

In 1765, with the passage of The Stamp Act, Lewis turned against the British government. He was appointed to the Stamp Act Congress, held in New York. In 1877, granddaughter Julia Delafield wrote, "On October 25 [1765] they met for the last time, and had the honor of being the first body to pass the resolution that the colonies ought to be united and act in common. Among the members of the New York committee we find the names of Francis Lewis and Robert R. Livingston. This Congress had not in its ranks a more consistent and energetic opponent of the tyranny of the mother country than Lewis."

During the crisis, Lewis moved his business and family to Whitestone, now part of Flushing, Queens County, New York. In 1771, he moved the business back to New York City and, with his son, Francis Lewis Jr., became one of the leading merchants under the banner of Francis Lewis and Son. He also became a founding member of the Sons of Liberty there.

To protest the closing of the port of Boston in 1774, New Yorkers formed the Committee of Fifty to oversee the city. Lewis, by unanimous consent, became the 51st member on May 16. The committee eventually included sixty members who established the colony's new government.

In 1775, sensing the risk of invasion, Lewis again moved the family and their belongings to Whitestone. He was elected to the Second Continental Congress on April 22, 1775, serving until November 19, 1779. He signed the Olive Branch Petition and used his own resources to help supply the army with clothing. On October 9, 1775, Lewis, John Alsop, and Philip Livingston were contracted by the Secret Committee of the Continental Congress to supply arms and ammunition. Benjamin Rush called Lewis "a very honest man and very useful in executive business."

When the vote for independence was called on July 2, 1776, New York's delegation abstained due to the lack of instructions from the provincial assembly. Thus, when independence was declared unanimously, 12 to 0, on July 4, New York was not among the colonies. Finally, the New York delegation received instructions to approve the measure, and Francis Lewis and the others signed the Declaration of Independence on August 2.

Only a few weeks later, on August 27, 1776, during the Battle of Brooklyn Heights, the British captured the Lewis estate at Whitestone. British Captain Birtch and a troop of light horsemen were sent to destroy the Lewis home. As the soldiers approached and a British warship opened fire on the house, Elizabeth remained calm. Thinking her shoe buckles were made of gold, a soldier bent down and tore them off.

"All that glitters is not gold," said Elizabeth to the young man. The buckles were just pinchbeck.

The soldiers ransacked the house, destroying books, papers, pictures, and furniture. They also took Elizabeth Lewis as a captive and imprisoned her without a bed or a change of clothes and little food.

Upon learning of this, General Washington ordered the arrest of two Loyalist women in Philadelphia and said these captives would receive the same treatment as Mrs. Lewis. Finally, an exchange was arranged, but Elizabeth's health was weakened.

That winter, while the troops were at Valley Forge, Lewis was a strong supporter of General Washington when the Conway Cabal became public. Meanwhile, in York, Pennsylvania, Lewis worked on the Articles of Confederation, which he signed in November 1778. He was just one of sixteen men to sign both the Declaration and the Articles.

He returned home in 1779 to be with his ailing wife. She passed in June 1779, and Lewis did not seek re-election after his term was up in November of that year. He then served as the chairman of the Continental Board of Admiralty until he retired from public service in 1781.

In his later years, from 1784 to 1786, Lewis was a vestryman at Trinity Church. He enjoyed the company of his family, especially his grandchildren. Lewis died on December 31, 1802, at age 89. He was buried in an unmarked grave at Trinity Church Cemetery in New York City. The descendants of the Signers of the Declaration of Independence added a granite marker and plaque in 1947.

Francis Lewis had many interesting descendants:

- His son Morgan served in the Continental Army during the Revolutionary War and later held many offices in New York, including governor (1804-1807). He was a major general in the War of 1812.
- Through Morgan, he was a grandfather of Margret Lewis (1780–1860), who married New York lawyer and politician Maturin Livingston and became parents to twelve children.
- Through his son Francis Jr., he was a grandfather of Gabriel Ludlow Lewis.
- Through his daughter Ann, he was a grandfather to Marianne Robertson (1779–1829), who married John Bird Sumner, the Archbishop of Canterbury and brother of Charles Richard Sumner, bishop of Winchester.
- Great-grandson Manny Livingston died at the Battle of Gettysburg during the Civil War.
- Great-great-great-grandson William A. Wellman was a Hollywood director.

Francis Lewis is also remembered in many ways:

- John Trumbull's 1819 painting *Declaration of Independence* includes Lewis, near Richard Stockton and John Witherspoon. This painting hangs in the Rotunda of the Capitol in Washington, D.C.

- A granite boulder bears his name in the memorial park of the 55 signers near the Washington Monument in Washington, D.C.
- Francis Lewis High School and P.S. 79, "The Francis Lewis School" in Queens, New York, are named after Lewis.
- Francis Lewis Boulevard, known locally as "Franny Lew" or "Franny Lewie," stretches almost the entire north/south length of Queens.
- Francis Lewis Park is located under the Queens approach of the Bronx-Whitestone Bridge, on the site of the Lewis home.
- A society of the Children of the American Revolution located in Queens, New York, is named for him.
- A Masonic lodge, Francis Lewis #273, is in Whitestone.

Grave of Francis Lewis

William Livingston
(1723–1790)

"First Governor of New Jersey"

Buried at Green-Wood Cemetery,
Brooklyn, New York.

Continental Association • Governor • Constitution

William Livingston is best known as the first Governor of New Jersey following the Declaration of Independence. He was the brother of Philip Livingston, who signed that document. Livingston also served in the Continental Congress, where he signed the Continental Association. He was a delegate to the Constitutional Convention and signed the US Constitution.

Livingston, born November 30, 1723, in Albany, New York, was a son of Philip Livingston (1686–1749), the 2nd Lord of Livingston Manor, and his wife, Catherine (née Van Brugh) Livingston, the only child of Pieter Van Brugh, the Mayor of Albany. Livingston's siblings included Robert Livingston (1708–1790), the 3rd Lord of Livingston Manor; Peter Van Brugh Livingston (1710–1792), the Treasurer of New York; and Philip Livingston (1716–1778), a future signer of the Declaration of Independence.

Livingston was educated by tutors and in the local schools. When he was 13, he lived among the Iroquois in the Mohawk Valley with Henry Barclay, an Anglican missionary and Yale graduate. Livingston then enrolled at Yale at age 14 in 1737 and graduated in 1741, having

William Livingston

studied multiple languages and writing. Following his father's wishes, he next studied law under James Alexander in New York City and became his clerk. Alexander was the father of William Alexander, who became known as Lord Stirling and was a prominent major general during the Revolution. Livingston soon found himself bored with his law studies, and in the spring of 1746, he wrote an anonymous article attacking his boss's wife, Mary Spratt Provoost Alexander, a successful merchant. Alexander terminated the apprenticeship.

During this time, the young Livingston continued his writing and, in 1747, penned the pastoral poem "Philosophic Solitude, or the Choice of a Rural Life." This was one of the first successful poems by an American and was published many times by the 1800s.

Not deterred, Livingston's father found legal work for his son with William Smith, Sr., another leading attorney. Livingston studied with William Smith, Jr., and was admitted to the New York bar in 1748. He then set up a practice in New York City and Albany.

Livingston married Susannah French, the daughter of Philip French III and Susanna (née Brockholst) French, in 1748. The couple had 13 children, seven of whom lived to adulthood. Livingston also developed business associations with William Alexander, Lord Stirling, and John Morin Scott, a future Continental Congressman.

In 1752, Livingston was appointed by the New York colonial legislature to publish a history of the statutes enacted since the colony's founding, entitled *Digest of the Laws of the Colony, 1691–1751*. With partners William Smith, Jr., and John Morin Scott, he started a weekly journal, the *Independent Reflector*, the first New York newspaper to be critical of Catholic and Anglican Church activities in the New York City area. The three owners, Presbyterians, were called "The Triumvirate" by their contemporaries, who met weekly at The King's Arms tavern in an association dubbed The Whig Club, drinking to the memories of Oliver Cromwell and John Hampden. Their activities may have prevented the installation of an Anglican bishop in New York and diminished investment in King's College, which ultimately became Columbia University, founded by Anglicans. This put them at odds with New York Chief Justice James DeLancey, James Alexander, and Reverend Henry Barclay, Livingston's tutor.

The *Independent Reflector* only lasted until late 1753, after which Livingston published independent essays in the *New York Mercury* under the heading "The Watch Tower." These were early writings opposing a state-sanctioned church. King's College opened on October 31, 1754, and never appointed a bishop.

In 1754, Livingston was a commissioner working on the boundaries between New York and Massachusetts. He also helped to found the New York Society Library, which is still in existence. He then served briefly in the New York Provincial Assembly from 1759 to 1761, representing Livingston Manor in a rotation of family members through the office. In 1764, Livingston was back at negotiating boundaries, this time between New Jersey and New York. He was elected to the American Philosophical Society in 1768.

Livingston was back to writing history in 1770, releasing a history of the French and Indian War from the British perspective. In 1772, at age 49, he retired to New Jersey, moving to his wife's home in Elizabethtown. That winter, a fifteen-year-old Alexander Hamilton stayed with them while attending Francis Barber's grammar school. Livingston purchased land in Elizabethtown and started construction of a mansion dubbed Liberty Hall. It was completed in 1773 and stands to this day.

As tensions mounted with England, in December 1773, Livingston was among the Elizabethtown Committee of Correspondence, including Stephen Crane, John De Hart, William P. Smith, Elias Boudinot, and John Chetwood. On July 23, 1774, the New York legislature appointed Livingston to the First Continental Congress. There, he signed the Continental Association. He was then appointed to the Second Continental Congress, serving until June 1776, before the signing of the Declaration of Independence. Rather, he returned to New Jersey, which had declared its statehood and appointed Livingston as its first governor.

Livingston remained the governor of New Jersey for the rest of his life. During the early years immediately following independence, with the British headquartered in New York City, New Jersey was in a precarious position. Livingston dealt with Loyalists attempting to trade with the British and the regular movements of British troops through its borders. Between 1776 and 1779, Livingston moved his family to the Bowers-Livingston-Osborn House in Parsippany to stay away from British sympathizers and to avoid capture. There was a significant bounty on Livington's head, and the British frequently visited and looted Liberty Hall in his absence.

In June 1777, Livingston helped start a newspaper called the *New Jersey Gazette* that would be loyal to the cause. He then contributed to it with polemics and articles written under fourteen different pseudonyms. Scholars have dubbed him one of the most important propagandists in the colonies and certainly in New Jersey.

In June 1779, Loyalists raided the Parsippany home based on false information that Livingston would be there. Fortunately, he was not, and the perpetrators were captured. It is surmised a distant relative, the Loyalist mayor of New York City, David Mathews, was behind the attempt. The Livingstons returned to Liberty Hall later in 1779 and began restoring the property. In 1782, Livingston was honored to be a fellow of the American Academy of the Arts and Sciences.

In 1787, Livingston was elected to attend the Constitutional Convention on behalf of New Jersey. At 63, as one of the older delegates, his health limited his participation, but he did support the New Jersey

Plan, which defended the representation of the smaller states. Livingston, along with David Brearly, William Paterson, and Jonathan Dayton, signed the Constitution on behalf of New Jersey. Livingston was asked, the following year, to be the Minister to the Netherlands, but he declined the position. He wrote a commentary (in French) comparing the government of England with the new US Constitution entitled *Examen du Gouvernement d'Angleterre comparé aux Constitutions des Etats-Unis*. At the outset of the French Revolution, Emmanuel-Joseph Sieyès cited Livingston's commentary in his pamphlet *What Is the Third Estate?*

The grave of William Livingston.

Susannah Livingston died in July 1789 and was initially buried in the Trinity Churchyard in lower Manhattan. Livingston "very much regretted" her passing, according to the local newspapers. Meanwhile, he oversaw the implementation of the new state and federal offices for New Jersey under the new US Constitution.

Livingston died in Elizabeth, New Jersey, on July 25, 1790. He was 66. Wrote the *Federal Gazette*, ". . . America bewails the loss of one of her most distinguished patriots . . ." Livingston was interred next to his wife at Trinity Churchyard in New York City. In 1844, both husband and wife were exhumed and moved to Green-Wood Cemetery in Brooklyn, New York.

William and Susannah's children included:

- Susannah Livingston (1748–1840) married John Cleves Symmes (1742–1814) and became the stepmother-in-law of President William Henry Harrison.
- Catherine Livingston (1751–1813) married Matthew Ridley (1746–1789) and later her cousin John Livingston (1750–1822), son of Robert Livingston.

- Mary Livingston (born 1753) married James Linn in May 1771.
- William Livingston Jr. (1754–1817) married Mary Lennington.
- Philip Van Brugh Livingston (born 1755) died unmarried.
- Sarah Livingston (1756–1802) was educated at home and raised to be politically aware, even serving as her father's secretary. At only 17, she married John Jay and accompanied him to Spain and Paris, where he helped negotiate the Treaty of Paris in 1783. Sarah is credited with writing the toast used to celebrate the treaty at the official dinner. Back in New York, Jay was appointed the Secretary of Foreign Affairs, and the couple established weekly diplomatic dinners in the new capital, New York City. She was also First Lady of New York when her husband was governor and then wife of the 1st Chief Justice of the Supreme Court.
- Henry Brockholst Livingston (1757–1823) was a lawyer who became a member of the US Supreme Court (1807–1823). He is buried in Green-Wood Cemetery.
- Judith Livingston (1758–1843) married John W. Watkins, an attorney.
- Philip French Livingston (1760–c. 1765) drowned in a boating accident in the Hackensack River.
- John Lawrence Livingston (1762–1781) died at sea aboard the USS *Saratoga*.

Other interesting descendants of William Livingston include:

- Julia Kean, the wife of Hamilton Fish, former Governor of New York and US Secretary of State.
- Thomas Kean, former Governor of New Jersey.
- Edwin Brockholst Livingston was a historian who focused on the Livingston family history.
- Henry Brockholst Ledyard, former Mayor of Detroit.

William Livingston is honored by the town of Livingston, New Jersey; Governor Livingston High School in Berkeley Heights, New Jersey; and the Livingston campus at Rutgers University.

Thomas Lynch
(1727 – 1776)

South Carolina Son of Liberty

Buried at Saint Anne's Churchyard,
Annapolis, Maryland.

Continental Association

Thomas Lynch, Sr., was a South Carolina planter who served in the Stamp Act Congress and Continental Congress, where he signed the Continental Association. Before signing the Declaration of Independence, he was stricken, and his son, Thomas Lynch, Jr., took his place.

Thomas Lynch was born circa 1727, in St. James Santee Parish, Berkeley County, South Carolina, the son of Thomas Lynch, a wealthy rice planter, and his wife, Sabina (née Vanderhorst) Lynch. This elder Lynch was likely the grandson of Jonack Lynch, who emigrated from Connaught Ireland, in the late 1600s. He had decided to forego planting silkworms and Indian corn instead planting rice and indigo. He had grants for fifteen thousand acres in Craven County, on the North and South Santee Rivers, between Charles Towne and Georgetown. By the time he died in 1738, he had amassed seven plantations and nearly two hundred slaves.

As the only surviving child, Lynch inherited his family's vast estates. Lynch first married Elizabeth Allston in 1745 and fathered three children. He married second Hannah Motte, the daughter of Jacob Motte

Thomas Lynch

and Elizabeth Martin, on March 6, 1755. This marriage produced a daughter and Thomas Lynch, Jr. Hannah's brother, Isaac Motte, was later a South Carolina Congressman. Following Hannah's death during childbirth, Lynch married Annabella Josephiné Dé'Illiard.

Lynch served as a representative for the Parish of St. James, Santee, in the House of Commons and Provincial Assembly from 1751 to 1757, 1761 to 1763, 1765, 1768, and 1772. He was the first president of the Winyah Indigo Society from 1755 to 1757 and was the second wealthiest person in the colony.

Upon passage of the Stamp Act in Parliament, Lynch was a delegate to the Stamp Act Congress of 1765 in New York. He served on a committee that drafted a petition to the House of Commons demanding the Act be repealed. In 1769, Lynch served on the General Committee of the Non-Importation Association. He then helped run the colony in

Thomas Lynch (1727 – 1776)

the years leading up to the Revolution while colonial governor Charles Montagu was absent.

Visiting Charleston in early 1773, the Massachusetts lawyer and patriot Josiah Quincy described Lynch as "a man of sense, and a patriot." Lynch was highly active with the Sons of Liberty in South Carolina. In July of 1774, Lynch, Henry Middleton, John Rutledge, Christopher Gadsden, and Edward Rutledge were sent to the Continental Congress to represent South Carolina in Philadelphia that September. Wrote Silas Deane to his wife about Lynch,

> I will now give you the character of the Delegates, beginning at South Carolina, as they are the Southernmost. Mr. Lynch is a gentleman about sixty, and could you see him; I need say nothing more. He has much the appearance of Mr. Ja[mes] Mumford, deceased; dresses as plain, or plainer; is of immense fortune, and has his family with him. He wears the manufacture of this country, is plain, sensible, above ceremony, and carries with him more fore in his very appearance than most powdered folks in their conversation. He wears his hair strait [sic], his clothes in the plainest order, and is highly esteemed.

Lynch was an active member of the First Continental Congress, earning the respect of his fellow delegates. While he returned home to South Carolina in October 1774 after signing the Continental Association, he was re-elected to the Congress on March 4, 1775, along with the same group.

The following month, shots were fired at Lexington and Concord. Lynch was a supporter of appointing George Washington as the Commander-in-Chief of the Continental Army. He was able, through John Adams, to convince the New England delegation and then convinced the Southern delegation. Congress then appointed Washington.

Lynch joined Benjamin Franklin and Benjamin Harrison on a committee sent to Cambridge, Massachusetts, to discuss with General George Washington about "the most effectual method of continuing, supporting, and regulating the Continental Army." Washington mentioned his plan to arm ships to raid the British supply lines. The committee liked the idea and recommended it to Congress, thereby establishing "George Washington's Navy," the nation's first organized naval force.

Back home, Lynch was elected by St. James Santee Parish to the Second Provincial Congress for 1775 to 1776 and the first South Carolina General Assembly for 1776 but did not participate. Lynch was back in Philadelphia in 1776 as a member of the Second Continental Congress. He participated in the discussions concerning independence but suffered a debilitating stroke, paralyzing him. Thomas Lynch, Jr., was dispatched to Congress as an additional delegate to assist his father at the signing of the Declaration of Independence. The fifty-five other delegates left a blank space between Heywood and Rutledge in the South Carolina section of the document in honor of the elder Lynch.

After the document was signed, the Lynches headed back to South Carolina, but Lynch suffered another stroke and died on the way in December 1776. An obituary from the time stated,

> From the announcement of the present struggle in favour of American freedom, this gentleman acted a distinguished part and proved himself the firm, intrepid patriot. In private life, he was not less conspicuous, a warm and steady friend, hospitable, generous, and benevolent. He died in the fiftieth year of his age, greatly regretted by his relations and countrymen.

Rather than transporting his father's body hundreds of miles, Lynch Jr. buried him in St. Anne's Churchyard in Annapolis, Maryland. The younger Lynch followed in his father's footsteps in Congress until he was lost at sea in 1779.

After Lynch's death, his widow Annabella married South Carolina Governor William Moultrie. Lynch's daughter Elizabeth married James Hamilton. Their son, James Hamilton Jr., was elected governor of South Carolina in 1830 and led the state through the Nullification crisis through 1832.

Joseph Plumb Martin
(1760 – 1850)

Private Yankee Doodle

Buried at Sandy Point Cemetery.
Stockton Springs, Maine.

Military

Joseph Plumb Martin was a Connecticut militiaman and member of the Continental Army who served mostly in the Northern Theater during the American Revolution. He was lost to history until his detailed memoir from 1830 was rediscovered in the 1950s, providing a priceless primary source for the day-to-day experiences of the common soldier.

Martin was born on November 21, 1760, in Becket, Massachusetts, the son of Reverend Ebenezer Martin and his wife, Susannah (née Plumb) Martin. His father was Yale-educated and from a well-to-do family.

When young Joseph was seven years old, he was sent to live in Milford, Connecticut, with his affluent grandparents. Milford was ninety miles south of Becket, on the Long Island Sound. Here, Martin received a well-rounded education, including reading and writing.

On April 19, 1775, the Battle of Lexington and Concord occurred near Boston, Massachusetts, harkening "The Shot Heard 'Round the World." Young Joseph, approaching his 15th birthday, wanted to fight with the rebels, but his grandparents resisted the idea. When Joseph threatened to run away and join an American privateer to fight the British

Navy, they relented and allowed him to join the Connecticut Militia. He enlisted in June 1776, aged fifteen, as a private.

Martin's first tour of duty took him to the New York City area, serving under George Washington, at the start of the British Long Island Campaign. This was disastrous for the Americans, highlighted by Washington's escape across the East River to Manhattan in the fog on August 19, 1776. Martin participated in the Battles of Harlem Heights and White Plains before his tour ended in December 1776, just before Washington's crossing of the Delaware River and the Battles of Trenton and Princeton. Instead, Martin returned to his grandparents in Connecticut.

Joseph Plumb Martin photograph

The following spring, still itching to join the fight, Martin joined the Continental Army on April 22, 1777, and served until the end of the war. He was initially assigned to the 17th Continental Regiment, formerly the 8th Connecticut Regiment, under Brigadier General James Mitchell Varnum.

In 1777, Martin participated in the Siege of Fort Mifflin near Philadelphia and the Battle of Germantown prior to encamping at Valley Forge for the winter.

The following year, Martin was assigned to the Light Infantry and was promoted to corporal. He participated in the Battle of Monmouth that summer.

In 1779, Martin camped with Washington at Morristown. During the summer of 1780, Martin was promoted to sergeant and was assigned to the Corps of Sappers and Miners upon recommendation from his superior officers. He then witnessed John André being escorted to his execution that fall.

At the decisive Battle of Yorktown during the fall of 1781, Martin's unit was the vanguard for Alexander Hamilton's regiment, digging

Joseph Plumb Martin (1760–1850)

parallel entrenchments and clearing the field of defenses before Hamilton's capture of Redoubt #10. Martin's account of the action:

At dark the detachment was formed and advanced beyond the trenches and lay down on the ground to await the signal for advancing to the attack, which was to be three shells from a certain battery near where we were lying. All the batteries in our line were silent, and we lay anxiously waiting for the signal. The two brilliant planets, Jupiter and Venus, were in close contact in the western hemisphere, the same direction that the sig-

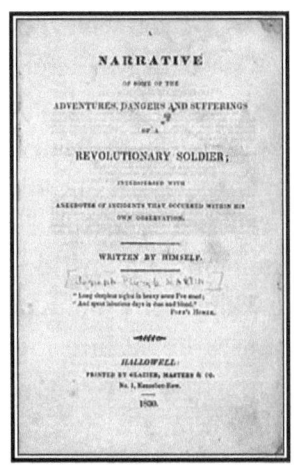

Martin's memoir

nal was to be made in. When I happened to cast my eyes to that quarter, which was often, and I caught a glance of them, I was ready to spring on my feet, thinking they were the signal for starting. Our watchword was "Rochambeau," the commander of the French forces' name, a good watchword, for being pronounced Ro-sham-bow, it sounded, when pronounced quick, like rush-on-boys.

We had not lain here long before the expected signal was given, for us and the French, who were to storm the other redoubt, by the three shells with their fiery trains mounting the air in quick succession. The word up, up, was then reiterated through the detachment. We immediately moved silently on toward the redoubt we were to attack, with unloaded muskets. Just as we arrived at the abatis, the enemy discovered us and directly opened a sharp fire upon us. We were now at a place where many of our large shells had burst in the ground, making holes sufficient to bury an ox in. The men, having their eyes fixed upon what was transacting before them, were every now and then falling into these holes. I thought the British were killing us off at a great rate. At length, one of the holes happening to pick me up, I found out the mystery of the huge slaughter.

As soon as the firing began, our people began to cry, "The fort's our own!" and it was "Rush on boys." The Sappers and Miners soon cleared a passage for the infantry, who entered it rapidly. Our Miners were ordered not to enter the fort, but there was no stopping them. "We will go," said they. "Then go to the d———," said the commanding officer of our corps, "if you will." I could not pass at the entrance we had made, it was so crowded. I therefore forced a passage at a place where I saw our shot had cut away some of the abatis; several others entered at the same place. While passing, a man at my side received a ball in his head and fell under my feet, crying out bitterly. While crossing the trench, the enemy threw hand grenades (small shells) into it. They were so thick that I at first thought them cartridge papers on fire, but was soon undeceived by their cracking. As I mounted the breastwork, I met an old associate hitching himself down into the trench. I knew him by the light of the enemy's musketry, it was so vivid. The fort was taken and all quiet in a very short time. Immediately after the firing ceased, I went out to see what had become of my wounded friend and the other that fell in the passage. They were both dead. In the heat of the action, I saw a British soldier jump over the walls of the fort next to the river and go down the bank, which was almost perpendicular and twenty or thirty feet high. When he came to the beach he made off for the town, and if he did not make good use of his legs, I never saw a man that did.

Following the victory at Yorktown, Martin accompanied Washington's army back to New York and was discharged in June 1783, before the British evacuated and the Continental Army mustered out that fall.

Next, Martin taught school in New York before settling on Maine's frontier as one of the founders of the town of Prospect, near modern-day Stockton Springs. There, in 1794, he married Lucy Clewley (born 1776). The couple had five children, including Joseph, born 1799; Nathan and Thomas, twins born 1803; James Sullivan, born 1810; and Susan, born 1812.

Also in 1794, Martin's modest 100-acre farm was embroiled in a dispute with former Major General Henry Knox, who as a land speculator, claiming 600,000 acres in what is now known as Waldo County, Maine. Martin's farm was within this claim, and Martin sued to be able to farm his land.

In 1797, Knox's claim was upheld, and Martin's land was appraised at $170, payable over six years in three installments of either cash or farm products. Martin had no money and begged Knox to keep the land, but the general ignored him. However, there is no record of Knox even responding to Martin, and Martin stayed on his land, farming only eight acres.

Over the years, Martin became well-known locally as a farmer, selectman, justice of the peace, and town clerk, a role he held for over twenty-five years.

General Knox died in 1806 and never demanded payment from Martin. However, by 1811, his farmland was reduced to fifty acres and then to nothing in 1818, when he appeared in Massachusetts General Court with other veterans seeking his pension. Martin then received $96 per year for the rest of his life.

Knowing other veterans were having difficulty achieving their pensions, as the nation passed its fiftieth birthday since the Declaration of Independence, Martin began writing about his experiences to call attention to their service. He had written stories and poems over the years, but in 1830, he completed a memoir based on his now-lost journals. This memoir, entitled *A Narrative of Some of the Adventures, Dangers, and Sufferings of a Revolutionary Soldier, Interspersed with Anecdotes of Incidents that Occurred Within His Own Observations*, was published anonymously in Hallowell, Maine, but received little attention. In 1835, the Federal government began offering pensions to enlisted soldiers or their surviving families.

In 1836, on the sixtieth anniversary, a platoon of United States Light Infantry, passing through Prospect, Maine, learned of Plumb and his location. They stopped outside his house and fired a salute in honor of the seventy-five-year-old veteran.

Martin died on May 2, 1850, at age 89. He was buried at the Sandy Point Cemetery, near Stockton Springs, Maine, next to his wife.

In the 1950s, a copy of Martin's book was donated to the Morristown National Historical Park. Little, Brown then published a new edition in 1962 under the title *Private Yankee Doodle*. Other editions have followed with various introductions and forewords by famous historians.

Often cited by scholars and used by re-enactors, Martin's memoir is also critiqued for potential bias or embellishment. However, he does convey in detail the daily experiences of the common soldiers, especially at difficult times such as the winter at Valley Forge.

Martin has since been portrayed in various television documentaries about the American Revolution. Copies of his first edition book reside at the Library of Congress, the US Army Military History Institute at Carlisle, Pennsylvania, and at the Morristown National Historical Park. The Valley Forge National Historical Park has a trail named in his honor that encircles the park.

Martin's grave

John Marshall
(1755 – 1835)

The Great Chief Justice

Buried at Shockoe Hill Cemetery,
Richmond, Virginia.

Supreme Court — Secretary of State — House of Representatives

John Marshall was a Virginia attorney who was a distant relation of Thomas Jefferson. Marshall is one of few Americans who has served in all three branches of the Federal Government. He served briefly as Secretary of State under John Adams and was a US House Representative from Virginia, prior to becoming the longest-tenured and most influential Chief Justice of the Supreme Court in American history.

Marshall was born in a two-room log cabin on September 24, 1755, in Germantown, Fauquier County, Virginia, near present-day Midland, the son of Thomas Marshall, a surveyor and land agent for Lord Fairfax, and Mary Randolph (née Kieth) Marshall, who was the daughter of Thomas Randolph of Tuckahoe Plantation and a second cousin of Thomas Jefferson. In the 1760s, the increasing family moved to Markham, Virginia. John Marshall was the first of fifteen children. Younger brother James Markham Marshall later became a federal judge. Marshall was also the first cousin of Kentucky Senator Humphrey Marshall, and first cousin, three generations removed, of George C. Marshall, Army Chief of Staff, Secretary of Defense, and Secretary of State.

Marshall was not formally educated, except for one year during which he befriended James Monroe. Otherwise, Marshall was encouraged to

John Marshall

read widely and greatly respected his parents. Father Thomas Marshall purchased the Oak Hill Plantation in the early 1770s, and the family moved there.

At the outbreak of the American Revolution in 1775, Thomas and John enrolled in the 3rd Virginia Regiment. The following year, Marshall was a lieutenant in the Continental Army's 11th Virginia Regiment. He fought at the Battles of Brandywine, Germantown, and Monmouth, and was at Valley Forge during the bitter winter of 1777/8.

Following his furlough from the Army, Marshall attended the College of William and Mary and read law under George Wythe. He was admitted to the bar in 1780 and after a brief return to the Army in the Yorktown area, he was elected to the Virginia House of Delegates in 1782. During his time in Yorktown, he met Mary Ambler, the daughter of Jaquelyn "Jack" Ambler, a member if Virginia's Council of State. He married Mary on January 3, 1783.

John Marshall (1755–1835)

At the Virginia House, Marshall was well-connected thanks to friends such as James Monroe and Richard Henry Lee and his father-in-law. Soon, Marshall, too, was elected to the Council of State as his father-in-law became Treasurer. Marshall was the youngest to serve on the Council up to that point, at only 28.

In 1785, Marshall also became the Recorded of the Richmond City Hustings Court and began to build his law practice. In 1786, he purchased his cousin's, Edmund Randolph's, practice when he became Governor of Virginia. His reputation grew, especially when he represented the heirs of Lord Fairfax in *Hite v. Fairfax*.

A strong supporter of the new Constitution, Marshall was elected to the Virginia Ratifying Convention in 1788, siding with James Madison on convincing delegates to approve, winning 89 to 79.

During the early days of the Washington Administration, Marshall rebuffed an offer to become the US Attorney for Virginia despite being confirmed by the Senate. Instead, he focused on his law practice and building the Federalist Party within the state, counter to his cousin, Thomas Jefferson, who led the opposing Democratic-Republicans. He was also the Grand Master of Masons in Virginia during 1794 and 1795. He again rebuffed Washington in 1795 when asked to be US Attorney General. Instead, he continued to serve Virginia in a variety of roles. The following year, he appeared before the same court to argue the *Ware v. Hylton* case, and though he lost, he acquitted himself well.

Early in the Adams administration, in 1797, the relations with Revolutionary France were tenuous and Marshall was one of three delegates, including Charles Cotesworth Pinckney and Elbridge Gerry, who were sent to France to negotiate. After a fifteen-minute meeting with French Foreign Minister Talleyrand, they were met by three of Talleyrand's subordinates who demanded bribes. Pinckney and Gerry left immediately, but Marshall lingered for two months and sent secret correspondence to Adams. He then returned to the US in April 1798, and Congress demanded to see the correspondence. When the public learned of the bribes in what was known as the XYZ Affair, Congress imposed an embargo on France in July 1798 and the two sides harassed each other's ships. During this Quasi-War, Marshall supported most of

Congress's measures but opposed the Alien and Sedition Acts that were meant to suppress dissent.

In September 1798, at the urging of George Washington and Patrick Henry and owing to his popularity in the XYZ Affair, Marshall ran for and won Virginia's 13th Congressional District, defeating Democratic-Republican incumbent John Clopton. During the campaign, Marshall declined an appointment to be an associate justice on the US Supreme Court. Instead, his friend, Bushrod Washington, the nephew of the president, was selected.

Next, in May 1800, President Adams first nominated Marshall to be the Secretary of War but changed his mind and switched to Secretary of State. He was confirmed by the Senate on May 13, 1800, and took office on June 6, replacing the fired Timothy Pickering. Adams now wanted peace with France. This was achieved in October.

The 1800 presidential election was a very close affair, with the Democratic-Republican ticket of Thomas Jefferson and Aaron Burr defeating the incumbent Federalist ticket of John Adams and Charles Cotesworth Pinckney, 73 electoral votes to 65. In the Electoral College of the time, the top two vote-getters would be president and vice-president, respectively. During the 1796 election, Adams and Jefferson, despite being in separate parties, were elected. This time, each elector had two votes and placed one vote each on their two candidates on the ticket. The plan was to have one or two electors not vote for the intended vice presidential candidate, instead voting for a candidate unlikely to win. But this did not happen as expected, and both Jefferson and Burr had the same number of electoral votes. The election then went to the House of Representatives where each state had one vote. After thirty-six ballots and a deal struck by Alexander Hamilton, Jefferson was named the President and Burr the Vice President.

Meanwhile, during this lame-duck period, President Adams and the Congress passed the Judiciary Act of 1801, later known as the Midnight Judges Act, expanding the federal judiciary and reducing the number of Supreme Court justices from six to five upon the next vacancy. This was intended to deny the next president an opportunity to appoint a justice until a second vacancy had occurred. However, Chief Justice Oliver Ellsworth suddenly resigned due to poor health, Adams needed to replace him. At first, he offered it to John Jay, who had held the position in the past. Jay refused. Secretary of State Marshall suggested that Justice William Paterson be elevated to Chief Justice, but Adams rejected the idea, stating, "I believe I must nominate you."

The Senate confirmed Marshall on January 27, 1801, and he took office on February 4. President Adams also requested he stay on as Secretary of State until the inauguration on March 4. Of course, it had yet to be determined who would be President. The 36th ballot occurred two weeks later, on February 17. Thus, had that ballot not been successful, and the controversy continued, it was possible that Marshall, still next in line at Secretary of State and now Chief Justice, would have been the active president. Marshall now set about implementing the Midnight Judges Act and its appointments. Critics saw this as a court-packing maneuver as judges had to be approved for the new lower-level courts. Marshall raced against the inauguration clock and ran out of time on the last day to complete them all due to not being able to "carry all the documents."

Marshall quickly rose to prominence in his new role. He changed the way rulings were presented, preferring to provide a majority opinion rather than seriatim opinions (from each justice). He implemented the process of judicial review via the 1803 case of *Marbury v. Madison*, creating the independent judiciary. The Supreme Court helped define the separation of powers, permitting the court to strike down federal and state laws deemed unconstitutional.

Prior to Marshall, the Supreme Court had made only 63 decisions. For the next thirty-four years, Marshall oversaw over 1000 decisions, laying the precedents for countless future cases. It was the practice of the time that the justices worked in their circuits for six months out of the year and sequestered in Washington, DC, the rest of the time, staying in the same hotel. There, they would meet together acting as their own clerks and hammer out their decisions. Marshall was known for building consensus and allowing his justices to form their majority opinion before weighing in. Justice Oliver Wolcott described Marshall's knack for "putting his own ideas into the minds of others, unconsciously to them."

One of the Associate Justices of the Supreme Court was Marshall's friend, Bushrod Washington, the nephew of the former president. The nephew inherited the papers of his uncle and asked Marshall to assist in writing a biography of George Washington based on them. The first two volumes were completed in 1804, with the set growing to five volumes when complete.

During his tenure on the court, Marshall also oversaw the impeachment hearing of Associate Justice Samuel Chase, who was acquitted by the Senate, the treason trial of Aaron Burr, for allegedly attempting to create an independent republic in the western United States. When Thomas Jefferson declared his correspondence with General James Wilkinson as protected by executive privilege, Marshall ruled most of the evidence against Burr was inadmissible, and Burr was acquitted, much to the chagrin of Jefferson and the Democratic-Republicans. Towards the end of his tenure, during the Jackson administration, Marshall was often at odds with the President, a Democrat, and found his influence waning as his colleagues on the court were gradually replaced. After the passing of Associate Justice Bushrod Washington, Marshall was alone of all the justices he had originally worked with.

In December 1831, Marshall's wife, Polly passed away at Richmond, Virginia. Marshall focused on an abridgment of his Washington biography for schools, completing it in 1833. However, his health was gradually

Grave of John Marshall

failing, and on July 6, 1835, he died in Philadelphia while seeking medical treatment. He was 79 years old and had served as the Chief Justice for 34 years. Oddly, Marshall's son Thomas had died in Baltimore two days earlier when a chimney collapsed in a storm while he was on his way to Philadelphia to be with his father. Marshall never learned of this death.

The Liberty Bell was rung at Philadelphia in honor of his death. One story claimed it was the last time the bell was rung because it cracked. Marshall was returned to Richmond where he was interred at Shockoe Hill Cemetery, next to his wife.

Marshall was the last surviving cabinet member from the first Adams administration and the last to have served in the 1700s. Andrew Jackson nominated Roger Taney to replace him.

Marshall is remembered in many ways. His homestead and birthplace are national historic parks. He has appeared on currency, postage stamps, painting, and statues, and his name has been used for many places and institutions. If it has Marshall in the name, it is likely named for John Marshall.

James McHenry
(1753–1816)

Secretary of War

Buried at Westminster Hall and Burying Ground,
Baltimore, Maryland.

U.S. Constitution

James McHenry was a military surgeon and statesman who signed the U.S. Constitution on behalf of Maryland. He was a member of the Continental Congress, secretary to General George Washington, aide-de-camp to Marquis de Lafayette, and secretary of war bridging the Washington and Adams administrations.

James McHenry was born November 16, 1753, in Ballymena, in County Antrim, Ireland, the son of Daniel McHenry, a merchant, and his wife, Agnes. The family was Scotch Irish Presbyterian.

McHenry was sent to Dublin as a boy to receive a classical education. However, he became ill while at school and was sent to America in 1771 to improve his health. McHenry was placed in the care of family friend Captain William Allison of Philadelphia. There, he met Allison's stepdaughter, Margaret Caldwell, whom he subsequently married. McHenry's parents and siblings joined him in Baltimore soon after. McHenry's father opened a merchant shop with his son John called McHenry and Son.

McHenry finished his preparatory education at Newark Academy, now the University of Delaware. He then returned to Philadelphia to

James McHenry (1753–1816)

James McHenry

study medicine as an apprentice to Benjamin Rush. McHenry became a physician.

When the Revolution broke out in 1775, McHenry traveled to Cambridge, Massachusetts, and met with George Washington to offer his medical services. In January 1776, he was assigned to the military hospital in Cambridge and was recognized for his skill by the Continental Congress. On August 10, McHenry was named the surgeon for Colonel Robert Magaw's 5th Pennsylvania Battalion, but he was captured at the fall of Fort Washington in November. McHenry was paroled on January 27, 1777, but remained in Philadelphia and Baltimore until a prisoner exchange was completed in March 1778.

Upon his return to service, McHenry was the senior surgeon at Valley Forge until May 15, 1778, when he was appointed the secretary to Washington. He held this position until 1780, when he was named Lafayette's aide-de-camp. McHenry remained in this position until the end of the war.

Back in Maryland in 1781, McHenry was elected to the Maryland State Senate, where he served until 1786. He was elected by the Maryland

General Assembly to the Continental Congress on May 12, 1783, serving through 1785. He was elected a member of the American Philosophical Society in January 1786.

In 1787, Maryland selected as delegates to the U.S. Constitutional Convention Daniel Carroll, Daniel of St. Thomas Jenifer, Luther Martin, John Francis Mercer, and James McHenry. At the convention held in Philadelphia in the summer of 1787, McHenry took copious notes on all matters debated before and by the delegates. His notations provide historians a moment-by-moment examination of how the U.S. Constitution came together. For instance, at the opening of the parley, he wrote:

> On the 25th [of May], seven states being represented viz. In New York, New Jersey, Pennsylvania, Delaware, Virginia, North Carolina, and South Carolina, George Washington was elected (unanimously) president of the convention. The convention appoint a committee to prepare and report rules for conducting business which were reported, debated, and in general agreed to on the 28th.
>
> 29 [May]. Governor Randolph opened the business of the convention. (2) He observed that the confederation fulfilled none of the objects for which it was framed. 1st. It does not provide against foreign invasions. 2dly. It does not secure harmony to the States. 3d. It is incapable of producing certain blessings to the States. 4. It cannot defend itself against encroachments. 5th. It is not superior to State constitutions.
>
> 1st. It does not provide against foreign invasion. If a State acts against a foreign power contrary to the laws of nations or violates a treaty, it cannot punish that State, or compel its obedience to the treaty. It can only leave the offending State to the operations of the offended power. It, therefore, cannot prevent a war. If the rights of an ambassador be invaded by any citizen, it is only in a few States that any laws exist to punish the offender. A State may encroach on foreign possessions in its neighborhood, and Congress cannot

prevent it. Disputes that respect naturalization cannot be adjusted. None of the judges in the several States under the obligation of an oath to support the confederation, in which view this writing will be made to yield to State constitutions.

McHenry missed much of the convention due to his brother's illness but was an active speaker when present. He signed the Constitution and then helped to see it ratified by Maryland. He returned to state politics in 1788 when he was elected to the Maryland House of Delegates on October 10. After two years in the role, he spent a year in the mercantile business before accepting a term in the Maryland Senate on November 15, 1791. He served five years.

In 1792, McHenry purchased a 95-acre tract from Ridgely's Delight near Baltimore and named it Fayetteville in honor of his friend, the Marquis de Lafayette.

During President Washington's second term, in 1796, McHenry was appointed secretary of war, a cabinet position overseeing the entire American military establishment, Indian affairs, and naval activity. His initial task was to transition Western military posts ceded from Great Britain under the terms of the Jay Treaty. Subsequently, McHenry's primary focus was to prepare for a possible war with either France or England.

When the Adams administration followed in 1797, McHenry continued in his role as secretary of war. However, he had a strained relationship with him. After a stormy cabinet meeting in May 1800, Adams requested McHenry's resignation. He resigned on May 13. In a letter to his friend Hugh Williamson, dated May 29, 1800, McHenry wrote of his being relieved of his services:

> I have not now time to communicate to you the particulars which [unintelligible] to the late changes in the Executive offices. Perhaps you will discover some of the causes in the man stabs evidently taken by the President to receive its diction. He has certainly acted and is daily acting in a manner to break up the federal party [sic] and destroy any remaining confidence many may have in him.

Ft. Henry bombardment 1814

He cannot hear Washington praised without intolerable pain and hates with inconceivable acrimony those who consider that great man to have outstripped him in virtuous and honorable reputation. It is certain that all of our courtesies to the opposition and measures to secure votes will not divert a single one from Jefferson.

During the election of 1800, McHenry urged Alexander Hamilton to release a pamphlet questioning Adams's loyalty and patriotism. This was controversial and paved the way for Thomas Jefferson to become president.

Now retired at his home, McHenry kept up his correspondence with his friends and associates. He frequently conversed with Timothy Pickering and Benjamin Tallmadge about the Federalists and the War of 1812. In 1812, Fort McHenry was erected in Baltimore Harbor and named in his honor. He was also elected president of the Bible Society of Baltimore in 1813.

James McHenry (1753–1816)

In 1814, McHenry was stricken by an attack of paralysis from which he was in severe pain and lost the use of his legs. On September 13, 1814, British naval vessels bombarded Fort McHenry during the War of 1812. This event was the basis for Francis Scott Key's "Star-Spangled Banner."

The grave of James McHenry

Despite his failing health, McHenry was elected a member of the American Antiquarian Society in July 1815. On May 3, 1816, he died at his estate and was buried in the Westminster Presbyterian Churchyard in Baltimore. His gravestone reads, "James McHenry. Signer of the Constitution." Upon the death of her beloved husband, Mrs. McHenry wrote:

> Here we come to the end of a life of a courteous, high-minded, keen-spirited, Christian gentleman. He was not a great man but participated in great events, and great men loved him, while all men appreciated his goodness and purity of soul. His highest titles to remembrance are that he was faithful to every duty and that he was the intimate and trusted friend of Lafayette, of Hamilton, and of Washington.

Biographer Karen Robbins wrote in 1994,

> James McHenry was a man of integrity and talent, with successes and failures, who served his country to the best of his ability, and whose story sheds light on the problems within the Federalist Party during the Adams administration. From an early point, this Scots-Irish immigrant emerged as a cautious man, slow to decide but steadfast once committed, who was transformed into a colonist, a patriot, a politician, and, finally, a Federalist.

James McHenry has been honored by Henry Street in Madison, Wisconsin, and the town of McHenry, Maryland, in Garrett County, was named after him. He was also memorialized at Independence Hall and the National Constitution Center in Philadelphia.

Thomas McKean
(1735–1817)

"First Elected President of the Confederation"

Buried at Laurel Hill Cemetery,
Philadelphia, Pennsylvania.

**Military • Declaration of Independence
Articles of Confederation**

This founder was known for his very brusque take-charge attitude that at times upset his fellow patriots. This may have contributed to the fact that while serving in the Stamp Act Congress, two other delegates challenged him to duels which he speedily accepted. Only the departure of one representative and the existence of cooler heads avoided the shedding of blood. His resume is lengthy and in addition to service in Congress included service in the military. He also served as Governor of Delaware and as Chief Justice of Pennsylvania at the same time. He would later attend the Pennsylvania convention that ratified the United States Constitution and serve as the Governor of that state. He also affixed his signature to both the Declaration of Independence and the Articles of Confederation. Some contend that he served as one of the first Presidents of the United States under those Articles. His name was Thomas McKean.

McKean was born on March 19, 1734, in New London Township located in Chester County, Pennsylvania. His parents were both Irish born Ulster-Scots who came to America from Ballymoney, County

Thomas McKean

Antrim, Ireland. When McKean was 16 years of age, he traveled to New Castle, Delaware to study the law under one of his cousins. By 1756 he had been admitted to the bar in both Delaware and Pennsylvania. By the mid-1760s he was serving in the Delaware General Assembly and as a judge of the Court of Common Pleas. Delaware at the time had two political factions which were commonly referred to as the "Court Party" and the "Country Party." The former party urged reconciliation with England while the latter, of which McKean was a leading member, supported American independence.

In 1765, Mckean and Caesar Rodney represented Delaware at the Stamp Act Congress. McKean was an active member of this group and along with John Rutledge and Philip Livingston served on the committee that drafted the Declaration of Rights and Grievances. Timothy Ruggles, a delegate from Massachusetts who served as president of the body, refused to sign the Memorial. Ruggles also declined to state the reasons for his objection. McKean wouldn't let the matter drop and demanded that Ruggles explain himself. The Massachusetts delegate then explained that his conscience would not permit him to address complaints to the king. McKean responded with scorn twice bellowing out the word conscience in a sarcastic manner that Ruggles viewed as an insult. He challenged McKean to a duel which was immediately accepted. Early the next morning Ruggles returned to his home state, so no duel was fought. The Massachusetts legislature officially censured Ruggles for "a neglect of duty." Ruggles wasn't the only delegate at the gathering to draw McKean's ire. Robert Ogden, a representative from New Jersey, also challenged McKean to a meeting on the field of honor. McKean accepted this invitation but cooler heads in attendance interceded, and the quarrel was settled without a shot being fired.

McKean would marry twice and father eleven children. His first wife, Mary Borden, passed away in 1773. A year later he married Sarah Armitage and moved his family to Philadelphia. Despite his Pennsylvania residence he was elected to represent Delaware in the Continental Congress. As a member of Congress, McKean is remembered for the part he played in fellow delegate Caesar Rodney's midnight ride. On July 1, 1776, McKean concluded that another delegate from Delaware, George Read, intended to vote against declaring American independence. Rodney, who like McKean favored independence, was absent from Congress due to a severe illness. Realizing that Rodney's vote would be needed McKean sent a messenger to Rodney who had returned to his home in Dover, Delaware. The message urged his fellow delegate to return to Philadelphia at once. Rodney immediately mounted a horse and began the eighty-mile trip back to Congress. As McKean later remembered in a letter to one of Rodney's nephews, he met Rodney "at the State-house door in his boots and spurs as the members were assembling; after a friendly salutation (without a word on the business) we went into the Hall of Congress together, and found we were among the latest: proceedings immediately commenced, and after a few minutes the great question was put; when the vote for Delaware was called, your uncle arose and said: 'As I believe the voice of my constituents and of all the sensible & honest men is in favor of Independence & my own judgment concurs with them I vote for Independence." Read voted nay but by a margin of two to one Delaware favored independence.

McKean did not get to sign the Declaration of Independence with his fellow members of Congress. Soon after casting his vote he led a militia group to assist George Washington during the unsuccessful defense of New York City. As a result of this military duty, McKean is considered to be the last signer of the Declaration of Independence. McKean insisted that he signed the document sometime in 1776 though most historians believe he affixed his signature to the document between 1777 and 1781.

The war years weren't quiet ones for McKean. He had been placed on the English hit list and wrote in a letter to John Adams that "he was being hunted like a fox." When the British captured the rebel governor of Delaware, McKean assumed the post. At the same time he was serving quite capably as Chief Justice of Pennsylvania in a post he filled from 1777 until 1799. According to his biographer John Coleman, "only the historiographical difficultly of reviewing court records and other scattered documents prevents recognition that McKean, rather than John Marshall, did more than anyone else to establish an independent judiciary in the United States. As Chief Justice under a Pennsylvania constitution he considered flawed, he assumed it the right of the court to strike down legislative acts it deemed unconstitutional, preceding by ten years the U.S. Supreme Court's establishment of the doctrine of judicial review."

In October of 1776 the during what was viewed as a conservative reaction against independence, the Delaware General Assembly did not re-elect McKean to the newly declared nation's Congress. Within a year British occupation of the state changed public opinion, and McKean was returned to Congress in 1777. He would serve in this body until 1783. He helped draft the Articles of Confederation and voted for their adoption in 1781. That same year he was elected to the position of President of Congress. Though primarily a ceremonial position with little authority some have argued that McKean served as President of the United States.

Though he did not attend the Constitutional Convention, McKean took a leading role in securing Pennsylvania's ratification of the United

States Constitution. He argued in favor of a strong executive and was a member of the state convention that voted to ratify the document. When American political parties came into being, he allied himself initially with the Federalists. By the mid-1790s he broke with that party because of disagreements with compromises that the administration in Philadelphia made with Great Britain. He became an outspoken Jeffersonian Republican.

In 1799 McKean was elected to the first of three terms he would serve as Governor of Pennsylvania. As Governor, he demanded that things be done his way. He removed his critics from government posts and rewarded his supporters with jobs. His administration was so stormy

The grave of Thomas McKean.

that he had to survive an impeachment attempt by his political foes in 1807. In this, he proved successful.

McKean passed away in 1817 at the age of 83. He was initially laid to rest in the First Presbyterian Church Cemetery, but his remains were moved to Philadelphia's Laurel Hill Cemetery in 1843. In a letter to one of McKean's sons, John Adams described his fellow founder as "among the best tried and firmest pillars of the Revolution."

McKean County, Pennsylvania is named in his honor. There is also a McKean Street in Philadelphia. Both the University of Delaware and Penn State University have buildings named for him.

Samuel Meredith
(1741 – 1817)

Silk Stockings Associator

Buried at Samuel Meredith Monument,
Pleasant Mount, Pennsylvania.

Military • 1st Treasurer of U.S.A.

Samuel Meredith partnered with his father, Reese Meredith, and founder George Clymer in a successful merchant business in Philadelphia, Meredith and Clymer. At the outset of the Revolution, Samuel enlisted in the Continental Army and rose to brigadier general before returning to his business pursuits. He then became a Continental Congressman and later served as the first Treasurer of the post-Constitution United States during the entire Washington and Adams administrations and the beginning of the Jefferson administration, from 1789 to 1801.

Born in Philadelphia, Pennsylvania, in 1741, Samuel Meredith was the son of Reese Meredith (1705–1778) and his wife, Martha (née Carpenter). The elder Meredith was from Leominster, Herefordshire, England. He was educated at Oxford and married into the Carpenter family of prosperous merchants. Reese and Martha emigrated to Philadelphia in February 1730, following the death of his father, John Meredith, where he later became a friend of George Washington.

Young Samuel attended Doctor Francis Allison's Academy in Philadelphia before becoming engaged in mercantile pursuits. Allison

Samuel Meredith

also had as pupils Thomas McKean, George Read, James Smith, Charles Thomson, and the siblings of John Dickinson.

During the Stamp Act controversy of 1765, both Samuel and his father Reese signed the non-importation resolutions in Philadelphia that were similar to other protests throughout the colonies regarding "taxation without representation." During this time, Samuel partnered with his father and another Philadelphia merchant, George Clymer, to expand their enterprise, including the mercantile business and land speculation in northeastern Pennsylvania, Delaware, New York, Kentucky, and Virginia. Clymer later married Samuel's sister, Elizabeth, to further cement the relationship.

In 1772, Meredith married Margaret Cadwalader, the daughter of Doctor Thomas and Hannah Cadwalader. The father-in-law was a well-known physician who was also a member of the American Philosophical

Society. The Merediths had six children. A daughter, Martha, later married John Read, the son of Constitution and Declaration of Independence signer George Read.

By 1775, Meredith was involved in politics as a delegate to the Pennsylvania Provincial Congress, held in Philadelphia. He also served as the chairman of the Committee of Safety. After shots were fired that spring at Lexington and Concord, Meredith volunteered for military service. He was assigned to the 3rd Battalion of Associators, also known as the "Silk Stockings Company" because of the upper-class social standing of the men. As a major in this brigade, he saw action at the battles of Trenton and Princeton. He led a different brigade at the battles of Brandywine and Germantown, earning him a promotion to brigadier general. However, only a few months later, in January 1778, he resigned his commission and returned to Philadelphia to deal with the repercussions of the British invasion of that city on his family and property.

Meredith then served three terms in the Pennsylvania Colonial Assembly, from 1778 to 1779, 1781 to 1782, and 1782 to 1783. William Duer wrote to Robert Morris from Rhinebeck, New York on July 11, 1781:

> "I have just received your Favor of the 29th May on my Return last Night from Camp, where I had the Pleasure of seeing the Chevalier de la Luzerne, and our Mutual Friend Mr. Meredith."

That November, Meredith was elected as a director of the Bank of North America.

On October 31, 1786, Meredith, a Federalist, was appointed by the Pennsylvania legislature to the Continental Congress. He served through 1788, focusing mainly on financial matters. During this time, in December 1787, Meredith took in part in Pennsylvania's ratifying convention along with Thomas McKean, Anthony Wayne, Stephen Chambers, and Timothy Pickering.

With the new federal government underway in early 1789, Meredith petitioned President George Washington for a position:

"As the Unanimous voice of America will very soon call you to a Station which I flatter myself you will not decline filling, I hope this application (which perhaps I ought to have deferred till this universally wished for event had realy [sic] taken place) may not appear indelicate in your Eyes—The Fall of Landed property, added to losses occasioned by a too great confidence in Continental money, have so extreemly [sic] diminished my income as to render it necessary I should do something for the present support of my Family, I, therefore, take the Liberty of requesting the favour [sic] of your Interest in order to procure some office under Congress, in which I may be of service to the Publick [sic], & at the same time benefit myself—It is generally supposed the import will immediately in the meeting of Congress engage their attention, and as an Officer will be required for that department; I should esteem myself very fortunate if thro [sic] your Influence I could be appointed, and be assured Sir I shall endeavour by a faithful discharge of the duties of the Office to make some returns for the Obligation your friendship will lay me under on this particular occasion1—As for the unspeakable one I and all America owe you as the Preserver of your Country they must ever remain in full force."

President Washington appointed Meredith as the surveyor of the Port of Philadelphia on August 1, 1789, and then weeks later, nominated him to serve as the first Treasurer of the United States. With the Senate's consent, Meredith took office on September 11, 1789. During this time, Meredith was responsible for managing the money of the new republic, settling its many bills, working in concert with Secretary of the Treasury Alexander Hamilton. He often gave his personal funds to do so, including over a hundred thousand dollars never repaid to him or his heirs. He developed a system for managing his duties and was retained through the entire Washington and Adams administrations.

On October 31, 1801, only months after the inauguration of Thomas Jefferson as the third President of the United States, Meredith resigned his post. He had written Jefferson on August 29, 1801:

"The precarious state of Mrs. Meredith's health, which has been injured by change of situation, the anxious desire she and the family have to be with their Friends & relations, as well as the necessary attention to my private affairs, which are suffering by my absence from Philada.; have induced me to offer you my resignation, to take place if you think proper about the last of October, or beginning of November, which I think will give me time to receive returns from the most distant Banks, make up my Quarterly Accounts to the 30th: September, and hand them to the Auditor for settlement: And for you Sir, to fix on a successor, to whom I may deliver over the funds in my hands, giving him every information I am capable of . . ."

Upon leaving office on December 1, 1801, Meredith headed to his country estate, Belmont Manor, near Pleasant Mount, Wayne County, Pennsylvania. There he lived the rest of his days, passing on February 10, 1817, at the age of 65 or 66. Recorded one newspaper at the time:

"Meredith, at the commencement of the revolution, took an active and decided part with his country. A native of Philadelphia, he was among the foremost of the Patriots of that day who encountered hazards, and endured the privations, attendant on the crisis of the times, being personally engaged at the cannonade of Trenton, the battle of Princeton, and afterwards with his family suffering in exile on the occupation of Philadelphia by the British."

Meredith was initially laid to rest in the family plot at Belmont Manor. His wife, Margaret, followed in 1820.

In 1904, thanks to local efforts and a Commonwealth grant, Mr. and Mrs. Meredith's remains were removed to a plot in the town of Pleasant Mount, where a monument with a life-sized statue was erected to honor him. It reads, "Samuel Meredith. First Treasurer of the U.S.A."

Said one of the speakers honoring Meredith at the dedication of the memorial:

"The name of Samuel Meredith 'was not born to die,' else we should not be here today, nearly a century after he breathed his last sign among the hills of Wayne, to unveil a monument to his memory. If that name had been doomed to oblivion, surely it would have long since passed from the minds of men. Rarely in the history of public benefactors has there been such tardy recognition of their merit as this demonstration discloses."

The grave of Samuel Meredith

Lewis Morris III
(1726 – 1798)

"The Last Lord of Morrisania"

Buried at St. Ann's Church of Morrisania,
Bronx, New York.

Declaration of Independence

Lewis Morris was a wealthy landowner in what is now Bronx County, New York. As a Continental Congressman from New York, he signed the Declaration of Independence. He was the older half-brother of Gouverneur Morris and the last "Lord of Morrisania Manor."

Morris, born April 8, 1726, at the family's estate, Morrisania (now part of Bronx County), New York, was the oldest son of Lewis Morris II (1698-1762) and his wife, Katrintje (née Staats) Morris. Morris had two brothers, Staats Long Morris (1728-1800) and Richard Morris (1730-1810). After his mother died in 1731, his father married Sarah Gouverneur (1714-1786). Half-siblings Mary Lawrence, Gouverneur Morris (1752-1816), Isabella, and Catherine were issues of this marriage. Morris was the nephew of Robert Hunter Morris (1700-1764), the colonial governor of Pennsylvania. He was also the cousin, by marriage, of New Jersey Governor William Paterson and father-in-law of New York Lieutenant Governor Stephen Van Rensselaer, the brother of Albany Mayor Philip Schuyler Van Rensselaer. General Anthony Walton White of the Continental Army was also a cousin, the son of his aunt Elizabeth.

Lewis Morris III

Morrisania had its origins with Morris's great-grandfather, Richard Morris, who came to New York via Barbados following the restoration of Charles II after the English Civil War. Richard, who had been in Cromwell's rebel army, purchased over 2,000 acres that are now within Bronx County, New York. His son, Lewis I, inherited and expanded the estate. Lewis I, the first royal governor of New Jersey, was very popular. Morristown, New Jersey, was named in his honor. His eldest son, Lewis II, was, for a time, the Speaker of the New York Assembly.

Lewis Morris III was educated by private tutors before attending Yale College. He graduated with an A.B. degree in 1746. That same year, following the death of his grandfather, his father became "Lord of Morrisania Manor." Young Morris returned from Yale to assist in the running of the estate. He married Mary Walton on September 24, 1749. The couple eventually had ten children:

- Catherine Morris (1751–1835) married Thomas Lawrence (1744–1823).
- Mary Morris (1752–1776).
- Colonel Lewis V. Morris (1754–1824) married Ann B. Elliott (1762–1848), sister-in-law of Congressman Daniel Huger.
- General Jacob Morris (1755–1844) married Mary Cox (1758–1827) (Morris, New York, is named after him).
- Sarah Morris (born in 1757) died young.
- Lieutenant William Walton Morris (1760–1832), aide-de-camp to General Anthony Wayne, married Sarah Carpender.
- Helena Magdalena Morris (1762–1840) married John Rutherfurd (1760–1840), a Senator from New Jersey.
- James Morris (1764–1827) married Helen Van Cortlandt (1768–1812), daughter of Augustus Van Cortlandt and granddaughter of Frederick Van Cortlandt.
- Captain Staats Morris (1765–1826) married Everarda van Braam Houckgeest (1765–1816), the daughter of Andreas van Braam Houckgeest and Baroness Catharina C.G. van Reeds van Oudtshoorn.
- Captain Richard Valentine Morris (1768–1815) married Anne Walton (1773–1858).

Morris was named as a judge of the Court of Admiralty, which oversaw shipping matters, in 1760. Upon the death of his father in 1762, Morris inherited the bulk of the family estate, becoming the third and final "Lord of Morrisania Manor."

Given his newfound wealth and influence, Morris was elected to the New York General Assembly in 1769 as part of the Livingston/DeLancey feud for power in the state. Morris was allied with his brother Richard, who was loyal to the Livingstons. Morris only lasted one term.

As tensions increased with Britain, he resigned from the Admiralty Court in 1774. In March 1775, countering the DeLanceys' power in the General Assembly, Morris led the call for a new Provincial Assembly, its purpose to elect delegates to the Continental Congress. Despite strong resistance, the meeting was held in White Plains on April 1. The elections were held on April 22 to select the delegates. Lewis Morris was one of them, serving until April 18, 1777.

While in Congress, Morris signed the open letter to the King of England. He was also involved in negotiations with the "Western Indians" in Virginia and was the chairman of the committee involved with financing and supplying the army. In 1776, Morris signed the Declaration of Independence. According to Howard Caine's 1972 film *1776*, based on the 1969 Broadway musical, Lewis, as chairman of the New York delegation, was reluctant to agree to anything because the New York Provincial Congress did not provide any instructions. When Morris learns of the destruction of his estates by the British from George Washington, he decides to sign the Declaration. In reality, when his brother General Staats Morris, who was in the British army, warned of the consequences of signing, Morris said, "Damn the consequences. Give me the pen." Within months, the British invaded Long Island and New York. Morrisania was looted and burned.

At the end of his term in 1777, Morris returned to Westchester, New York, and served as a county judge and New York State Senator until July 1, 1781.

After the war, he returned to Morrisania and began rebuilding it. He returned to the New York State Senate in 1783 and served until 1790. In 1784, he was made an honorary member of the New York Society of Cincinnati and appointed to the Board of Regents of the University of the State of New York.

In 1787, his half-brother Gouverneur Morris signed the Constitution after being credited with writing much of it. Morris then backed the Constitution in the New York ratifying convention, pushing for its narrow passage, 30 to 27. This pair of brothers are the only two brothers to sign both key founding documents, the Declaration and the Constitution.

In 1790, Morris offered Morrisania as the site of the new U.S. capital, replacing Philadelphia. Manhattan was chosen instead until Washington, D.C., was founded. In 1796, Morris was a presidential elector, voting for John Adams and Charles Cotesworth Pinckney.

According to the historian James J. Kirschke, by the end of Morris's life, Morrisania was in a 'leaky and ruinous' condition. "The estate house,

Grave of Lewis Morris III

servants' quarters, and grounds . . . had been used by the British as a horse park through most of the Revolution. An attack by the Continentals late in the war had caused further extensive damage. And Lewis had been too ill in the last several years of his life to manage and restore the place." Morris died at Morrisania on January 22, 1798, at age 71. He was buried in the Morris vault on the former Morrisania, now St. Ann's Church in the Bronx. His half-brother Gouverneur also rests there.

Some of Morris's noteworthy descendants include:

- Through his eldest son, Lewis V. Morris, he was grandfather to Lewis Morris (1785–1863), the father of Charles Manigault Morris (1820–1895), a Confederate officer.
- Also, through Lewis V. Morris, granddaughter Sabina Elliott Morris (1789–1857) married her first cousin, Robert Walter Rutherfurd (1788–1852), the son of John Rutherfurd and Helena Morris, and was the mother of Lewis Morris Rutherfurd (1816–1892), a pioneering astrophotographer who took the first

telescopic photographs of the moon and sun, as well as many stars and planets.
- Through his son, Staats Morris, his great-grandson was Daniel François van Braam Morris (b. 1840), a Dutchman and governor of Celebes in the Dutch East Indies.
- A great-granddaughter of his grandfather, Lewis Morris, named Mary Antill, was married to Gerrit G. Lansing, himself a brother of Congressman John Lansing. John Lansing's daughter, Sarah, was married to Edward Livingston, a great-grandson of Philip Livingston.

William Moultrie
(1730–1805)

Hero of Sullivan's Island

Buried at Fort Moultrie Grounds,
Charleston, South Carolina.

Military Commander • Governor

William Moultrie was an American slave-owning planter and politician who became a general in the American Revolutionary War. He became a war hero when he successfully defended Charleston during the Battle of Sullivan's Island on June 28, 1776, in which he dealt the Royal Navy a crushing defeat. After the war, Moultrie returned to the South Carolina General Assembly in 1783. Two years later, he was elected Governor. In 1792, he was again elected governor. Fort Moultrie is named in his honor.

William Moultrie was born in Charleston, South Carolina, on November 23, 1730, to Dr. John and Lucretia Cooper Moultrie. His father was a prominent physician, exceptionally skilled in obstetrics. Little is known about William's early life and education, other than that he was baptized in December 1730 and married in 1749 at the age of 19. He married Damaris Elizabeth de St. Julien, a wealthy descendant of French immigrants whose family owned a large plantation. The couple had three children, one dying in infancy. Because of English laws that denied married women's rights to control property, he became an influential

MAJOR GENERAL WILLIAM MOULTRIE.

member of his community. He soon purchased a 1020-acre plantation and owned about 200 slaves.

In 1752, he was elected to the South Carolina Commons House of Assembly, beginning a political career that lasted until 1794. In 1758, after a decade of tension between the colonists and the Cherokee tribe, war broke out. Moultrie was appointed a captain of the South Carolina militia. He was active in the invasion of Cherokee County and rose to the rank of colonel in 1774.

As the revolution approached, Moultrie was chosen as a delegate to the First Continental Congress; however, he declined to serve. Instead, Moultrie stayed in South Carolina serving as deputy to both the First and Second South Carolina Provincial Congresses. He was a member of the First South Carolina General Assembly after the adoption of the state constitution in 1776. During this time, he was a staunch patriot and supporter of the revolutionary cause.

In 1776, the British mounted an attack on Charleston, the fourth-largest port in the colonies. Moultrie defended a small fort on Sullivan's Island at the entrance to Charleston Harbor. On June 28, 1776, the British attacked Sullivan's Island. Against impossible odds and outnumbered 2,200 British troops to 435 soldiers within the fort, Moultrie successfully prevented land and sea invasions of Charleston. The small fort on Sullivan's Island was named Fort Moultrie in his honor, and the Continental Congress passed a resolution thanking Moultrie. He was promoted to brigadier general, and his regiment was taken into the Continental Army.

In February 1779, at the Battle of Beaufort, Moultrie commanded a largely militia force and defeated the British. This boosted patriot morale after the British capture of Savannah, Georgia. In the spring of 1779, Major General Benjamin Lincoln, the commander of the Continental Army's Southern Department, took the bulk of the Southern Army to threaten Augusta, Georgia. Seizing the initiative, the British advanced on Charleston from Savannah. Moultrie led a skillful withdrawal from Black Swamp, where Lincoln had left him with a small force. That small force garrisoned Charleston and held off a brief British siege before Lincoln's force returned.

In the spring of 1780, a series of engagements led to the surrender of Charleston by General Lincoln and the capture of more than 5,000 Continental soldiers, the largest loss during the war. Moultrie was one of them, and he was left in command of the American prisoners and frequently negotiated on their behalf for better conditions.

While a prisoner, Lord Charles Montague, the British Governor of South Carolina, offered an opportunity to desert to the British to regain his freedom and lost property. He replied to Montague, "Could I be guilty of so much baseness I should hate myself and shun mankind?" He was exchanged for British General John Burgoyne in 1782. When he returned to American lines, Congress made him a major general.

After the war, Moultrie returned to the General Assembly in 1783. Two years later, the new State Legislature elected him Governor of South Carolina. He served until 1787, and because the South Carolina Constitution prevented governors from serving two consecutive terms,

Grave of William Moultrie

he was elected to the state senate in 1787. During this time, he served as a member of the South Carolina Convention to ratify the US Constitution. He again served as governor starting in 1792 and ending in 1794. He ran again for governor in 1798 but lost decisively to Federalist Edward Rutledge.

Financial misadventures left Moultrie practically destitute in his later years. Yet, in 1802, he managed to publish his papers as the two-volume *Memoirs of the American Revolution*. This important primary source is often quoted in other works and is still regarded as one of the best personal accounts of the Revolutionary War.

William Moultrie died on September 27, 1805, in Charleston, South Carolina, at the age of 74. His slaves had a varied and complex fate, as some were sold to settle debts, some were hired out to work for the Santee Canal Company, and some escaped.

Moultrie was initially buried in the family cemetery. His remains were later moved to Fort Moultrie in 1978.

Andrew Pickens
(1739 – 1817)

The Wizard Owl

Buried at Old Stone Church Cemetery,
Clemson, Pickens County, South Carolina.

Military

This founder was a Revolutionary War South Carolina Militia General. He initially led troops against the Cherokee Indians in the French and Indian War and later against the British during the American Revolution. He was largely successful in both cases, though at one point he was captured by the British. The Continental Congress honored him for his service by awarding him a sword. Though he had fought Native Americans after the war, the sides mended fences, and he was held in high regard. The Indians he dealt with gave him the name Skyagunsta, "The Wizard Owl," a name said to be based on a highly regarded previous chief of the Cherokee. The nickname resulted from his ability to exploit the weaknesses of those he faced in battle. He was elected to the third United States Congress. His name was Andrew Pickens.

Pickens was born in 1739 in Bucks County, Pennsylvania. His parents were immigrants who had come to America from what is now Northern Ireland. The Pickens family moved from Pennsylvania following the Great Wagon Road that took them to Virginia's Shenandoah Valley. In 1752, they moved again, settling on the South Carolina frontier.

Andrew Pickens (1739–1817)

Andrew Pickens

Pickens moved to Abbeville County, South Carolina, where he purchased land in 1764. The following year, he married Rebecca Calhoun, and they started a family. It was here that Pickens became acquainted with the Cherokee Indians. He built the Hopewell Plantation on the Keowee River. Just across the river was a Cherokee settlement known as Seneca.

Pickens' military career began during the Anglo-Cherokee War, which was part of the French and Indian War. The conflict broke out in 1758, when the Virginia militia attacked the Cherokees for the alleged theft of horses. Pickens was a member of the South Carolina militia and served in the war in 1760 and 1761.

When the American Revolution began, Pickens was a captain in the militia. The Cherokee had allied with the loyalists, and Pickens emerged as a military leader fighting them at Long Cane. On February 14, 1779, Pickens, who was now a colonel, led his 300-man militia against a Loyalist force of approximately 800 under Colonel James Boyd at the Battle of Kettle Creek in Georgia. As described by Rick Atkinson in his work *The Fate of the Day: The War for America, Fort Ticonderoga to Charleston, 1777-1780,* Pickens, despite being outnumbered, ordered a frontal lunge accompanied by attacks on both flanks. During the fighting, Boyd fell mortally wounded. On his deathbed, Boyd asked Pickens to send his wife a brooch he had saved for her. When she received it, she exclaimed, "It's a lie. No damned rebel ever killed my husband." But not only had her husband been killed, Pickens and his troops had killed sixty others as well, while losing nine of their own. The rebels had also captured more than 150 men and six hundred horses. Pickens described the victory as "the severest check and chastisement the Tories ever received in Georgia or South Carolina." The outcome of the battle slowed the successful recruitment of Loyalists.

In 1780, things did not go as well for Pickens. The British defeated the Southern Continental Army in the Siege of Charleston. Pickens surrendered a fort in the Ninety-Six District. He and his 300-man militia were captured and then paroled after taking an oath to sit out the war. For Pickens, the oath proved to be of a short duration. Tories destroyed much of his property and frightened his family. At this point, he informed the British that they had violated the terms of his parole, and he rejoined the war, serving with Francis Marion and Thomas Sumter.

After his return to the fighting, Pickens saw action in several engagements, including the Battle of Cowpens. The battle took place in Cowpens, South Carolina. Brigadier General Daniel Morgan led the Americans. The British troops were under the command of Lieutenant Colonel Banastre Tarleton. Tarleton had a simple plan: he would have his infantry attack Morgan directly while dragoon units would protect his left and right flanks. He would use his two-hundred-man cavalry to attack the Americans when they broke and ran.

Shortly before sunrise on January 17, 1781, the attack began. Morgan had given Pickens command of the militia. When the British soldiers reached the militia, they were greeted by two volleys of fire, with commanders specifically targeted. This resulted in forty percent of the British casualties being officers, leaving the attackers surprised and confused. As planned, Pickens' men seemed to flee after firing the second volley. Tarleton believed he was seeing a hasty retreat. He ordered his men to charge, and the Americans drew them into a double envelopment. Pickens' militia had reorganized and charged. The British forces were soundly defeated. South Carolina Governor John Rutledge promoted Pickens to brigadier general, and Congress awarded him a sword.

After the American victory in the Revolution, Pickens was elected to the South Carolina House of Representatives. During the winter of 1785/86, negotiations took place for 45 days at his Hopewell Plantation

Grave of Andrew Pickens

involving representatives of the United States and leaders of the Cherokee, Choctaw and Chickasaw Indians. This resulted in three agreements, each one known as the Treaty of Hopewell. The treaties defined boundaries between tribal lands and those opened for settlement. They included provisions for the exchange of prisoners, punishment of crimes against Native Americans and the regulation of trade.

Pickens served in the Third United States Congress from 1793 to 1795. He was an anti-administration member who opposed the policies championed by the Secretary of the Treasury, Alexander Hamilton. He was one of nine representatives, and the only member of the anti-administration party, to vote against the Eleventh Amendment to the United States Constitution. This amendment restricts the ability of individuals to sue in federal court the states in which they are not citizens.

Pickens passed away in South Carolina on August 11, 1817. He was laid to rest in the Old Stone Church Cemetery in Clemson, South Carolina. One of his descendants, Marion Scherger, wrote a children's book titled *Courageous Uncle Andrew: The Story of Andrew Pickens, Revolutionary War Hero*, that quotes from a journal written by Pickens' sister, Katherine, on the day he died. She wrote, "My brother was a Revolutionary War Hero, a successful merchant, planter, respected judge and legislator. However, my brother Andrew, as a man of honor, I will miss you."

Pickens' heroics in the Revolution serve as one of the models for the fictional character Benjamin Martin in the film *The Patriot*. In one scene, Martin asks the militia for two rounds prior to retreating, similar to the orders Pickens and his men carried out in the Battle of Cowpens.

David Rittenhouse
(1732–1796)

Scientist, Surveyor, and First Mint Director

Buried at Laurel Hill Cemetery,
Philadelphia, Pennsylvania.

Scientist • Surveyor • U.S. Mint

David Rittenhouse was an important figure at the founding of our nation. He was a friend of many of the founders in his role as a surveyor, clockmaker, astronomer, inventor, mathematician, and scientist. During the Revolutionary War, he served on the Council of Safety and in the Pennsylvania Constitution convention. He accurately surveyed many state boundaries and was a member of the American Philosophical Society with Ben Franklin. Rittenhouse was also the first director of the United States Mint and may be the reason we have stars on a field of blue on our flag.

David Rittenhouse was born April 8, 1732, near Germantown, Pennsylvania, then a separate village from Philadelphia. His parents, Matthias and Elizabeth Williams Rittenhouse, were farmers in a little village called Rittenhousetown in Roxborough Township, Philadelphia County. His father was of German Mennonite descent while his mother was Welsh Quaker; however, neither denomination was emphasized in the home.

William Rittenhouse, his great grandfather, had built the first paper mill in the British colonies in Germantown in 1690. When his uncle

David Rittenhouse

William, also a miller, died, David inherited his tools and instructional books from which he gained much of his early informal education. As a lad, young David was adept at building mechanical models and demonstrating mathematical skills. At only eight years of age, he made a model of a water mill.

Soon, at only 13 years of age, Rittenhouse acquired other books like Newton's *Principia,* which helped him master Newton's laws of motion and gravity. Rittenhouse began to construct clocks, making a wooden one when he was seventeen and one of brass soon after. By age 19, in 1751, he opened a shop on the road that ran by his father's farm where he sold clocks, mathematical instruments, and mechanical models of the solar system. This was in what is now East Norriton Township near the Valley Forge Medical Center and Hospital.

David Rittenhouse (1732–1796)

Rittenhouse became very skilled at constructing astronomical instruments by 1756, experimenting with telescopes and mechanical models. He made surveyors' compasses, levels, transits, and zenith sectors as well as thermometers, barometers, at least one hygrometer, and occasional eyeglasses. During 1763 to 1764, Rittenhouse surveyed the boundary between Pennsylvania and Delaware, measuring a 12-mile circle from the New Castle, Delaware courthouse. This measurement was so precise that it was included without modification into the work by Mason and Dixon for the Pennsylvania-Maryland border.

On February 20, 1766, Rittenhouse took time away from his tinkering to marry Eleanor Coulston with whom he eventually had two daughters: Elizabeth (born 1767) and Ester (born 1769).

In 1768, Rittenhouse was admitted as a member of the American Philosophical Society, eventually serving as librarian and secretary. After Ben Franklin's passing in 1790, Rittenhouse became vice president and then president until 1796. The Society thought Rittenhouse the perfect person to study the upcoming transit of Venus. Rittenhouse had built an observatory in his backyard having constructed his telescope. To observe the transit, he thought he needed 22 of them set up at various locations. The legislature funded this.

When the transit of Venus occurred on June 3, 1769, Rittenhouse and his team were ready to make their observations. Rittenhouse was so excited as he lay under his telescope that he momentarily fainted. He had been ill the week prior and was still weak, though he recovered to continue his work. Rittenhouse also noticed that Venus had an atmosphere, a fact that was not previously known. He also calculated the average distance between the earth and the sun at 93 million miles. The American Philosophical Society subsequently published the results of the transit though no mention was made of his fainting and the significance of the atmospheric finding was not recognized for over a century.

Due to his balky health, perhaps to a duodenal ulcer, Rittenhouse moved his family to Philadelphia permanently in 1770. Around this time, he built an advanced orrery (a scale model of the solar system) for the College of New Jersey (now Princeton). Later, he made a more advanced model that he gave to the College of Philadelphia (now the

University of Pennsylvania). Rittenhouse earned honorary degrees from both institutions, and the orreries still exist in their collections.

Tragically, Eleanor Rittenhouse died in 1771 at the age of 35 while in childbirth. The baby also did not survive. David remarried the following year Hannah Jacobs with whom he had no surviving children. Hannah lived until 1799 and may be the reason Rittenhouse was a Presbyterian later in life.

From 1773 and onward, it was Rittenhouse's astronomical observations that were utilized by almanacs in Pennsylvania, Maryland, and Virginia.

During the American Revolution, Rittenhouse was the engineer and vice president of the Committee of Safety and served on the Board of War. Rittenhouse was concerned with the production of saltpeter and guns and helped to design the Delaware River defenses. He also experimented with telescopic sights for rifles and rifled cannon. Rittenhouse participated in the creation of the Pennsylvania Constitution of 1776. He was then the treasurer of Pennsylvania from 1777 to 1789.

Francis Hopkinson, a close friend and colleague who was on the Navy Board, wrote the Flag Act of 1777 in which he explained the blue field of stars as a "new constellation." Some attribute this thought to Rittenhouse.

Amid the tensions with Britain, Rittenhouse also continued his academic work. From 1779 to 1782 he was a Professor of Astronomy at what is now the University of Pennsylvania. He was subsequently vice-provost of the university from 1780 to 1782 and trustee from 1782 until his death. In 1781, he was the first American to spot the planet Uranus. The next year he was elected a Fellow of the American Academy of Arts and Sciences.

Rittenhouse's first work with coinage was regarding the Nova Constellatio (New Constellation) pattern coins which were minted in Philadelphia in 1783 at the behest of Robert Morris. Rittenhouse was consulted on the design which resembles the stars on the flag.

In 1784, Rittenhouse and Andrew Ellicott finished the Mason-Dixon line to the southwest corner of Pennsylvania. This was the last of his surveying work. Previously, he had also helped locate other boundaries between

David Rittenhouse (1732–1796)

Pennsylvania, New York, New Jersey, and the Northwest Territory. He also worked on borders for Massachusetts.

In 1786, next to the octagonal observatory he had built previously, Rittenhouse constructed a new Georgian-style house at 4th and Arch Streets in Philadelphia. Every Wednesday he held a salon meeting with such luminaries as Ben Franklin, Francis Hopkinson, Pierre Eugene du Simitiere, Thomas Jefferson (when in town), and others. Jefferson once wrote he would rather attend one of these meetings "than spend a whole week in Paris." In his *Notes on the State of Virginia* published a few years prior Jefferson listed Rittenhouse, Franklin, and Washington as examples of New World genius when refuting French naturalist Georges-Louis Leclerc, Comte de Buffon's claim that the intellects of the people living there were stunted by the environment and climate of North America.

During the Washington administration, the need for a national coinage came to the forefront. Rittenhouse was selected the first Director of the Mint, and set about to issue coins, opening the first mint on April 2, 1792. On the morning of July 30, 1792, Washington provided the silver flatware himself that was melted to become the first coin planchettes. Rittenhouse then personally tested the equipment, hand striking the

The grave of Rittenhouse

first coins which were given to Washington in appreciation of his many contributions. Coin production on a large scale was begun in 1793. Rittenhouse remained the Mint Director until June 30, 1795, when he resigned due to declining health.

In his later years, Rittenhouse founded the Democratic-Republican Societies in Philadelphia in 1793. In 1795, he was honored to become a member of the Royal Society of London, a rare recognition for an American scientist.

David Rittenhouse died at his home on June 26, 1796. He is now buried at Laurel Hill Cemetery in Philadelphia.

There are several tributes to David Rittenhouse:
- There is a crater on the moon named Rittenhouse Crater.
- In 1825, Southwest Square in Philadelphia was renamed Rittenhouse Square.
- The University of Pennsylvania has the David Rittenhouse Laboratory.
- The David Rittenhouse Junior High School is in Norristown, Pennsylvania.

Daniel Roberdeau
(1727 – 1795)

Pennsylvania Associator

Buried at Mount Hebron Cemetery,
Winchester, Virginia.

Articles of Confederation • Military

Daniel Roberdeau was a Philadelphia merchant and brigadier general who led the Pennsylvania Associators, a branch of the militia. He was also a political leader in Philadelphia who was elected to the Second Continental Congress, where he signed the Articles of Confederation as a Pennsylvania delegate.

Roberdeau was born in 1727 on the Island of St. Chrisopher, also known as St. Kitts, in the West Indies, east of Puerto Rico. He was the son of a French Huguenot father, Isaac Roberdeau, and his wife, Mary (née Cunningham) Roberdeau, of Scottish origin. When his father died, the family moved to Philadelphia.

Roberdeau was initially educated in England, but then learned the merchant trade in Philadelphia, where he became a timber merchant, leveraging his connections in the Caribbean.

Circa 1749 to 1754, as an early adherent of Freemasonry in Philadelphia, Roberdeau became established among the leadership of that colonial city, including Benjamin Franklin. He was elected as a city warden in 1756 and served on the hospital board with Franklin. He was then elected to the Pennsylvania Assembly from 1756 to 1760.

Daniel Roberdeau

On October 3, 1761, Roberdeau married Mary Bostwick of Philadelphia and joined in her Presbyterian faith. The couple ultimately had nine children, and Roberdeau became an elder of the church. He was again elected to the Pennsylvania Assembly, serving from 1766 to 1776, serving on the Committee of Finance and actively engaging the negotiations with the Native Americans.

Despite being involved in importing and exporting goods, Roberdeau was in favor of the non-importation protests of the early 1770s. After railing for the replacement of the current members of the Pennsylvania delegation in the Continental Congress, Roberdeau was appointed to the Pennsylvania Council of Safety in 1775 and chaired a protest against the king in May 1776 in Philadelphia that caught the attention of John Adams, who was attending the Continental Congress. Roberdeau signed as chairman of the committee that declared the King a mortal enemy.

Adams wrote to James Warren on May 20, 1776, about the event, noting how orderly it was run. Roberdeau was a staunch supporter of independence and was appointed as a brigadier general in the Pennsylvania Militia, in charge of the Pennsylvania Associators.

Following the fall of New York in the summer of 1776, Roberdeau and his Associators engaged the British in New Jersey. Said Roberdeau to his men in a speech made on August 19, 1776: "As it hath pleased Providence, for the exercise of our patience, and for the defense of that freedom which we inherit from the great Giver of all things, to call us from our families to the field; and as I have the honor of being your General officer, I trust you will take it well in me to endeavor to point out to you whatever appears necessary, either for your own particular good, or the more noble object — the good of all."

Roberdeau's ability to lead and motivate was widely evident. Unfortunately, he became ill and was evacuated to Lancaster, Pennsylvania to recover. Meanwhile, the Pennsylvania Associators disbanded following the Battles of Trenton and Princeton. The colony then formalized the Pennsylvania Militia in March 1777.

Recovered from his illness, Roberdeau was elected to the Continental Congress on February 5, 1777, serving for two years. During the winter of 1777/78, when General Washington was at Valley Forge, Roberdeau set up and commanded what became known as the Flying Camp, an attempt to rally and organize state militias to the cause. Ultimately, the Flying Camp concept gave way to a centralized Continental Army.

In November 1777, Roberdeau was among the Continental Congressman who adopted the Articles of Confederation. Sadly, wife Mary Roberdeau passed away this year.

In April 1778, Roberdeau decided to deal with the shortage of ammunition in the army and left Congress for several months on an expedition into western Pennsylvania at his own expense to discover and establish a lead mine in what is now Blair County. He also built a timber palisade fort to protect it that became known as Fort Roberdeau or "Lead Mine Fort."

Roberdeau married his second wife, Jane Milligan, on December 3, 1778, and the mine produced 1000 pounds of lead. The mine ran into

The grave of Daniel Roberdeau

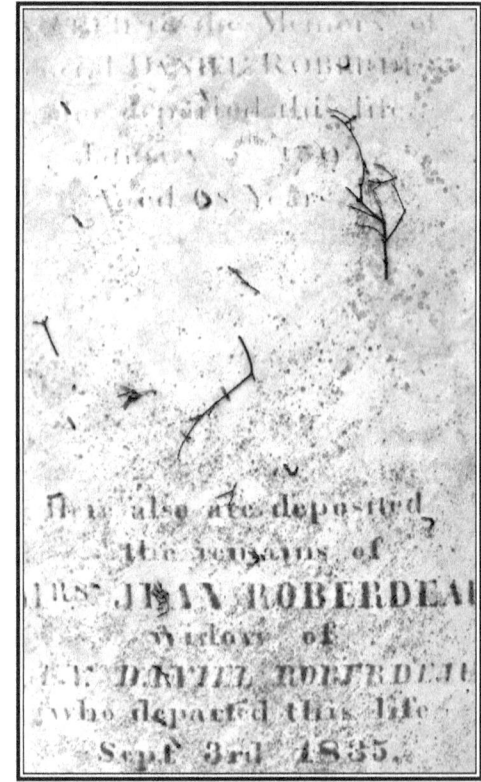

1780, when production halted, and the fort became a haven for local settlers.

Following the war, in 1783, Roberdeau traveled to England with his son, Isaac, to arrange his education. He then returned to Philadelphia in 1784, but did not stay long. Instead, he moved to Alexandria, Virginia, where he established a wharf and distillery.

As his health began to fail, Roberdeau moved to Winchester, Virginia, to be near his daughter. He died there on January 5, 1795. The *Aurora General Advertiser* of Philadelphia noted, "Died . . . in this town, on Monday last, after a lingering illness, which he bore with great Christian fortitude, and patient resignation to the Divine Will, General Daniel Roberdeau. He formerly resigned in Alexandria, and was a man universally esteemed, not only on account of the meritorious services [that] he rendered this country in a military capacity, but also for his strict integrity, piety, benevolence and philanthropy."

Roberdeau was buried in Mount Hebron Cemetery in Winchester.

Son Isaac Roberdeau was an Army officer and civil engineer who assisted Pierre L'Enfant with the plan for Washington, D.C.

Fort Roberdeau was reconstructed in the 1930s and remains a historic site near Altoona, Pennsylvania.

Betsy Ross
(1752 – 1836)

American Seamstress

Buried at Betsy Ross House Grounds,
Philadelphia, Pennsylvania.

Legendary Patriot Figure

This founder's grandson, William Canby, wrote about her association with the American flag in the 1870s. According to Canby, his account was based on conversations with family members, including his grandmother. In a speech to the Historical Society of Pennsylvania, he spoke of a visit made by George Washington and two members of the Continental Congress to a seamstress shop on Arch Street in Philadelphia. Their purpose was to create a flag proclaiming the independence of the United States. They met with the seamstress and showed her a rough sketch of what they had in mind. The four talked over ideas and agreed on a rectangular banner of red, white, and blue distinguished by an unusual field of five-pointed stars. The woman was an enterprising Quaker who would produce the first American flag and distinguish herself as one of just a handful of Revolutionary heroines. Her name was Betsy Ross.

Ross was born on January 1, 1752, in Philadelphia as Elizabeth Griscom. "Betsy" was the eighth of seventeen children and one of nine that survived childhood. She grew up in a strict Quaker household and

Betsy Ross (1752–1836)

Betsy Ross

was educated at a Quaker-run state school. It was an aunt who taught her the art of sewing—a skill that would lead to the part she played in the history of the United States of America.

In 1773 the then Betsy Griscom eloped and married John Ross, the nephew of, George Ross, a future signer of the Declaration of Independence and the son of an Episcopal minister. As a result of the marriage, she was expelled from the Quaker congregation. The union also resulted in a split in the Griscom family. The young couple started their own upholstery business and joined the city-parish of Christ Church. On occasion, their worship services were joined by a Virginia militia commander by the name of George Washington.

When the American Revolution began, John Ross was a member of the Pennsylvania Provincial Militia and was assigned to guard munitions. He passed away in 1775. Some claim his death came as a result of an explosion involving gunpowder though this has never been verified. After his death, his wife stayed busy in the upholstery business working on uniforms and tents to help supply the Continental Army. She was also known to be one of several flag makers in Philadelphia

Ross would marry twice more in her lifetime. Her second husband was a mariner whose ship was captured by the British. Charged with treason, he was imprisoned in England where he died. Her third husband had met her second husband in jail and brought her the news of his death. These three marriages produced seven daughters, five of whom survived childhood.

Ross worked as a seamstress until her retirement in 1827. She spent her final years in the care of one of her daughters. She passed away on January 30, 1836, at the age of 84. She was initially buried in the Free Quaker Burial Ground in Philadelphia. Twenty years later her remains were moved to the Mt. Moriah Cemetery in Philadelphia. In 1875 as part of the coming American Centennial celebration, the city fathers decided to remove her remains to the Betsy Ross House where she was believed to have resided. Workers found no remains under her tombstone. There were other bones found in the family plot that were deemed to be hers. These bones were buried in the tomb at the Betsy Ross House—a tourist attraction that attracts thousands of visitors each year.

There is no doubt that Ross was hired to make flags for the American Navy during the Revolution. Records of the Pennsylvania Navy Board includes orders to pay her for this work. Historians have disputed the account made by William Canby holding that his story is unsubstantiated and that it came at a time when Americans were eager for tales highlighting the heroes and heroines of the struggle for American Independence. A history buff by the name of Robert Morris spent five years investigating the story. He concluded that while Ross didn't design the flag, she did suggest some changes to the design made by Francis Hopkinson and presented to her by Washington. Morris believes that Ross suggested that the flag's stars be five-pointed rather than six-pointed. He also believes that it was Ross who proposed that the flag be a rectangle rather than a square. As a result of his work, Morris came to believe that Ross was a hardworking, patriotic woman who played a noteworthy role in American history. He also believes that on the recommendation of George Ross, her first husband's uncle, Congress decided to have Betsy Ross sew the first the American flag.

Betsy Ross (1752–1836)

The Betsy Ross Bridge that connects Philadelphia with Pennsauken Township, New Jersey is named in her honor. In 1952 the United States Post Office issued a commemorative stamp showing her presenting the completed flag to George Washington with Robert Morris and George Ross present at the event. Biographer Maria Miller wrote that in her opinion Ross is representative of more than a single flag. Instead, her story reflects and is a symbol of the lives of many working men and women who contributed to the cause of independence.

The grave of Betsy Ross

Nathaniel Scudder
(1733 – 1781)

"The Only Congressman to Die in Battle"

Buried at Old Tennent Churchyard,
Tennent, New Jersey.

Articles of Confederation • Military

Nathaniel Scudder was a physician and Continental Congressman who signed the Articles of Confederation. He was also an officer in the New Jersey Militia during the American Revolution and was killed in action. Scudder was the only former member of the Continental Congress killed in battle.

Scudder, born May 10, 1733, in Monmouth Court House, New Jersey, was the son of Jacob Scudder and his wife, Abia (née Rowe) Scudder.

Scudder was a 1751 graduate of the College of New Jersey (now Princeton University). He studied medicine and then opened a practice in Monmouth County. He married Isabella Anderson with whom he had five children. He was also, as of December 1766, one of the board members of Mattisonia Grammar School in Lower Freehold, New Jersey, along with Reverand William Tennent and Reverand Charles M. Knight.

In 1774, as hostilities increased with England, Scudder joined the county's Committee of Safety and was elected to attend the Provincial Congress of New Jersey. By 1776, Scudder was elevated to the New

Nathaniel Scudder (1733–1781)

Portrait of Nathaniel Scudder.

Jersey Committee of Safety and became the Speaker of the New Jersey Assembly. He also joined the New Jersey Militia as a lieutenant colonel.

On November 20, 1777, Scudder was elected to the Continental Congress which met in York, Pennsylvania. He was re-elected the following year, serving with Abraham Clark, Elias Boudinot, Jonathan Elmer, and John Witherspoon back in Philadelphia.

The summer of 1778 was especially busy for Scudder, who had abandoned his medical practice and was splitting his time between Congress and the New Jersey Militia. On June 28, 1778, he led his regiment at the Battle of Monmouth, very close to his birthplace. He also wrote a series of impassioned letters about the progress of the Articles of Confederation. In a letter to John Hart on July 13, 1778, he worried about the delay in the ratification of the Articles of Confederation:

> I do myself the Honor to address you upon an Affair to me one of the most serious and alarming Importance. The Honorable

Council and Assembly of this State have not thought proper to invest their Delegates with Power to ratify and sign the [Articles of] Confederation; and it is obvious that unless every [one] of the thirteen States shall accede to it, we remain an unconfederated [sic] People. These States have actually entered into a Treaty with the Court of Versailles as a Confederated People and Monsieur Girard their ambassador Plenipotentiary to Congress is now on our Coast with a powerfull [sic] Fleet of Ships, which have taken Pilots on Board for Delaware. He probably may be landed by this Time, and will at all Events be in Philadelphia in a few Days. How must he be astonished & confounded? [A]nd what may be the fatal Consequences to America, when he discovers (which he will immediately do) that we are ipso facto unconfederated [sic], and consequently, what our Enemies have called us, 'a Rope of Sand'? Will he not have just Cause to resent the Deception? [A]nd may not insidious Britain, knowing the same, take Advantage of our Disunion? For my own Part I am of Opinion She will never desist from her nefarious Designs, nor ever consider her Attempts upon our Liberties fruitless and vain, untill [sic] she knows the golden knot is actually tied. I left Congress last Wednesday Evening. The Affair of Confederation was to be taken up next Day. The Magna Charta of America was amply engrossed and prepared for signing. Ten States had actually authorised [sic] their Delegates to ratify; a Delegate from an eleventh (vizt. Georgia) declared he was so fully possessed of the Sense of his Constituents, that he should not hesitate to subscribe it.

New Jersey ratified the Articles of Confederation on November 19, 1778. John Witherspoon signed with Nathaniel Scudder. Scudder was elected to the Continental Congress again in 1779.

Finished in the Continental Congress, Scudder next served in the New Jersey General Assembly in 1780. He also continued his military service and was promoted to colonel in 1781. On October 17, 1781, he led part of his regiment to counter a foraging party from the British Army near Shrewsbury, New Jersey and was killed in the skirmish at

Blacks Point. He was buried at the Tennent Church Graveyard in Tennent, Monmouth County, New Jersey, three days later, the same day the British surrendered at Yorktown.

Scudder was the only member of the Continental Congress to die in battle. He was also the last colonel to die in battle during the American Revolution.

Scudder's tombstone reads, "In Memory of the Honorable Nathaniel Scudder, Who Fell in Defence of His Country October the 16th 1781 Aged 48 Years."

The grave of Nathaniel Scudder.

Jonathan Bayard Smith
(1742 – 1812)

Quaker Educator

Buried at Mount Vernon Cemetery,
Philadelphia, Pennsylvania.

Military • Articles of Confederation

This founder was a native Pennsylvanian born and bred in Philadelphia. A graduate of Princeton, he entered the mercantile business owned and operated by his father. An ardent patriot he embraced the at times unpopular stance, especially among Quaker Pennsylvania, of taking up arms against the British. Elected to the Continental Congress, he endorsed and signed the Articles of Confederation. He was a great promoter of education in the new nation. His name was Jonathan Bayard Smith.

Smith was born on February 21, 1742. His father Samuel Smith moved to Philadelphia from New Hampshire. Once settled in Pennsylvania he opened a business and quickly became a prosperous and respected merchant. The elder Smith saw to it that his son received a quality education. In 1760 he graduated from Princeton, a university he would later serve as a trustee. It may have been his father who instilled in Smith his devotion to education that he exhibited throughout his life.

By 1775 Smith was already supporting independence for the American colonies. That same year he was elected secretary of the committee of public safety. An election to the Continental Congress followed

Jonathan Bayard Smith (1742–1812)

Jonathan Bayard Smith

in 1777. He served in Congress until November of 1778 and signed the Articles of Confederation on behalf of Pennsylvania. The Articles were finally ratified in 1781which for the first time formally formed the states into a union.

During this same time, he put his money where his mouth was. On December 1, 1777, Smith presided at a public meeting in Philadelphia where it was resolved, "That it be recommended to the council of safety that in this great emergency . . . every person between the age of 16 and 50 be ordered out under arms." Smith joined the militia becoming a lieutenant colonel in John Bayard's regiment. His commanding officer was his brother- in- law. It was after marrying Susannah Bayard that Smith took his wife's maiden name as his middle name.

After leaving Congress, Smith returned to running his business though he remained active in civic affairs. He promoted education and in 1779 was one of the founders of the University of the State of

Pennsylvania. In 1795 when it merged with two other schools to form the University of Pennsylvania Smith became a trustee—a position he would hold until his death. He also put in thirty years of service as a trustee at his alma mater, Princeton.

He remained active almost to his last days. When the War of 1812 broke out public meetings were held in Philadelphia sponsored by the Democratic Young Men, but it was the 70-year-old Smith who headed these meetings as the organization's president. He passed away on June 16, 1812, and was laid to rest with Masonic honors in the Cemetery of the Second Presbyterian Church. When that cemetery closed in 1867 Smith's was one of the approximately 2,500 graves moved to the Mount Vernon Cemetery where he now rests behind locked gates. We were unable to visit his grave because the cemetery, though still in operation, is not open to the public, has suffered from neglect and is widely overgrown. It is our understanding that local volunteers are looking at taking action to clean up what was once, and could be again a beautiful cemetery.

The locked gateway to Mount Vernon Cemetery, Philadelphia.

Richard Dobbs Spaight
(1758–1802)

The Dueling Signer

Buried at Clermont Estate Cemetery,
New Bern, North Carolina.

Military • US Constitution

This founder was a successful politician and planter born and bred in his native state of North Carolina. He fought in the American Revolution. He represented his state in the Continental Congress from 1782 to 1785. He was one of the delegates chosen to represent North Carolina at the 1787 Constitutional Convention held in Philadelphia. He was also a signer of the document that gathering produced. He also served as governor of his state and in the United States House of Representatives. He would become the first of two signers of the Constitution to be killed in a duel. Similar to Alexander Hamilton, his opponent in the duel was a political rival. His name was Richard Dobbs Spaight.

As told by Denise Kiernan and Joseph D'Agnese in their work *Signing Their Rights Away,* Spaight was born on March 25, 1758, in the coastal town of New Bern, North Carolina. His mother was the sister of the royal governor, and his father was a wealthy planter. By the time he was eight, both his parents had died, and the orphan was sent to live with relatives in Northern Ireland. When the American Revolutionary War broke out, Spaight was attending the University of Glasgow. After he graduated, he returned to North Carolina.

Upon his arrival in America, Spaight served as an aide-de-camp to Major General Richard Caswell at the Battle of Camden, also known as

Richard Dobbs Spaight

the Battle of Camden Court House. The fighting took place on August 16, 1780, north of Camden, South Carolina. Lord Cornwallis commanded the British forces while the Americans were led by the American general who had defeated the British at Saratoga three years earlier. In his work, *Patriots*, A. J. Langguth writes that when Gates embarked on his first mission in the southern theater, his friend Charles Lee told him, "Take care lest your Northern laurels turn to Southern willows." Despite having a significant numerical superiority, the American forces were routed, and Gates never held a field command again.

After the Revolution, Spaight, armed with his considerable wealth and war record, entered politics. The North Carolina General Assembly elected him to serve in the Congress of Confederation between 1782 and 1785. Here, Spaight played a key role relative to the Land Ordinance of 1784. This ordinance called for the land in the recently created United States, located west of the Appalachian Mountains, north of the Ohio

Richard Dobbs Spaight (1758–1802)

River, and east of the Mississippi River, to be divided into separate states. Thomas Jefferson was the principal author of the proposal considered by Congress. One of the articles proposed by Jefferson was that after the year 1800, there shall be neither slavery nor involuntary servitude in any of the new states. Spaight, seconded by Jacob Read of South Carolina, moved to strike out this article. In a letter dated April 25, 1784, from Jefferson to James Madison, the future president wrote, "The clause was lost by one individual vote only." Jefferson blamed the defeat on Spaight and never forgave him, and would describe him as the man who permitted slavery to expand westward.

From 1785 to 1787, Spaight served in the North Carolina House of Commons, where he was named Speaker of the House. In 1787, he represented his state at the Constitutional Convention in Philadelphia. As noted by Clinton Rossiter in his work, *1787: The Grand Convention*, Spaight, at 29, was one of the youngest delegates to attend the gathering. Rossiter describes Spaight as somewhat of a straddler on critical issues who was thought to lean toward a more powerful federal government. To the best of our knowledge, he attended every session. In assessing Spaight's performance, Rossiter calls him "one of the usefuls who had several small triumphs as the plugger of holes." One example is that Spaight was successful in persuading the convention to give the President the power to make recess appointments. At the convention's conclusion, he added his signature to the Constitution.

In 1788, Spaight was a delegate to North Carolina's ratifying convention. He supported ratification, but the convention voted against ratification. In that same year, he married Mary Leach, who had the distinction of being the First Lady to dance with George Washington at a ball held in Washington's honor at the Governor's Palace, New Bern, in 1791.

Spaight retired from politics for several years, citing health reasons. He returned to public service in 1792, when he was elected to the state House of Representatives. That same year, the General Assembly elected him as the first native-born governor of North Carolina. He would be reelected for two further one-year terms. He moved the state capital to Raleigh and played a key role in the founding of the University of North Carolina at Chapel Hill.

Spaight was elected to the United States House of Representatives in 1798, filling the unexpired term of Nathan Bryan, who had passed away. A year later, he was elected to a two-year term. He tried for a second full term but lost to his Federalist opponent, John Stanly. Upon returning to North Carolina, Spaight served in the North Carolina Senate. Stanly began to criticize his predecessor, saying that Spaight wasn't sickly but used health as an excuse to avoid taking a position on controversial issues. The situation escalated, resulting in a duel. The duel took place at 5:30 in the afternoon on September 5, 1802, behind New Bern's Masonic Hall. Approximately three hundred people witnessed the event. The two men aimed and fired, but both missed their target. The men reloaded and fired again with the same result. Some of the townspeople implored the two to call a truce, but Spaight refused. The third shots also missed, but on the fourth attempt, Spaight was struck in the side and mortally wounded, and he died the next day. Stanly was charged with murder but pardoned by the governor.

Spaight was laid to rest in Clermont Cemetery in New Bern, North Carolina. There is a local legend saying that Union soldiers desecrated his grave during the Civil War. The authors believe this to be unlikely.

Duel between Spaight and John Stanly

Richard Dobbs Spaight (1758–1802)

Grave of Richard Dobbs Spaight

John Stark
(1728 – 1822)

"Hero of Bennington"

Buried at Stark Cemetery,
Manchester, New Hampshire.

Military Commander

John Stark was a tough guy, a true warrior. He possessed an incredible ability to lead men in battle and a fierce independence and stubbornness that served him well during the French and Indian War and the Revolutionary War. He became known as the "Hero of Bennington" for his service at the Battle of Bennington in 1777.

He was born in Londonderry, New Hampshire, on August 28, 1728. His father, Archibald, was born in Scotland and met his mother, Elizabeth, when he moved to Ireland. They emigrated from Ireland in 1720 and settled in Nutfield, New Hampshire. When Stark was eight years old, the family moved to Manchester, New Hampshire, formerly known as Derryfield. The couple had children who died during passage from Ireland and had six children born here.

The family home was destroyed by fire, and John and his brothers grew up on the wilderness frontier, becoming active hunters and trappers. They were accustomed to staying in forest camps, becoming inured to hardships and learning lessons of self-dependence. They had frequent

John Stark (1728–1822)

John Stark

contact with Indians from whom they obtained knowledge of their language and customs, and as a result, they became excellent marksmen.

On April 28, 1752, while on a hunting and trapping trip along the Baker River, Stark was captured by Abenaki warriors and taken to the village of St. Francis in Quebec. While a captive, Stark was treated well by the Abenaki, who adopted him into the tribe. They admired his spunk and defiance. In later years, John would comment that he "had experienced more genuine kindness from the savages of St. Francis than he ever knew prisoners of war to receive from more civilized nations." In July, John was sold for $103 to a Mr. Wheelwright of Boston, hired to purchase white captives of Native Americans. He safely returned to New Hampshire.

Stark married Elizabeth (Molly) Page on August 20, 1758. The couple had eleven children, the oldest of whom, Caleb, served with his father in the 1st New Hampshire Regiment at the Battles of Bunker Hill, Trenton, and Princeton. He rose to the rank of Major and served in the New Hampshire Senate.

During the French and Indian War, Stark served as a second Lieutenant and member of Rogers' Rangers, a bold troop of colonial militia under Captain Robert Rogers' command. He fought in the Battle of Lake George and Bloody Pond and many others but would not participate in Rogers' October 4, 1759 raid against the Abenaki at St. Francis out of respect for his Indian foster parents who lived there. At the end of the war, Stark retired as a captain and returned to Derryfield. His time with the Rangers taught him tactics that would serve him well in the revolution to come.

Stark was at his sawmill when he heard of the battles at Lexington and Concord. He immediately went home, gathered his belongings and set out on the road towards Medford, Massachusetts. According to historian Thomas Fleming, within six hours, he enlisted half his regiment. Once he arrived in Medford, just outside of Boston, the New Hampshire men gathered to select a leader. On April 23, Stark accepted a Colonelcy in the New Hampshire militia and was given command of the 1st New Hampshire Regiment. The regiment consisted of 800 men. Thomas Fleming writes that Stark's men were "the best troops in the amorphous American army. Stark's men were much more used to handling guns than the majority of the Grand American Army. They were also considerably tougher".

During the siege of Boston, Stark's regiment was assigned to the northern flank of the Charlestown peninsula. Stark anticipated his opponent's, British General William Howe, next move by building a breastwork along the beach to prevent being flanked by Howe's light infantry. Stark predicted correctly as about 350 light infantrymen charged Stark's regiment. The 1st New Hampshire laid waste to several waves of British attackers until the remaining British troops retreated, losing one-third of their force. The day's New Hampshire dead were buried in Salem Street Burying Grounds in Medford.

Soon after the Battle of Bunker Hill, Washington offered Stark a command in the Continental Army, and he accepted. He and his New Hampshire regiment agreed to join the Continental Army. They were sent to Canada as reinforcements in the spring of 1776. The invasion failed, and Stark and his men joined Washington's main army. He successfully commanded his men at the Battles of Trenton and Princeton, after which he was sent home to recruit more troops, as the regiment was now half its original size. He was successful in recruitment but discovered that Congress had overlooked him for a promotion to the rank of brigadier general. Feeling outraged and betrayed, he tendered his resignation. When other generals tried to talk him out of it, he replied that a new British threat would be coming from Canada, and he would be ready to face it from New Hampshire. Four months later, he was offered the position of Brigadier General of the New Hampshire Militia, which he accepted on the condition that he not be answerable to the Continental Army.

John Stark statue in the US Capitol

Stark was right; as soon as British General John Burgoyne, heading south from Canada, sent an expedition to capture American supplies at Bennington, Vermont. Stark learned of the approaching British troops and assembled his men at Bennington on August 13, 1777. On the 16th, the battle began when Stark's men attacked the British at Walloomsac, New York, ten miles from Bennington. Stark claimed it was "the hottest engagement I have ever witnessed." Darkness brought the battle to a halt, and it ended in an American victory. Stark's action contributed to the surrender of Burgoyne's northern army on October 17, following the Battles of Saratoga, by raising American morale, preventing the British from obtaining supplies, and eliminating several hundred enemy soldiers. Stark lost 14 men killed and 42 wounded. The British had 374 professional soldiers, and only 9 men escaped. For this feat, Stark was promoted to brigadier general in the Continental Army.

Burgoyne's surrender is regarded as a pivotal turning point in the Revolutionary War, as it marked the first major defeat of a British general and convinced the French that the Americans were worthy of military aid.

In September 1780, Stark sat as a judge in the court-martial that found British Major John André guilty of spying and aiding in Benedict Arnold's conspiracy to surrender West Point to the British.

Stark remained active throughout the remainder of the Revolutionary War, and Congress recognized his service on September 30, 1783, when he was promoted to the rank of major general.

Once the war ended, Stark chose to retire entirely. He returned to his farm in Manchester, New Hampshire, where he remained tending to it until he became too ill to do so. In 1809, a group of "Bennington" veterans gathered to commemorate the battle. Stark was not well enough to travel, but he sent a letter to his comrades, which closed with "Live free or die: death is not the worst of evils." New Hampshire would later (1945) adopt "Live free or die" as the state's motto.

Stark died at home on May 8, 1822, at the age of 93. He was buried in Stark Park in Manchester. He is memorialized in many ways and places. There is a New Hampshire historical marker near his birthplace, as well as a stone marker at the actual homestead location. The Daughters of the American Revolution owns his childhood home, and it is a National Historic Landmark. There is a bronze statue of General Stark in front of the New Hampshire statehouse in Concord and another in front of the West Annex of Manchester's City Hall. Stark and the Battle of Bennington are commemorated with a 306-foot-tall Bennington Battle Monument and a statue of Stark in Bennington, Vermont. In 1894, the State of New Hampshire donated a statue of General Stark for the National Statuary Hall of the United States Capitol.

Stark's grave

William Alexander, Lord Stirling
(1725–1783)

"The Bravest Man in America"

Buried at Albany Rural Cemetery,
Menands, New York.

Major General

William Alexander, also known as Lord Stirling, was a major general during the American Revolution who was a close friend of George Washington, ranking third or fourth in the chain of command in the Continental Army. Alexander was a wealthy man who often self-funded his military units. He was known for his courage on the battlefield and was dubbed "The Bravest Man in America" by a newspaper following his actions on Long Island. He was the general who unraveled the Conway Cabal. His claim to a Scottish earldom was dubious, but he used the title throughout his life.

Alexander, born December 27, 1725, in New York, New York, was the son of James Alexander (1691–1756), the Attorney General of New York, and his wife, Mary (née Spratt Provoost) Alexander (1693–1760). The elder Alexander was a distant relative of Henry Alexander, the 5th Earl of Sterling, who died in 1739, but he never pursued the title. He had fled Scotland after the failed Jacobite uprising and had success in America, emigrating with his wife in 1716. Mother Mary was a successful merchant, descended from the Spratt and de Peyster families and

William Alexander, Lord Stirling (1725–1783)

William Alexander, Lord Stirling

the stepdaughter of David Provoost, a successful Huguenot merchant in New York. Mary took over the Provoost business and grew it to the point where she was one of the largest merchants in New York City, especially during the time of the French and Indian War.

Young Alexander was educated privately, studying law under his father's direction, and demonstrated aptitudes in mathematics and astronomy. He assisted his mother in her import business. In 1748, Alexander married Sarah Livingston, the daughter of Philip Livingston, the 2nd Lord of Livingston Manor, and the sister of William Livingston, the Governor of New Jersey. The couple eventually had two daughters and one son: Mary Alexander (1749–1820), who married the merchant Robert Watts (1743–1814), the son of John Watts of New York; Catherine Alexander (1755–1826), who married Continental Congressman William Duer (1743–1799); and William Alexander, who died in infancy.

Alexander struck up a partnership with his brother-in-law, Hendrick "Henry" Livingston, who was based in Jamaica. They imported goods from England into the Hudson Valley, purchasing two ships for this purpose. William was also a captain in the local militia and routinely drilled his recruits.

In June 1754, Alexander attended the Albany Congress on behalf of his father, who was ill. There, he witnessed the presentation of Benjamin Franklin's Albany Plan of Union, the first plan to unify the colonies under a national government. He also met with representatives of the Iroquois Confederacy to discuss the Livingston family land claims in dispute. He offered lands back to the Iroquois that he would likely not accrue to him as part of his father-in-law's estate. Alexander also represented the Penns in their efforts to purchase more land for Pennsylvania.

After the conference, Massachusetts Governor William Shirley, who supported an attack on the French, asked Alexander to help him plan an attack on Fort Niagara, near present-day Buffalo, New York. Alexander procured provisions and boats and prepared for the attack. When William Johnson began planning an attack on the French at Lake George, the two began competing for the same resources, which led to disagreement. Neither attack was successful, and Shirley was replaced as the British military leader in North America.

In 1756, Alexander accompanied Shirley to England to testify on the latter's behalf as he defended his actions. Alexander ended up staying for nearly five years in England. While there, he learned of the vacant earldom in Scotland. At the encouragement of two Scottish lords, Archibald Campbell, the 3rd Duke of Argyll, and John Stuart, the 3rd Earl of Bute, Alexander pursued the Earldom of Stirling. The last earl had died in 1739, and the peerage was extinct unless filled. Alexander's sponsors believed Alexander stood to inherit vast lands in if approved, and they awaited their cut as a reward. The lands included large sections of Nantucket, Long Island, New Brunswick, Martha's Vineyard, Nova Scotia, and a large portion of what is now Maine. The Duke of York had purchased Long Island from the late earl's estate for 7,000 British pounds, but the sum had not been transferred due to the line dying out. While Alexander was descended from the 1st Earl of Stirling, he was a distant relation of the late 5th Earl. In 1759, a Scottish court in Edinburgh ruled unanimously in favor of the case, and Alexander adopted the title. However, against the advice of his sponsors, Alexander sought validation

William Alexander, Lord Stirling (1725–1783)

in the House of Lords as required by British law. They denied the claim, and though the lands were not acquired, Alexander kept using the title in America without their approval.

Regardless, Alexander returned to New York in 1761 on the same ship as his friend Philip Schuyler, having inherited a large fortune from his father, including mining and agricultural enterprises. Using the title Lord Stirling, he lived an extravagant lifestyle and built a grand estate in Basking Ridge, Bernards Township, New Jersey. Upon its completion, he moved there from New York City. When his mother passed away in 1763, he also inherited her fortune.

In New Jersey, Lord Stirling entertained often and lavishly. He was a member of the New Jersey Provincial Council and the Surveyor General. George Washington was a frequent guest, and he gave away Alexander's daughter at her wedding. Due to his successful attempts at winemaking in New Jersey, the Royal Society of Arts awarded Alexander a gold medal for winning the challenge of making wine in America. Alexander had planted 2100 grapevines on his estate. He was elected to the American Philosophical Society in 1770.

As tensions arose with England, Alexander sided with the Patriots, joining the New Jersey Council of Safety. He was expelled from the Royal Militia units he had been part of in New York and New Jersey.

In November 1775, he was appointed colonel of the 1st New Jersey Regiment of militia, which he funded himself. In January 1776, he led a group of volunteers to successfully capture a British transport ship in New York Bay.

In March 1776, Congress appointed Alexander as a brigadier general in the Continental Army upon the recommendation of Major General Charles Lee. He was initially in command at New York City where he supervised the fortifications of the city and harbor under the commander of the Northern Department, Philip Schuyler, based in Albany. He was then assigned to the 1st Maryland Regiment in Sullivan's division during the Battle of Long Island in August 1776. Alexander and his men faced repeated attacks and heavy losses from British General James Grant at the Old Stone House near Gowanus Creek. Realizing the British were overwhelming his forces; he implemented a rear-guard action that delayed the British attacks while the bulk of his troops escaped Brooklyn

Heights. Alexander himself stayed behind to lead a counterattack, allowing Washington and his troops to eventually evacuate to Manhattan in the fog overnight. Said Washington at the time, "Good God! What brave fellows I must this day lose." The fighting devolved to hand-to-hand combat, and only ten Americans survived. Two of the survivors, Generals Sullivan and Alexander, were captured by the British and spent several months as prisoners in New York City in the company of the Howe brothers. Both Washington and the British praised Alexander for his courage, audacity, and leadership. The British said he "fought like a wolf." An American newspaper described him as "the bravest man in America."

During their captivity, the Howes tried to turn the generals to the British to no avail, though some British officers quipped Alexander should be returned in order to preserve the supply of good wine. Alexander was returned in a prisoner exchange for Governor (of British West Florida) Montfort Browne and fought at the Battle of Trenton in December 1776, where he received the surrender of a Hessian regiment.

On February 19, 1777, Alexander was promoted to major general and initially served in the Hudson Highlands. For the balance of the Revolution, Alexander ranked third or fourth in the Continental Army, fighting at Metuchen, Brandywine, and Germantown.

During the bitter winter of 1777/78, the Continental Army was at Valley Forge. The British had occupied Philadelphia, and the Congress was in York, Pennsylvania. At this time, a young major named James Monroe was Alexander's aide-de-camp stationed at his headquarters. In later years, Aaron Burr criticized Monroe, saying his duty was to refill Alexander's tankard and listen to his stories about himself. Also during this time, General Horatio Gates was whispered as a possible replacement for George Washington. While one of Gates's aides, James Wilkinson, was at Alexander's headquarters in Tredyffrin Township, Chester County, Pennsylvania, he got drunk over dinner and began berating Washington, sharing criticisms from other officers. He revealed to Alexander he had read a letter from Thomas Conway to Gates urging him to "save the country." Alexander wrote to Washington (and other members of Congress) the next day, sharing what Wilkinson had said. Washington then confronted Conway, who called Alexander a liar and denied the note's existence. However, Gates made statements that betrayed his guilt. The Conway Cabal then unraveled.

On June 12, 1778, while at the Continental Congress in York, brother-in-law and Declaration of Independence signer Philip Livingston died. Alexander was away in New Jersey. On June 28, 1778, at the Battle of Monmouth, he led the Left Wing of the Army, holding off a critical British flanking maneuver. Then, from July 4 to August 12, Alexander presided over the court martial of Major General Charles Lee. Lee, the 2nd in command at Monmouth, had disobeyed Washington's orders to attack. Lee was found guilty and suspended from command.

From December 21, 1778, until February 5, 1779, while George Washington was with Congress in Philadelphia, he put Alexander in charge of the Army while encamped at Middlebrook, New Jersey, headquartered at the Van Horne House.

In August 1779, with "Lighthorse Harry" Lee, Alexander supported a successful raid on Paulus Hook, now Jersey City, New Jersey. He then managed the Staten Island expedition of January 14 to 15, 1780. Later that year, he sat on the board of inquiry regarding the actions of British spy Major John André. This exposed Benedict Arnold's treachery and led to André's execution by hanging on October 2, 1780.

As the focus of the war shifted South to Yorktown, Washington awarded Alexander command of the Northern Department, headquartered in Albany, New York, in October 1781. There, he countered a British attack from Lake George that fizzled after the Yorktown surrender.

During the interim period from the victory in Virginia at Yorktown until the Treaty of Paris, Alexander was stationed in Albany. There, he continued his lavish eating and drinking, leading to severe gout and rheumatism. By November 1782, his health had deteriorated rapidly. He was losing the use of his hands. By December, he was fervid and bedridden. His wife and daughter cared for him. Major General William Alexander died at Albany on January 15, 1783.

Alexander was initially buried at Trinity Churchyard in New York City. A memorial tablet to the Alexander family there faces the historic Wall Street district adjoining St. Paul's Chapel.

The grave of William Alexander.

Eventually, Alexander was reinterred at Albany Rural Cemetery in Menands, New York, in the Church Grounds, Section 49, Lot 12.

Ninety years after the Battle of Brooklyn, a commemorative monument was erected to honor the brave men who fought and died there in the Revolution. While excavating the monument, known as Prospect Park, the bones of many soldiers were discovered. This hallowed ground in New York was deeded to the State of Maryland in honor of the blood-soaked ground on which their soldiers had fallen.

William Alexander, Lord Stirling, is honored in many ways, including schools and parks in New Jersey. The town of Sterling, Massachusetts, and Sterling Place in Brooklyn, New York, are named after him.

William Alexander, Lord Stirling (1725–1783)

Through his daughter Catherine, his descendants include Columbia University president William Alexander Duer, lawyer and jurist John Duer, U.S. Congressman William Duer, and writer and suffragette Alice Duer Miller.

Through his daughter Mary, his descendants include General Stephen Watts Kearny and General Philip Kearny, Jr., who was killed in action during the Civil War.

Edward Telfair
(1738 – 1807)

Master of Sharon

Buried at Bonaventure Cemetery,
Savannah, Georgia.

Articles of Confederation • Governor

Edward Telfair was a native of Scotland who moved to Virginia, Nova Scotia, North Carolina, and then Georgia, where he became a merchant involved in the slave trade. He was also a state legislator, Continental Congressman, and two-time governor of the state. While in the Continental Congress, he signed the Articles of Confederation.

Telfair was born, according to most sources, in 1735, on the family's farm near Kirkcudbright, Galloway, Scotland. The names of his parents are no longer known. He attended the local grammar school and later studied commercial trade.

According to most sources, Telfair, a young man in 1758, was an agent for a commission house that sent him to the colonies, where he first settled in Virginia. He then hopped to Halifax, Nova Scotia and North Carolina, before joining his brother in Savannah, Georgia, in 1766. Telfair partnered with Basil Cowper in their own commission house which was very successful. The primary focus of the operation was the importation of enslaved people. Telfair wrote about methods to manage enslaved people best and the challenges owners faced, including

Edward Telfair (1738–1807)

Edward Telfair

runaways, mortality, dealing with those who were closely related, and relations between whites and freedmen.

In 1768, Telfair was elected to Georgia's Commons House of Assembly while also serving in lower-level offices in Savannah.

In 1774, Telfair married Sarah Gibbons, age 16, at her mother's plantation, Sharon, west of Savannah. The couple ultimately had six children, three sons and three daughters.

When hostilities began with Great Britain, Telfair sided with the rebels. He participated in the "general meeting of inhabitants" in Savannah on August 10, 1774, which passed several resolutions in protest.

The following year, Telfair was appointed to the Georgia Committee of Safety and the Provincial Congress. After the Battle of Lexington and Concord, Telfair participated in an attack on the British garrison at Savannah to seize arms and ammunition on May 11, 1775. In 1776, he was added to the Georgia Committee of Intelligence.

Next, Telfair was elected to the Continental Congress four times: February 26, 1778; January 11, 1780; August 17, 1781; and February 10, 1782. Having arrived in Philadelphia on July 8, 1778, he, Edward Langworthy, and John Walton signed the Articles of Confederation on behalf of Georgia. He then served in the Congress between July 13 and

November 16, 1778, after the Congress had returned from York. Telfair was rarely mentioned in the correspondence of the Congress and appears to have been uninvolved in most of the debates. His service ended in January 1783.

The following month, February 1783, Georgia commissioned Telfair to negotiate a treaty with the Chickamauga Cherokee Indians in a bid to end the Cherokee-American wars. He also helped settle a boundary dispute between North and South Carolina and attended Georgia's ratification of the Articles of Confederation.

On January 9, 1786, Telfair was elected as the 19th governor of Georgia and the first under the new state constitution, succeeding Samuel Elbert, serving until January 9, 1787, when he was succeeded by George Mathews.

In 1788, Telfair served as a delegate to the state constitutional convention and represented Burke County at the ratifying convention of the US Constitution in 1789. Telfair was one of only twelve people to receive electoral votes in the nation's first presidential election.

On November 9, 1790, Telfair was again elected to the governor's office, succeeding George Walton. He then served two full terms through

Grave of Edward Telfair

November 7, 1793. During his tenure, he dealt with Native tribes and was involved in illegal land sales to speculators as part of the Yazoo land scandal.

In 1794, Telfair was unsuccessful in his attempt to run for the US Senate from Georgia, losing to incumbent James Gunn. He then retired from public service until he was appointed as a justice in the Inferior Court in Chatham County, Georgia, on February 14, 1799.

Telfair died on September 17, 1807, and was initially interred in the family vault on the Sharon Plantation. Soon after, Telfair County, Georgia, was named in his honor.

Son Thoms Telfair (1780–1818) was a member of the US House of Representatives for two terms from 1813 to 1817.

Decades later, Telfair's remains were transferred to a large sarcophagus at Bonaventure Cemetery in Savannah. It was engraved "Edward Telfair of Georgia, who Died Sept. 17, 1807. Aged 64." This age is likely in error because it would infer his birth year as 1743. Most historians believe the age on the sarcophagus is incorrect given that it was carved many years later.

Daughter Mary Telfair (1791–1875) outlived her siblings and, upon her death, donated her Savannah home as the first public art museum in the South, now a complex of buildings known as the Telfair Museums. She also endowed the founding of the Telfair Hospital for Females. Today, it continues as Mary Telfair Women's Hospital.

After Mary Telfair's death, St. James Square in Savannah, near the Telfair Museums, was renamed to Telfair Square in honor of the family.

Mary Telfair

Matthew Thornton
(1714–1803)

First Speaker of the New Hampshire Assembly

Buried at Thornton Family Burying Ground,
Merrimack, New Hampshire.

Continental Congress • Declaration of Independence • Military

Matthew Thornton was a physician, judge, and member of the New Hampshire Provincial Congress. As a member of the Continental Congress from late 1776 until May 1777, he was a signer of the Declaration of Independence on behalf of New Hampshire. For a time, he was the Speaker of the New Hampshire House of Representatives.

Thornton was born on March 3, 1714, in Lisburn, County Antrim, Ireland (now in Northern Ireland), the son of James Thornton and Elizabeth (née Jenkins) Thornton, poor Irish farmers near Belfast.

When Thornton was about three years old, the family emigrated to North America and settled first in Wiscasset, Massachusetts Bay Colony (now Maine). Following an Indian attack on July 11, 1722, the family fled their burning home and resettled in Worcester, Massachusetts.

Thorton was educated in the local schools of Worcester and then studied medicine under Dr. Grout. In approximately 1740, he completed these studies and moved to Londonderry, New Hampshire, to establish a medical practice.

Early in his career as a physician, Thornton served as a surgeon in the New Hampshire Militia in the successful expedition to capture Fortress

Matthew Thornton (1714–1803)

Matthew Thornton

Louisbourg on Cape Breton in 1745. Upon his return, he focused on building his medical practice and acquiring land.

From 1758 through 1762, Thornton served in the New Hampshire Provincial Assembly. During this period, in 1760, at age 46, he married eighteen-year-old Hannah Jack. The couple ultimately had five children.

On July 6, 1763, Thornton was granted a township in his name by Benning Wentworth, then the Governor of New Hampshire. However, in 1765, with the announcement of the Stamp Act, Thornton voiced his opinion against it. Regardless, Governor Wentworth still named Thornton a colonel in the militia. By 1771, Thornton was also a justice of the peace for the County of Hillsborough, New Hampshire.

As the Revolutionary War commenced in 1775, Thornton sided with the rebels, denouncing the royal government in New Hampshire. Thornton was then appointed the President of the Provincial Congress, which met on June 14, 1775, to fill the vacuum left by the flight of Governor Wentworth. Said Thornton, now the presiding officer of the whole state, to the Congress:

> Friends and brethren, you must all be sensible that the affairs of America have, at length, come to a very affecting and alarming crisis. The horrors and Distresses of a Civil War, which, till of late, we only had in contemplation, we now find ourselves obliged to realize. Painful, beyond expression, have been those Scenes of blood and devastation, which the barbarous cruelty of British troops have placed before our eyes. Duty to God—to ourselves—to Posterity—enforced by the cries of slaughtered Innocents, have urged us to take up arms in our own defence. Such a day as this, was never before known, either to us or to our Fathers. You will give u leave, therefore, in whom you have reposed special confidence as your representative body, to suggest a few things, which call for the serious attention of every northeast, who has the true interest of America at Heart. We would therefore recommend to the colony at large to cultivate that christian [sic] Union, Harmony and tender affection, which is the only foundation upon which our invaluable privileges can rest, with any security; or our publick measures be pursued with the least prospect of success . . . We seriously and earnestly recommend the practice of that pure and undefiled religion, which embalmed the memory of our pious ancestors, as that alone upon which we can build a solid hope and confidence in the Divine protection and favour, without whose blessing all the measures of safety we have, or can propose, will end in our shame and disappointment.

That November, at the second Provincial Congress, Thornton was renewed as a colonel in the militia, a position he held until November 1779. He also oversaw the drafting of the first state constitution for New Hampshire, which was adopted on January 5, 1776, the first for any rebelling colony. The delegates then elected Thornton as the first Speaker of the New Hampshire Assembly.

Thornton was elected to an open seat in the Continental Congress on September 12, 1776. He arrived in Philadelphia on November 4, 1776, four months after the Declaration of Independence was passed. On that date, he became the third person from New Hampshire to sign

Matthew Thornton (1714–1803)

the document, following Josiah Bartlett and William Whipple. Thornton was reelected to the Continental Congress on December 24, 1776, but only served until May 2, 1777.

John Adams, in a letter to his wife, Abigail, wrote of Thornton:

> We have from New Hampshire a Col. Thornton, a Physician by Profession, a Man of Humour. He has a large Budget of droll Stories, with which he entertains Company Perpetually. I heard about Twenty or five and twenty Years ago, a Story of a Physician in Londonderry, who accidentally [met] with one of our new England Enthusiasts, call'd [Exhorters]. The Fanatic soon began to examine the Dr. [concerning] the Articles of his Faith, and what he thought of original Sin? Why, says the Dr., I satisfy myself about it in this manner. Either original Sin is divisible or indivisible. If it was divisible every descendant of Adam and Eve must have a Part, and the share which falls to each Individual at this Day, is so small a Particle, that I think it is not worth considering. If indivisible, then the whole Quantity must have descended in a right Line, and must now be possessed by one Person only, and the Chances are Millions and Millions to one that that Person is now in Asia or Africa, and that I have nothing to do with it. I told Thornton the story and that I suspected him to be the Man. He said he was. He belongs to Londonderry.

Thornton should not be confused with his namesake nephew. Captain Matthew Thornton was charged with treason before the Battle of Bennington in 1777. Daniel Webster's father, Ebenezer Webster, investigated the allegations. Thornton was found not guilty and was discharged.

Following his service in the Continental Congress, Thornton, now in his sixties, served as a judge on the New Hampshire Superior Court until 1782. During this time, he wrote political essays and retired from his medical practice to Merrimack, New Hampshire. There, he operated a farm and a ferry with his family.

In his later years, Thornton remained involved in politics. He served as the representative of Merrimack and Bedford in the New Hampshire

House of Representatives in 1783, and in the New Hampshire Senate from 1784 to 1787, while also serving as a state counselor from 1785 to 1786, and again as the representative for Merrimack in 1786.

Sadly, his wife Hannah, 28 years his junior, died in 1786, perhaps signaling the end of his public life.

While visiting his daughter in Newburyport, Massachusetts, Thornton died on June 24, 1803, at age 89. *The Farmer's Cabinet* stated:

> His Character needs not the aid of a newspaper panegyric: His life is its best eulogium. It exhibited at once the Christian and the Patriot, and was a proof that he united the love of God with the

Grave of Matthew Thornton

love of his country. He engaged early in the cause of American Independence, and continued to his death a firm friend to the constitution and government of his country. His private virtues were a model for imitation, and, while memory does her office, will be had in grateful recollection.

Thornton was buried next to his wife at the Thornton Family Burying Ground in Merrimack, New Hampshire.

Thornton is honored in several ways, including the naming of a town and an elementary school after him. His former home is on the National Register of Historic Places, and a historical marker featuring him was erected on US Route 3 in Merrimack. In 1873, his great-grandson, US Navy Captain James S. Thornton of the *Kearsarge*, donated a portrait of Thornton to the state of New Hampshire.

George Walton
1749?–1804

The Orphaned Founder

Buried at Courthouse Grounds,
Augusta, Georgia.

Declaration of Independence

This founder was orphaned at a young age. Many signers of the Declaration of Independence served in state militias, but few participated in any battles during the Revolutionary War. Not only did this founder see action, but he was wounded, captured, and imprisoned by the British. In addition to serving in the Continental Congress, he would also serve as governor and a United States senator from Georgia. His name was George Walton.

Walton was born in Cumberland County, Virginia. The exact year of his birth is unknown. The *New Georgia Encyclopedia* states that it is believed he was born in 1749; however, some researchers have placed his birth as early as 1740. What is known is that he was orphaned at a young age and adopted by an uncle who apprenticed Walton to a carpenter.

Like the date of his birth, there is confusion about his experience as an apprentice. In their book, *Signing Their Lives Away,* Denise Kiernan and Joseph D'Agnese write that there are two stories about how the carpenter treated him. One describes the carpenter as a mean man who was against Walton seeking to educate himself, so he refused to provide a candle so Walton could read his books. In this version, the resourceful Walton

George Walton 1749?–1804

George Walton

gathers wood chips, which he sets ablaze to provide some light to read by. In another, very different version, the carpenter is a kindly gentleman who lets Walton miss work to attend school. The authors conclude that it is difficult to determine which version is accurate, but do note that he was educated enough to study with an attorney when he moved to Savannah, Georgia, in his twenties. He was admitted to the bar in 1774.

Walton became active in supporting the patriots' cause. He was elected secretary of the Georgia Provincial Congress and became president of the Council of Safety. However, his views did not represent those in the majority in Georgia, as evidenced by the fact that Georgia was the only colony that did not send representatives to the First Continental Congress.

It was only when armed conflict between the colonists and the English ensued that the tide turned in Georgia. In 1775, the colony sent delegates to Philadelphia, and in 1776, Walton was elected to join them. Here, he joined Lyman Hall and Button Gwinnett, both considered to be more radical than he was. He would serve honorably and remain in Congress longer than his two colleagues and fellow signers of the Declaration of Independence. If you believe the account of signer Benjamin Rush, Walton was the youngest signer. Rush wrote, "He (Walton) was the youngest member of Congress, not quite being three and twenty when he signed the Declaration of Independence." Thus, Rush added to the possible year of Walton's birth, 1753. However, without additional evidence, the youngest signer must continue to be recognized as Edward Rutledge of South Carolina.

Signers Monument in Augusta, Georgia.

George Walton 1749?–1804

Walton took leave from Congress in 1778 to assume the role of colonel in the militia and fight in the Revolution. During the siege of Savannah, he was shot and fell off his horse. The British quickly captured him. He was not treated harshly and was permitted to seek private medical care to treat the wound in his thigh. Some speculate that the reason for this is that he was a prized prisoner due to his service in Congress and could be used in a prisoner exchange for a high-ranking British officer. He was held prisoner for a year before being exchanged for an English naval captain.

After leaving Congress, Walton continued to serve the people of Georgia as the state's chief justice, governor, and United States senator. He was elected to serve as a delegate to the 1787 Constitutional Convention but declined due to his duties at the state level. In 1789, he served as a presidential elector. He was also the founder and trustee of the Academy of Richmond County in Augusta and of Franklin College, now the University of Georgia in Athens. After serving as governor, he became a judge of the superior court from 1790 until his death.

Walton died in 1804 and was originally buried in Augusta's Rosney Cemetery. His remains were later reinterred in 1848 beneath the signer's monument on the approach to the Augusta municipal building. Lyman Hall is also buried here, and Button Gwinnett is memorialized.

Grave of George Walton

Samuel Ward
(1725 – 1776)

Colonial Governor and Continental Congressman

Buried at Common Burial Ground,
Newport, Rhode Island.

Governor • Continental Association

The son of Royal Governor of Rhode Island Richard Ward, Samuel Ward, a farmer, was also a governor and later a Continental Congressman who signed the Continental Association.

Ward was born on May 27, 1725, in Newport, Rhode Island, the son of Richard Ward, the Royal Governor of Rhode Island, and Mary (née Tillinghast) Ward, who was the daughter of John Tillinghast and Isabel Sayles and great-granddaughter of Roger Williams, the founder of the colony. Ward, on his father's side, was the great-grandson of John Ward, a cavalry officer in Cromwell's army, who came to America following the restoration of Charles II. Richard Ward's sister Mary Ward married Sion Arnold, a grandson of Governor Benedict Arnold II, the grandfather of the infamous traitor.

Ward was the ninth of fourteen children who grew up in a wealthy household. He was educated in the local grammar school and may have been tutored by his older brother Thomas, a Harvard graduate.

In 1745, only twenty years of age, Ward married Anna Ray, the daughter of a plantation owner on Block Island. The dowry included

Samuel Ward (1725–1776)

Samuel Ward

land on the island on which the young couple settled and began farming and racing livestock, including Narraganset Pacers, a breed of racehorse. The couple had eleven children, including five sons and six daughters.

As a young man of thirty-one, Ward was elected a deputy from Westerly in the colonial assembly in 1756, siding on the hard money (specie) side of the ongoing paper money debate in the colony. This put him at odds with rival Stephen Hopkins of Providence, who favored paper money. The vitriol between the two was bitter, leading to a lawsuit filed by Hopkins against Ward for slander. The case was moved to Massachusetts to find an impartial court, where Ward prevailed in 1759.

Over the next ten years, Ward and Hopkins switch off in the governor's seat. In 1761, when Hopkins defeated Ward for governor, the assembly appointed Ward the chief justice of the Rhode Island Supreme Court. He held this post for one year until he was again elected governor. Ward was a proponent of the Rhode Island College, which later became Brown University. In 1765, Ward was one of the college's founding trustees.

Despite being the Royal Governor in 1765 and 1766, Ward railed against the Stamp Act, opposing Parliament. When Rhode Island citizens protested the British tax authorities, Governor Ward did nothing to stop them and was the only colonial governor to do so. This led to the forfeiture of his position as governor, despite the act being repealed.

Hopkins won the governorship in 1767, and Ward returned home to his farm and served as a trustee of the college. As both Hopkins and Ward were no longer governors after 1768, they eventually established friendly relations.

On August 5, 1769, Ward was baptized at the age of 44 as a Seventh Day Baptist. He remained out of politics for several years.

Mrs. Anna Ward died in 1770, followed by the Boston Massacre later that year. Tensions continued to rise in Boston between the British authorities and the colonists. Following the Boston Tea Party in December 1773, the British passed the Boston Port Bill, closing the port to commerce. This led to a call for a congress to meet in Philadelphia. Both Ward and Hopkins were appointed delegates to the First Continental Congress in Philadelphia that summer, in 1774.

When the First Continental Congress met in Philadelphia, Ward kept a diary. He recapped the first day on September 5, 1774:

> Met at the New Tavern; went to Carpenter's Hall, and, liking the place, agreed to hold the Congress there; took a list of the Delegates, chose the Honorable Peyton Randolph Esq. President, and Mr. Charles Thompson Secretary; read the appointments of the Delegates; considered of the manner of each Colony's voting and rules for regulating the business; but adjourned until ten o'clock tomorrow.

Two days later, he wrote:

> Mr. [Jacob] Duché read prayers and lessons, and concluded with one of the most sublime, catholic [*sic*], well-adapted prayers I ever heard. Thanks for it and presented by Mr. [Thomas] Cushing [of Massachusetts] and Mr. [Artemas] Ward [of Massachusetts]. A

Committee of two from each Colony appointed to prepare a statement of those rights of the Colonists, the infringements of those rights and the means of redress. A committee to report what Acts of Parliament affect the trade of the Colonies. (45 members present.) Door keepers appointed.

Ward signed the Continental Association on October 20, 1774. He and Hopkins were then re-appointed to the Congress, attending the Continental Congress beginning in May 1775 following the battles at Lexington and Concord. Wrote Ward, "'Heaven save my country,' is my

Grave of Samuel Ward.

first, my last, and almost my only prayer." Ward devoted all of his time to the Continental Congress and served on the Committee on Secrets, and the Committee of the Whole.

In March 1776, while in Philadelphia, Ward contracted smallpox. He died on March 26, 1776, at the age of 50. Initially, Ward was buried at the First Baptist Church in Philadelphia. He was reinterred in the Common Burial Ground in Newport, Rhode Island, in 1860.

Ward's second son, Samuel Ward Jr. was a lieutenant colonel of the 1st Rhode Island Regiment in the Continental Army. Great-granddaughter Julia Ward Howe composed the "Battle Hymn of the Republic."

Westerly, Rhode Island, named its high school after Ward in 1937, but changed it to Westerly High School late in the 20th century, leaving his name on the main auditorium.

Close-up view of Samuel Ward's grave.

John Wentworth Jr.
(1745–1787)

New Hampshire Scion

Buried at Pine Hill Cemetery,
Dover, New Hampshire.

Continental Congress • Articles of Confederation

John Wentworth Jr. was an attorney from a famous New Hampshire family. As a member of the Continental Congress from 1778 until 1779, he was a signer of the Articles of Confederation on behalf of New Hampshire.

Wentworth was born on July 17, 1745, near the Salmon Falls River at Somersworth, Strafford County, New Hampshire, the son of Judge John Wentworth and Joanna (née Gilman) Wentworth, a descendant of "Elder" William Wentworth who emigrated to America in the mid-1600s and had blood ties to King Edward VI of England and Sir Thomas Wentworth, the Earl of Strafford, for whom Strafford County, New Hampshire, was named. Two other John Wentworths were descendants of "Elder" including John Wentworth (1672–1730), a lieutenant governor of New Hampshire, and Sir John Wentworth (1737–1820), the last colonial governor of New Hampshire, and a first cousin once removed to the signer.

Wentworth was tutored privately and then entered Harvard College, where he graduated in 1768. He then began studying law in Dover, New

Hampshire. He was admitted to the New Hampshire bar in 1771, but did not open a law practice. Instead, Governor John Wentworth appointed him as the register of probate for Strafford County from 1773 until his death.

On January 1, 1774, siding with the revolutionaries, Wentworth was named to the New Hampshire Committee of Correspondence against the wishes of his family. This put him at odds with the governor and other Loyalist family members. It was the various Committees of Correspondence that agreed to call for a Continental Congress.

On May 11, 1775, the New Hampshire Provincial Congress held a Convention of Deputies at Exeter, New Hampshire, of which young Wentworth, not yet thirty, was the chair. This committee elected John Langdon and John Sullivan to the First Continental Congress.

From 1776 through 1780, Wentworth, representing Dover, was elected to the New Hampshire House of Representatives, which succeeded the colonial government during the Revolution. In 1777, Wentworth was also named to the New Hampshire Committee of Safety.

On March 14, 1778, Wentworth was elected to the Continental Congress, still meeting in York, Pennsylvania, after the authoring of the Articles of Confederation. Wentworth attended the Congress from May

York Courthouse where the Continental Congress approved the Articles of Confederation.

30 to June 18, 1778, and then affixed his signature on behalf of New Hampshire on July 9, 1778. A letter from Josiah Bartlett, New Hampshire Congressman, to Meshech Weare, the President of New Hampshire, on July 11, 1778, stated, "Mr. Wentworth had a fever at York Town; it was pretty bad. I tarried with him for four days after the Congress adjourned; left him better Thursday the 2nd instant; have not heard from him since; hope he will be here the beginning of the week."

Grave of John Wentworth Jr.

On August 18, 1778, Bartlett wrote to William Whipple, "Mr. Wentworth is in town but does not attend public business." However, Wentworth was reelected to Congress the next day on August 19, 1778.

The following month, on September 8, 1778, Bartlett again wrote to Weare: "I have Reced [received] a Copy of the appointment of Delegates to attend Congress the first of November next, and I must beg leave inform you That I can by no means attend Congress after the last of october [sic] next. By reason of Mr. Wentworth's Sickness I have not Recd. the least assistance from him, and am obliged to attend so Closely to public business without any interval of Relaxation, that it will be necessary for my Constitution of body and mind to be relieved then, if I am able to hold out till that time."

It appears that Wentworth did not attend the Congress again. On April 3, 1779, Nathaniel Peabody and Woodbury Langdon were elected to the Congress in place of Bartlett and Wentworth, who had resigned. Rather, Wentworth remained in the New Hampshire House of Representatives. In 1781, he replaced his father as a member of the state executive council, in support of Meshech Weare. He was also a member of the New Hampshire Committee of Safety.

In 1783, Wentworth was elected to the New Hampshire Senate and left the executive council. He served through 1786.

Wentworth died at age 41 on January 10, 1787, at Dover, New Hampshire. He was interred at Pine Hill Cemetery in Dover.

William Whipple
(1730–1785)

Hero of Saratoga

Buried at Old North Cemetery,
Portsmouth, New Hampshire.

Continental Congress • Declaration of Independence • Military

William Whipple was a merchant and ship's captain who later became a judge. As a member of the Continental Congress from 1776 to 1779, he was a signer of the Declaration of Independence on behalf of New Hampshire. As a soldier, he commanded brigades in the New Hampshire Militia at Saratoga and during the Battle of Rhode Island.

Whipple was born on January 14, 1730, in Kittery, Massachusetts (now in Maine), the son of Captain William Whipple, Sr., and Mary (née Cutt) Whipple, the daughter of a wealthy shipbuilder. Some sources described Whipple Sr. as a brewer or "maltster." Regardless, they were an old Massachusetts Bay Colony family, descended from Samuel Appleton.

Master Whipple attended the common schools in Kittery and then went to sea. By age 21, he was a ship's master. Soon, he purchased his own ship and traded in commodities, engaging in the triangular trade between North America, Africa, and the West Indies, dealing in wood, rum, and slaves.

Circa 1759, Whipple went into business with his brother Joseph in Portsmouth and dropped the slave trade. He also later freed any slaves in

William Whipple

his household, including a servant named Prince Whipple, and refused to deal with the issue further. Whipple hoped for the abolition of the slave trade throughout America.

In 1767, Whipple married his first cousin, Catherine Moffat. They moved into the Moffatt-Ladd House in Portsmouth in 1769, but their only child, a son name William III, died as an infant.

Early in 1775, as the rebellion against the crown was starting, the people of New Hampshire elected a Provincial Congress. On February 6, 1775, it was reported that John Wentworth, Nathaniel Folsom, Meshech Weare, Josiah Bartlett, Christopher Toppan, Ebenezer Thompson, and William Whipple were elected to the committee. Whipple was also appointed to the Committee of Safety for New Hampshire and was elected to the Continental Congress along with Josiah Bartlett and John Langdon.

Prior to leaving for the Continental Congress, Whipple wrote to fellow Congressman Josiah Bartlett, anticipating the work ahead: "This year, my Friend, is big with mighty events. Nothing less than the fate of America depends on the virtue of her sons, and if they do not have virtue enough to support the most Glorious Cause ever human beings were engaged in, they don't deserve the blessings of freedom."

Whipple arrived at the Continental Congress in Philadelphia on February 29, 1776. He served through September 24, 1779. During the summer of 1776, Whipple and fellow New Hampshire delegates Josiah Bartlett and Matthew Thornton signed the Declaration of Independence. Whipple was also the second cousin of Stephen Hopkins, another signer from Rhode Island.

Early in 1777, with the war going poorly to the south, the New Hampshire Assembly established two brigades of militia for the defense of the state. Command of one was given to Whipple, and the other to John Stark. At this time, Whipple's servant, Prince Whipple, urged his master to allow him to also fight for the cause. "You are going to fight for liberty," he said, "but I have none to fight for." Whipple granted Prince's request to fight and emancipated Prince upon the conclusion of his military service.

Following service in the Continental Congress, during the summer of 1777, Whipple traveled back to New Hampshire with fellow Congressman William Ellery from Rhode Island. Whipple kept meticulous notes about his travels, which survive to this day.

The New Hampshire militia saw action that autumn at Saratoga in September and October. Whipple commanded four militia regiments, including Bellow's, Chase's, Moore's, and Welch's. Following the great victory, Major General Horatio Gates selected Whipple and Colonel James Wilkinson to negotiate the British surrender with two of their counterparts under General Burgoyne. Whipple was one of the signers of the Convention of Saratoga. Whipple then escorted Burgoyne and his army back to Winter Hill, Somerville, Massachusetts. He passed the news of the victory to Captain John Paul Jones, who later informed Benjamin Franklin in Paris.

The following year, during the Battle of Rhode Island, Whipple led three regiments under the command of General John Sullivan. This battle did not go as well, and when Sullivan ordered a retreat, Whipple and his men, who resided in a house near the battlefield, were within cannon shot of the advancing British. One cannonball tore through a horse outside the house and smashed the leg of one Whipple's subordinates, later requiring amputation.

Returning to the Continental Congress in 1779, Whipple was not shy in his letters to his colleagues, complaining about the difficulties of being in the Congress, according to one source:

> "Discontent over pay and allowances frequently resulted in delegates threatening to return home. As his ragged clothes fell off his back and his 'lady of the tub' badgered him over failure to pay for his freshly washed socks, [James] Lovell demanded 'ninety days of refreshment' from the Continental Congress. He admitted to Sam Adams that Congress, 'this political scene of drudgery,' had become too expensive for him to attend. In 1779, [John] Fell similarly observed that New Jersey's parsimony did not tempt him to stay in Congress 'longer than I had engaged for,' and William Whipple declared that 'there is no pecuniary temptation that will be a temptation to tarry through the summer.'"

That November, the Continental Congress appointed Whipple and Thomas Waring to the Board of Admiralty, but Whipple returned to New Hampshire and was elected to the New Hampshire Assembly in 1780, serving until 1784. During this time, he was elected one of the "Overseers of the Poor," and on October 11, 1782, he was one of the judges, along with David Brearly, William Churchill Houston, Cyrus Griffin, Joseph Jones, and Thomas Nelson, to help resolve the land dispute over the Wyoming Valley between Pennsylvania and Connecticut. The court was held in Trenton, New Jersey, on November 12, 1782. Also, in 1782, Whipple was appointed as a justice on the Supreme Court of New Hampshire, a position he held until his death.

It was while riding on his judicial circuit at only age 55 on November 28, 1785, that Justice Whipple suffered a cardiac episode and fainted, falling off his horse. Whipple died that day and was buried at the Old North Cemetery in Portsmouth, New Hampshire.

A Maryland newspaper declared him "a Gentleman of a very amiable Character."

Another newspaper in New Hampshire eulogized him: "On Monday, the 28th ultimo, died, universally lamented, the Hon. General William Whipple, a Judge of the Superior Court of this State. In him, concentrated every principle of the dignity of man. His disinterested patriotism and public services are now known to all; and when newspaper encomiums are lost in oblivion, the pen of the historian shall preserve the remembrance of his virtues in the breast of succeeding generations."

Whipple's original tombstone reads:

"Here are deposited the remains of the Honourable William Whipple, who departed this Life on the 28th day of November, 1785, in the 55th Year of his Age. He was often elected and thrice attended the Continental Congress, as Delegate for the State of New Hampshire, particularly in that memorable Year in which America declared itself independent of Great Britain. He was also at the Time of his decease a Judge of the Supreme Court of Judicature. In Him a firm and ardent Patriotism, was united with universal benevolence, and every social Virtue."

Grave of William Whipple

John Williams
(1731–1799)

North Carolina Speaker of the House

Buried at Montpelier Plantation Cemetery,
Henderson, North Carolina.

Articles of Confederation • Military • Judge

John Williams, of North Carolina, was a colonel in the North Carolina militia and a member of the North Carolina House of Commons, where he became speaker. He was also a land speculator, involved in the acquisition of Kentucky. As a member of the Continental Congress, he signed the Articles of Confederation. He was also a superior court judge during his later years and a founder of the University of North Carolina.

Williams was born on March 14, 1731, in Surry County, North Carolina, the son of John Williams, IV, a planter, and his wife, Mary (née Womack) Williams, of Granville County, Virginia. He studied law and established a practice near his North Carolina plantation with his cousin, Richard Henderson. On November 12, 1759, Williams married a widow named Agnes Keeling (née Bullock). They produced one daughter, Agatha.

In 1768, Williams was appointed Deputy Attorney General of North Carolina. He was also commissioned to the ceremonial position of colonel in the North Carolina militia. Meanwhile, his plantation, Montpelier, outside of the future Williamsborough, was one of the most substantial in Granville County.

John Williams (1731–1799)

John Williams

During the 1760s, cousins Williams and Henderson pursued land ventures. In 1769, they hired Daniel Boone to survey the land between the Cumberland and Kentucky Rivers. In August 1774, when founding the Louisa Company, Henderson employed Boone to "make contacts with influential Cherokees to learn their attitude toward the sale of some of their lands in the Kentucky area to white purchasers."

The following March, Henderson and Boone signed the Treaty of Sycamore Shoals, also known as the Treaty of Watauga, leading to the Transylvania Purchase from the Cherokees of "a tract of 20 million acres lying north of the Cumberland River, southeast of the Ohio River, and west of the Cumberland Mountains, with a narrow access route extending from Sycamore Shoals to Cumberland Gap."

Meanwhile, Williams was involved with the state legislature, representing Granville County. During the congress's meeting in Hillsborough from August 24 to September 10, 1775, the delegates reviewed an early draft of the "Articles of the Confederacy." During this time, on September 9, Williams was commissioned as a lieutenant colonel under Colonel James Thackston of the Orange County Minutemen Regiment.

Meanwhile, Williams was named a resident agent of Boonesborough, Kentucky, for the Transylvania Company on September 25, 1775. According to the company's minutes, he was "to transact their business in the said Colony; and he is accordingly invested with full power, by letter of Attorney. Mr. Williams shall proceed to Boonesborough, in the said Colony, as soon as possible, and continue there until the twelfth day of April next; and to be allowed, for his services, one hundred and fifty pounds, Proclamation money of North Carolina, out of the profits arising from the sale of lands, after discharging the Company's present engagements."

Pulled away from his land pursuits, Colonel Williams was at the Battle of Moore's Creek Bridge on February 27, 1776. The minutemen regiments were then disbanded on April 10, 1776. Williams continued as a colonel and commandant of the 9th North Carolina Regiment of the North Carolina Line from 1776 to 1778.

Williams was elected to the North Carolina House of Commons from 1777 to 1778 and was named Speaker of the House. In 1778, he was appointed to the Continental Congress and signed the Articles of Confederation in Philadelphia on July 21. However, Williams resigned from the Continental Congress on February 1, 1779, seeking to return home.

Upon his return to North Carolina in 1779, the village near his plantation was named Williamsborough in his honor. It served as the state's temporary capital during the skirmishes between Loyalists and the North Carolina militia, from the summer of 1781 to February 1782. It was formally incorporated in 1787.

Additionally, in 1779, Williams was appointed as a judge to the Court of Conference, which effectively served as the state's superior court. His most notable ruling was during *Bayard v. Singleton* in 1787, the first example of a court exercising judicial review in the United States. This case was widely published and was credited as setting a precedent for the US Supreme Court's *Marbury v. Madison*.

Williams served more than twelve years as a judge and then devoted the rest of his life to supporting education. He was one of the seven founding trustees of the University of North Carolina at Chapel Hill in 1792. Williams also donated many books to the library and an ostrich egg to the museum.

Williams died on October 10, 1799, and was buried in the family plot at his estate, Montpelier.

Hugh Williamson
(1735 – 1819)

"The Ben Franklin of North Carolina"

Buried at Trinity Church Cemetery,
New York, New York.

US Constitution • First US Congress

Hugh Williamson was a Pennsylvania-born physician, scholar, and politician who was elected to the Continental Congress, where he signed the US Constitution on behalf of North Carolina. He lived in several states during his lifetime and was known as North Carolina's Benjamin Franklin.

Williamson, born December 5, 1735, in West Nottingham Township, Chester County, Pennsylvania, was the son of John Williamson, a clothier, and his wife, Mary (née Davison) Williamson. The Williamsons were devout Presbyterians of Scots-Irish descent. Apparently too frail for the family's clothier business, Williamson was encouraged to become a minister and was sent to Francis Alison's New London Academy near Newark, Delaware, graduating in 1754.

Upon graduation, Williamson spent the next three years studying mathematics at the College of Philadelphia, the predecessor of the University of Pennsylvania. He graduated in the school's first class on May 17, 1757, five days before his father died.

Hugh Williamson

Over the next few years, as he settled his father's estate, he tutored Latin at the Philadelphia Academy and continued his theological studies with Reverend Samuel Finley, his neighbor in West Nottingham, who later became the president of the College of New Jersey. Williamson moved to Connecticut and obtained a preacher's license but was disillusioned by the divisions in the Presbyterian Church and burdened by ill health. He turned again to academics and completed a master's degree at the College of Philadelphia in 1760 and joined the faculty as a professor of mathematics.

However, Williamson continued to study and became interested in the human body and its functions. He studied medicine at the University of Edinburgh and the University of Utrecht in the Netherlands. He received his medical degree on August 6, 1764, and returned to Philadelphia to open a practice. A polymath, he also continued other scientific pursuits and projects, landing membership in the American Philosophical Society in 1768 and acclaim in Europe in intellectual circles for his work on the transits of Venus and Mercury and his papers "An Attempt to Account for the Change in Climate" and "An Essay on Comets." All contained original ideas, leading to an honorary doctorate from the University of Leyden in the Netherlands.

In 1773, to raise money for a new academy in Newark, Delaware, Williamson traveled to the West Indies and then to Europe, stopping in Boston in mid-December. There, he witnessed the Boston Tea Party on December 18, as Patriots disguised as Indians tossed crates of tea into the harbor in protest of Parliament's tax.

Upon reaching England a few weeks later, Williamson was summoned before the Privy Council to testify regarding the rebellion in Boston and colonial affairs generally. He warned the councilors that there would be further trouble if policies were not changed. At the time, he was collaborating with Benjamin Franklin in London on electrical experiments. Williamson published an anonymous "Plea of the Colonies," hoping to encourage sympathetic Whigs to side with the Americans. He also may have been involved in the controversy regarding Benjamin Franklin, the colonial postmaster, and the letters of Massachusetts Royal Governor Thomas Hutchinson which called for an abridgment of colonial rights. He stayed in England, in scientific circles, for a while before moving on to the Netherlands. He was there in July 1776 when the colonies declared independence.

Williamson returned to Philadelphia in early 1777 and volunteered as a doctor in the Continental Army. He thought his best contribution would be procuring medications, so he headed to Charleston, South Carolina, to open a business in partnership with his brother John. The goal was to obtain scarce items from the West Indies that would circumvent the British blockades.

Later, on his way to Baltimore, he was waylaid in Edenton, North Carolina, and decided to make his base of operations there. Williamson quickly became connected to the government in North Carolina, answering the call of Major General and Governor Richard Caswell to be the state's Physician and Surgeon General. Williamson accepted and held the post until the end of the Revolution.

By 1780, Williamson worked as a field surgeon, treating troops in South Carolina following the stunning defeat of American forces in Charleston. After the Battle of Camden, Williamson insisted on attending to victims on both sides of the conflict due to widespread smallpox.

He then joined Major General Nathanael Greene's campaign to liberate the South.

After the war, Williamson was elected to the North Carolina House of Commons and the Continental Congress in 1782. He brought with him a Federalist perspective. In 1786, North Carolina selected Williamson to attend the Annapolis Convention but arrived too late to have an impact. The following year, he was appointed to the Constitutional Convention in Philadelphia. There, he lodged with Alexander Hamilton and James Madison and led the North Carolina delegation. Though personally opposed to slavery, Williamson voted for the "Three-Fifths Compromise" that permitted its continuance. Near the end of the convention, Williamson wrote what was known as the "Letters of Sylvius," urging North Carolina to ratify the Constitution. The decision was whether the United States would remain a "system of patchwork and a series of expedients" or become "the most flourishing, independent, and happy nation on the face of the earth." Thomas Jefferson summed up Williamson's contributions, noting he was "a very useful member, of an acute mind, attentive to business, and of a high degree of erudition."

After he signed the US Constitution, Williamson returned to the Congress in New York to wrap up. He then returned to North Carolina to urge its ratification, saying it was "more free and more perfect than any form of government that has ever been adopted by any nation."

Williamson was elected to the First Federal Congress and served two terms. He opposed the establishment of the Bank of the United States, the federal government's assumption of state debt, the whiskey excise tax, and the Jay Treaty.

Williamson finally married Maria Apthorpe, the daughter of Charles Ward Apthorpe, in January 1789. The couple had two sons, but Maria died during the birth of their second child in 1790. The child died soon after. Williamson decided not to run again for Congress and retired to New York City. There, he continued to write and research and raise his son, who perished in 1811 at the age of 22.

Over the years, Williamson published a wide range of works, including a two-volume *History of North Carolina* (1812). He advocated for inland canals, leading later to the Erie Canal. He was also a trustee or founding member of the University of North Carolina, the New York College of Physicians and Surgeons, and the New York Literary and Philosophical Society. His philanthropy involved the support and development of an orphan asylum, the humane society, and a hospital dispensary. He was also a prominent member of the New York Historical Society, and in 1813, Williamson was elected to the American Antiquarian Society.

Williamson died suddenly in New York City on May 22, 1819, while driving his carriage. He was 83. He was buried in Trinity Churchyard in New York City, near the grave of Alexander Hamilton.

Williamson Counties in Tennessee and Illinois were named for him. Williamson Street in Madison, Wisconsin, also carries his name.

Grave of Hugh Williamson

Thomas Willing
(1731 – 1821)

Banker and Financier

Buried at Christ Church Burial Ground,
Philadelphia, Pennsylvania.

Financier

Thomas Willing was the son of Philadelphia mayor Charles Willing (1710-1754) and his wife, Anne Shippen, heir to one of the prominent families in Pennsylvania and the granddaughter of Edward Shippen, Philadelphia's second mayor. Willing was a delegate to the Continental Congress but refused to sign the Declaration of Independence. Instead, he focused on organizing the finances of the young republic and was president of the Bank of North American and the first president of the Bank of the United States.

Willing was born December 19, 1731, in Philadelphia, Pennsylvania. He first attended preparatory school at Bath, England, followed by law studies at the Inner Temple in London and business studies at Watts Academy.

His education completed, in 1749 Willing returned to Philadelphia where he worked in his father's mercantile business selling dry goods on short-term credit. Having developed a strong conservative business sense, the younger Willing was elevated to a partner in 1751. Upon his father's unexpected death in 1754, the 23-year-old became solely responsible

Thomas Willing (1731–1821)

Thomas Willing

for the family's financial interests, taking care of his mother and nine younger siblings. He also managed the estates, wills, and trusts of other wealthy families.

Willing continued to expand his business interests in the 1750s, adding wet goods such as alcohol to the mix as well as entering the slave trade. He also invested in real estate, traded in mortgages, and underwrote marine insurance at cheaper rates than the London firms. In 1757, Willing joined forces with Robert Morris to establish the firm Willing, Morris, and Company, which was one of the most successful businesses in the colonies, transporting, importing, and exporting goods between Maryland, Virginia, and Europe. Morris later became the financier of the American Revolution and was at one point considered by some to be second to only George Washington in influence. Unlike Morris, however, Willing was less of a risk-taker and did not suffer the economic collapse later experienced by his partner.

Willing was active in city politics before the Revolution, holding several offices in the 1750s and 1760s, including Common Councilman, Judge of the Orphan's Court, and Mayor of Philadelphia in 1763. On behalf of Pennsylvania, he attended the Albany Congress, oversaw trade with the Indians, and organized the survey of the boundary with Maryland. He was also a member of the Pennsylvania Assembly from 1764 to 1767. He resigned when appointed by the Penns to become a justice on the Pennsylvania Supreme Court where he served for ten years, along with Thomas Lawrence, as the last under colonial rule. For 31 years, from 1760 until 1791, Willing was a trustee of the College of Philadelphia, now the University of Pennsylvania, serving as treasurer of the board of trustees for a time.

On a personal note, in 1763, Willing married Anne McCall (1745-1781), daughter of Samuel McCall, one of the founders of the University of Philadelphia, and Anne Searle, the daughter of Captain John Searle. The couple produced thirteen children.

With the passage of the Stamp Act in 1765, Willing found his profits significantly impacted. He was a leader of the protest and was the first signer of the Nonimportation Resolution, creating an embargo of British goods pending the repeal of the Act.

With tensions rising between the colonies and the mother country, Willing became active in the Revolutionary cause speaking publicly about unfair taxation. In 1774, he became a member of the Committee of Correspondence. He was also president of the first Provincial Congress of Pennsylvania, which sent petitions to Britain asking for the restoration of constitutional liberties to the colonies. The following year, he was a member of the Committee of Safety. He was appointed to the Continental Congress for 1775 and 1776, but, given his respect for the Penn family and his belief the colonies were not prepared for war, voted against the Declaration of Independence. This effectively ended his political career. He was not re-elected to the Congress.

Still a patriot, Willing continued to work for the cause, obtaining supplies and funding. However, he was criticized for selling these goods and loaning money rather than donating to the army. He also remained in Philadelphia during the British occupation but refused to swear an oath of loyalty to the king. He continued to work secretly against British interests.

In 1778, Thomas's brother James Willing led a series of raids known as the Willing Expedition to take British holdings in British West Florida, along the Mississippi River, now Natchez, Mississippi. James, also a member of the Continental Congress, had traveled to Natchez to convince the residents to join the Revolutionary cause and secure the Mississippi River for the Americans as the fourteenth state. While well-received, James's proposal was rejected by the mostly loyalist residents. So, he returned to Philadelphia and was commissioned a captain. He then led the expedition against Natchez, funded mainly by Robert Morris, traveling with a

The grave of Thomas Willing

crew of 29 from Fort Pitt in the gunboat USS *Rattletrap*, down the Ohio and Mississippi Rivers to raid the settlements. After numerous raids, Willing's Expedition ran out of steam and sought refuge in New Orleans. On his return to Philadelphia, James was captured by the British. He was later exchanged for a British officer.

Meanwhile, in Philadelphia, Robert Morris and his partner Thomas Willing convinced the Congress to form a bank that could lend money to the colonies and stabilize the currency. In 1781, the Bank of North America was founded, and Willing was its president. Later, following the adoption of the U.S. Constitution, wholeheartedly supported by Willing, Alexander Hamilton implemented a new financial system. Thomas Willing led his Bank of the United States as president until he suffered a stroke in 1807. The Bank of the United States under Willing's leadership helped stabilize the U.S. economy through the War of 1812.

His ability to speak limited by the effects of the stroke, Willing retired from public life and his business activities. He lived in Philadelphia until his death on January 19, 1821, a few weeks after his eighty-ninth birthday. Willing was buried in the Christ Church graveyard.

Paine Wingate
(1739–1838)

Last Continental Congressman to Die

Buried at Stratham Cemetery,
Stratham, New Hampshire.

Continental Congress • US Senate • US House of Representatives

Paine Wingate had a long life, much of it in public service. He was an American preacher, farmer, and statesman from New Hampshire. He served in the Continental Congress and both the United States Senate, where he was an inaugural member, and the United States House of Representatives.

He was born in Amesburg, Massachusetts, on May 14, 1739, the sixth of twelve children. His father, Paine Sr., was a minister in Amesburg. The young Paine graduated from Harvard in 1759 and became a minister, too. He was ordained as pastor of the Congregational Church in 1763. His pastorate was not successful and was full of controversy. He resigned in 1776 to become a farmer.

He married Eunice Pickering, the sister of Timothy Pickering, on May 23, 1765, in Essex, Massachusetts. Records show they had at least three sons and five daughters. He was held in high esteem by members of his community and in 1775 was appointed to represent his town at the Fourth Provincial Congress of New Hampshire. At that time, Wingate expressed the opinion that pacification with England was still possible. He was elected to several terms in the New Hampshire House of Representatives and was a delegate to the state Constitutional Convention in 1781.

In 1788 he served in the Continental Congress and was a strong advocate of ratification of the United States Constitution writing, "Those who are well-wishers to their country, and best know the situation we are in, are most sensible of the necessity of its adoption, and great pains are taken to obtain the end."

New Hampshire appointed him to the first United States Senate, in which he served from March 4, 1789, until March 3, 1793. He was present when the first President, George Washington, took the oath

Grave of Paine Wingate

of office. At that time, the Senate's business was conducted in secret. Wingate supported this saying, "How would all the little domestic transactions of even the best regulated family appear if exposed to the world; and may not this apply to a larger body?" He believed secrecy promoted respect for the Senate. One of the big issues in the Senate at the time was the Judiciary Act of 1789, which established the federal court system. Wingate served on the committee that drafted the bill. Wingate voted against it, although it passed. He felt it left too much for the state courts to decide.

Wingate lost his bid for re-election to the Senate in 1792 but won a seat in the United States House of Representatives, where he served from March 4, 1793, to March 3, 1795.

Wingate lost his re-election bid in 1794. He then served in the State House of Representatives until 1798, when he became an Associate Justice of the New Hampshire Supreme Court, serving until 1808. Theophilus Parsons, a jurist who served with Wingate, said this about him, "It was of great importance that your judge Wingate forms a correct opinion before he pronounces it- for after that, law, reason, and authority will be unavailing."

When Wingate died on March 7, 1838, he was the oldest graduate of Harvard and the last surviving member of the first United States Congress. His wife, Eunice, lived past 100 and is reported to have worn her wedding dress to her 100th birthday party. They are both buried in Stratham Cemetery.

Oliver Wolcott
(1726 – 1797)

Connecticut Yankee

Buried at East Cemetery,
Litchfield, Connecticut.

Declaration of Independence • Articles of Confederation

Oliver Wolcott was a Revolutionary War hero who went on to serve as a member of the Continental Congress and sign the Declaration of Independence and later the Articles of Confederation. He commanded fourteen regiments of troops during the Revolutionary War and rose to the rank of Major General. He served for ten years as Connecticut's Lieutenant Governor beginning in 1786 and in 1796 became Governor until he died in 1797.

Wolcott was born in Windsor, Connecticut on November 20, 1726, the youngest of ten children to Colonial Governor Roger Wolcott and Sarah Drake Wolcott. He attended Yale College and graduated at the top of his class in 1747. Immediately upon graduating, he received a captain's commission from New York Governor George Clinton to fight in King George's War. He served on the northern frontier defending the Canadian border against the French until the Treaty of Aix-La-Chappelle of 1748. After the war, his regiment was disbanded and Wolcott returned to Connecticut to study medicine with his uncle, Dr. Alexander Wolcott. He completed his training but rather than pursue a career in medicine

Oliver Wolcott (1726–1797)

Oliver Wolcott

he settled in the newly developed area of Litchfield County where his father owned land and pursued an entirely different career. He was elected sheriff of the county at the age of twenty-five and founded a successful business. He served as Sheriff from 1751 to 1771. He also represented Litchfield in both houses of the colonial and state legislatures and later was appointed as judge of the Litchfield Probate and County Courts.

Wolcott married Lorraine (Laura) Collins, the daughter of a sea captain. The couple had five children, four of whom survived to adulthood. Wolcott remained active in the militia during the period leading up to the Revolutionary War, devoting portions of each year to militia duty. He rose through the ranks, serving as captain and then major in 1771, and was promoted to colonel in 1774, and later rose to Major General.

As tensions escalated between the colonies and Britain Wolcott became an active participant in the Patriot cause. He was elected to the Continental Congress in 1775 and was an ardent proponent of independence noting "a final separation between the countries I consider as unavoidable." The Congress named him a Commissioner of Indian Affairs and asked him to persuade the northern Indian nations to remain neutral. His experience in the French and Indian War led to that assignment.

In the summer of 1776, a brief illness and Wolcott's role in military affairs drew him away from his political responsibilities, resulting in his absence from Congress during the adoption of the Declaration of Independence. When he recovered from his illness, rather than returning to Philadelphia, the Connecticut Governor Jonathan Trumbull appointed him to command a detachment of fourteen regiments of Connecticut militia to defend New York, which he did.

On July 9, he was in New York City when George Washington read the Declaration of Independence to the troops. A demonstration followed and a group of soldiers toppled a large statue of King George III. The statue was made of lead and shattered into many pieces. The head was put on a spike outside a tavern. Wolcott arranged for the collection of the pieces and had them shipped off to the general's house. There, Wolcott, his family, and some local patriots melted the lead and made over 42,000 bullets for the war effort. In October 1777 he used some of these bullets in the defeat of General Burgoyne's troops at Saratoga, New

Wolcott's grave

York. The victory was a turning point in the war, bolstering American morale and convincing France to support the revolution.

In the fall of 1776, Wolcott returned to Philadelphia and signed the Declaration of Independence. After the victory at Saratoga Wolcott returned to Congress which was then meeting in York, Pennsylvania due to the British occupation of Philadelphia. There he signed the Articles of Confederation, the nation's first constitution.

In 1786 Wolcott was elected Lieutenant Governor of Connecticut, a post he would hold for ten years. He was a member of the Connecticut State Convention which ratified the Constitution of the United States in 1787. He became governor when Samuel Huntington died on January 5, 1796. He held the office until his own death at age 71. He died on December 1, 1797, and was buried at East Cemetery beside his wife.

Oliver Wolcott Jr, his son, served as Secretary of the Treasury under George Washington and John Adams and as Governor of Connecticut. A plaque commemorating Wolcott signing the Declaration of Independence can be found on the Signers Walk on the six hundred block of Chestnut Street in Philadelphia. His home in Litchfield, Connecticut was declared a National Historic Landmark in 1971. The town of Walcott, Connecticut was named in honor of Oliver and his son.

Sources

Books, Magazines, Journals, Files:
Alexander, Edward P. *Revolutionary Conservative: James Duane of New York*. New York: Ams Press, 1978.
Anthony, Katharine Susan. *First Lady of the Revolution; The Life of Mercy Otis Warren*. Port Washington, N.Y.: Kennikat Press, 1972.
Appleby, Joyce. *Inheriting the Revolution: The First Generation of Americans*. Cambridge, Massachusetts: Harvard University Press, 2000.
Atkinson, Rick. *The British Are Coming: The War for America, Lexington to Princeton, 1775-1777*. New York: Henry Holt & Co. 2019.
Bordewich, Fergus M. *The First Congress: How James Madison, George Washington, and a Group of Extraordinary Men Invented the Government*. New York: Simon and Schuster Paperbacks, 2016.
Boudreau, George W. *Independence: A Guide to Historic Philadelphia*. Yardley, Pennsylvania: Westholme Publishing, LLC. 2012.
Bowen, Catherine Drinker. *Miracle at Philadelphia: The Story of the Constitutional Convention May to September 1787*. Boston, Massachusetts: Little, Brown & Company, 1966.
Breen, T.H, *George Washington's Journey: The President Forges a New Nation*. New York: Simon & Schuster. 2016.
Brookhiser, Richard. *Gentleman Revolutionary: Gouverneur Morris The Rake Who Wrote the Constitution*. New York: Free Press, 2003.
———. *John Marshall: The Man Who Made the Supreme Court*. New York: Basic Books. 2018.
Brush, Edward Hale. *Rufus King and His Times*. New York: N.L. Brown, 1926.
Chadwick, Bruce. *I Am Murdered: George Wythe, Thomas Jefferson, and the Killing That Shocked a New Nation*. Hoboken, New Jersey: John Wiley & Sons, 2009.
Chambers, II, John Whiteclay. *The Oxford Companion to American Military History*. Oxford: Oxford University Press, 1999.
Commager, Henry Steele & Richard B. Morris. *The Spirit of 'Seventy-Six: The Story of the American Revolution as Told by Participants*. New York: Harper & Rowe, 1967.
Cole, Ryan. *Light-Horse Harry Lee: The Rise and Fall of a Revolutionary Hero*. Washington, D.C.: Regnery History. 2019.
Conlin, Joseph R. *The Morrow Book of Quotations in American History*. New York: William Morrow and Company, Inc., 1984.
Daniels, Jonathan. *Ordeal of Ambition*. Garden City, New York: Doubleday & Company, Inc., 1970.
Dann, John C. *The Revolution Remembered: Eyewitness Accounts of the War for Independence*. Chicago: University of Chicago Press, 1980.
DeRose, Chris. *Founding Rivals: Madison vs. Monroe: The Bill of Rights and the Election that Saved a Nation*. New York: MJF Books, 2011.

Drury, Bob & Tom Clavin. *Valley Forge.* New York: Simon & Schuster. 2018.
Ellis, Joseph J. *Revolutionary Summer: The Birth of American Independence.* New York: Alfred A. Knopf, 2013.
———. *The Quartet: Orchestrating the Second American Revolution, 1783-1789.* New York: Alfred A. Knopf, 2015.
———. *His Excellency: George Washington.* New York: Alfred A. Knopf, 2004.
Flexner, James Thomas. *George Washington in the American Revolution, 1775-1783.* Boston: Little, Brown & Company, 1967.
Flower, Lenore Embick. "Visit of President George Washington to Carlisle, 1794." Carlisle, Pennsylvania: The Hamilton Library and Cumberland County Historical Society, 1932.
Gerlach, Don R. *Proud Patriot: Philip Schuyler and the War of Independence, 1775-1783.* Syracuse, N.Y.: Syracuse University Press, 1987.
Goodrich, Charles A. *Lives of the Signers of the Declaration of Independence.* Charlotteville, N.Y.: SamHar Press, 1976.
Griffith, IV, William R. *The Battle of Lake George: England's First Triumph in the French and Indian War.* Charleston, South Carolina: The History Press, 2016.
Grossman, Mark. *Encyclopedia of the Continental Congress.* Armenia, New York: Grey House Publishing, 2015.
Hamilton, Edward P. *Fort Ticonderoga: Key to a Continent.* Boston: Little, Brown & Company, 1964.
Isenberg, Nancy. *Fallen Founder: The Life of Aaron Burr.* New York: Penguin Group, 2007.
Kennedy, Roger G. *Burr, Hamilton, and Jefferson: A Study in Character.* New York: Oxford University Press, 1999.
Kiernan, Denise & Joseph D'Agnese. *Signing Their Lives Away: The Fame and Misfortune of the Men Who Signed the Declaration of Independence.* Philadelphia: Quirk Books, 2008.
———. *Signing Their Rights Away: The Fame and Misfortune of the Men Who Signed the United States Constitution.* Philadelphia: Quirk Books, 2011.
Klarman, Michael J. *The Framers' Coup: The Making of the United States Constitution.* New York: Oxford University Press, 2016.
Langguth, A. J. *Patriots.* New York: Simon and Schuster, 1988.
Larson, Edward J. *A Magnificient Catastrophe.* New York: Free Press, 2007.
Lee, Mike. Written *Out of History: The Forgotten Founders Who Fought Big Government.* New York: Penguin Books, 2017.
Lewis, James E., Jr., *The Burr Conspiracy: Uncovering the Story of an Early American Crisis*, Princeton: Princeton University Press, 2017.
Lockridge, Ross Franklin. *The Harrisons.* 1941.
Lomask, Milton. *Aaron Burr: The Years from Princeton to Vice President, 1756-1805.* New York: Farrar Straus Giroux, 1979.
Lossing, Benson J. *Pictorial Field Book of the Revolution.* New York: Harper Brothers. 1851.
Maier, Pauline. *American Scripture: Making the Declaration of Independence.* New York: Alfred A. Knopf, Inc., 1997.

McCullough, David. *John Adams*. New York: Simon & Schuster, 2002.
Meltzer, Brad & Josh Mensch. *The First Conspiracy: The Secret Plot to Kill George Washington*. New York: Flat Iron Books. 2018.
Middlekauff, Robert. *The Glorious Cause: The American Revolution, 1763-1789*. Oxford: Oxford University Press, 2005.
Miller, Jr., Arthur P. & Marjorie L. Miller. *Pennsylvania Battlefields and Military Landmarks*. Mechanicsburg, Pennsylvania: Stackpole Books, 2000.
Millett, Allan R. & Peter Maslowski. *For the Common Defense: A Military History of the United States of America*. New York: The Free Press, 1984.
Moore, Charles. *The Family Life of George Washington*. New York: Houghton Mifflin, 1926.
Nagel, Paul C. *The Lees of Virginia: Seven Generations of an American Family*. Oxford: Oxford University Press, 1990.
O'Connell, Robert L. *Revolutionary: George Washington at War*. New York: Random House. 2019.
Racove, Jack N. *Revolutionaries: A New History of the Invention of America*. New York: Houghton Mifflin Harcourt, 2011.
Raphael, Ray. Founding Myths: *Stories That Hide Our Patriotic Past*. New York: MJF Books, 2004.
Rossiter, Clinton. *1787 The Grand Convention*. New York: The Macmillan Company, 1966.
Seymour, Joseph. *The Pennsylvania Associators, 1747-1777*. Yardley, Pennsylvania: Westholme Publishing, LLC. 2012.
Schweikart, Larry & Michael Allen. *A Patriot's History of the United States from Columbus's Great Discovery to the War on Terror*. New York: Penguin, 2004.
Sharp, Arthur G. *Not Your Father's Founders*. Avon, Massachusetts: Adams Media, 2012.
Stahr, Walter. *John Jay: Founding Father*. New York: Diversion Books, 2017.
Taafee, Stephen R. *The Philadelphia Campaign, 1777-1778*. Lawrence, Kansas: University of Kansas Press, 2003.
Tinkcom, Harry Marlin, *The Republicans and the Federalists in Pennsylvania, 1790-1801*. Harrisburg, Pennsylvania: Pennsylvania Historical and Museum Commission. 1950.
Ward, Matthew C. *Breaking the Backcountry: The Seven Years' War in Virginia and Pennsylvania, 1754-1765*. Pittsburgh, Pennsylvania: University of Pittsburgh Press, 2003.
Weisberger, Bernard A. *America Afire: Jefferson, Adams, and the Revolutionary Election of 1800*. New York: HarperCollins, 2000.
Wood, Gordon S. *The Radicalism of the American Revolution*. New York: Vintage Books, 1993.
———. *Empire of Liberty: A History of the Early Republic, 1789-1815*. New York: Penguin Books, 2004.
———. *Revolutionary Characters: What Made the Founders Different*. New York: Penguin Books, 2006.
———. *The Americanization of Benjamin Franklin*. Oxford: Oxford University Press, 2009.

Wright, Benjamin F. *The Federalist: The Famous Papers on the Principles of American Government: Alexander Hamilton, James Madison, John Jay*. New York: Metro Books, 2002.

Zobel, Hiller B. *The Boston Massacre*. New York: W. W. Norton & Company, 1970.

Video Resources:
Guelzo, Allen C. The Great Courses: *America's Founding Fathers* (Course N. 8525). Chantilly, Virginia: The Teaching Company, 2017.

Online Resources:
Archives.gov – for information on the Constitutional Convention.
CauseofLiberty.blogspot.com – for information on Daniel Carroll.
ColonialHall.com – for information about the signers of the Declaration of Independence.
DSDI1776.com – for information on many Founders.
FamousAmericans.net – for information on many Founders.
FindaGrave.com – for burial information, vital statistics and obituaries.
FirstLadies.org – for information on Abigail Adams.
Newspapers.com – Hundreds of newspaper articles were accessed—too numerous to mention here.
NPS.gov – for information on various park sites.
TeachingAmericanHistory.com – for information on Charles Pinckney and George Wythe.
TheHistoryJunkie.com – for information on multiple Founders.
USHistory.org – for information on multiple Founders.
Wikipedia.com – for general historical information.

Index

Adams, John, 11–13, 20, 24, 34, 47, 62, 77, 100, 109, 114, 124, 127, 136–37, 155, 163, 165–70, 173–74, 176, 180, 182–83, 186, 192, 212–13, 253, 293
Adams, John Quincy, 18, 24–25, 32, 34, 128
Adams, Samuel, 114, 272
Albany Rural Cemetery, 238, 244
Alexander, William, Lord Stirling, 238–45
Alien and Sedition Acts, 13, 166
Alsop, John, 144
Annapolis Convention, 62, 99, 280
Armstrong, John, 32
Arnold, Benedict, 115, 138, 236, 243
Articles of Confederation, 8, 10, 40, 42, 62, 75, 77, 89, 91–92, 102, 104–5, 113–15, 141, 144, 177, 180, 211, 213, 220–22, 224–25, 246–48, 265–66, 274, 276, 290, 293
Atkinson, Rick, 202
Audubon, James, 58

Baldwin, Abraham, 35–39
Baldwin, Henry, 35
Banister, John, 40–43
Banister, John Baptist, 40
Bank of the United States, 280, 282, 286
Bartlett, Josiah, 253, 267–68, 270–71
Battle of Alamance, 49, 81
Battle of Beaufort, 197
Battle of Bennington, 232, 237, 253
Battle of Brandywine, 61, 138, 164, 185, 242
Battle of Brooklyn Heights, 144, 244
Battle of Bunker Hill, 137, 233
Battle of Camden Court House, 52, 71, 227–28, 279
Battle of Cowpens, 202, 204
Battle of Germantown, 61, 138, 158, 164, 185, 242
Battle of Harlem Heights, 158
Battle of Kettle Creek, 202
Battle of Lake George and Bloody Pond, 234
Battle of Monmouth, 138, 158, 164, 221, 243
Battle of Moore's Creek, 276
Battle of Point Pleasant, 90
Battle of Princeton, 138, 158, 185, 187, 213, 233–34
Battle of Rhode Island, 269, 271
Battle of Saratoga, 228, 236, 269, 271, 292
Battle of Springfield, 65
Battle of Sullivan's Island, 195, 197
Battle of Trenton, 158, 185, 187, 213, 233–34, 242
Battle of Quebec, 67

Battle of White Plains, 158
Battle of Yorktown, 42, 99, 122, 138, 158, 160, 223, 243
Bayard, John, 225
Bethesda Presbyterian Churchyard, 71, 73
Betsy Ross House Grounds, 216, 218
Bill of Rights, 5, 9–11, 31, 92, 100, 115, 123
Bingham, William, 128
Blair, John Jr., 42
Bland, Richard, 41
Bland, Theodorick, 41
Boerum, Simon, 44–46
Bonaventure Cemetery, 246, 249
Boone, Daniel, 55, 276
Boston, 7, 50, 96, 135–37, 143, 233–34, 262, 279
Boston Massacre, 96, 136, 262
Boston Tea Party, 7, 96, 118, 132, 279
Boudinot, Elias, 221
Boyd, James, 202
Brearly, David, 151
Brodie, Fawn, 12
Brooks, Victor, 137
Brown University, 261
Burgoyne, John, 198, 236, 271, 292
Burnett, Edmund Cody, 62
Burr, Aaron, 13–14, 23, 31, 58, 166, 168, 242

Calhoun, John C., 16
Campbell, John P., 58
Canby, William, 218
Carroll, Daniel, 172
Carson, Hampton, L., 119
Caswell Memorial Cemetery, 47, 52
Caswell, Richard, 47–52, 279
Cave Hill Cemetery, 53, 58
Chamberlain, Mellon, 114
Chambers, Stephen, 185
Chase, Samuel, 168
Cheney, Lynne, 6, 16, 19, 22–23, 25
Christ Church Burial Ground, 60, 63, 108, 111, 125, 130, 282, 286
Clark, Abraham, 69, 221
Clark, George Rogers, 53–59
Clark, William, 53, 58
Clay, Henry, 16
Clermont Estate Cemetery, 227, 230
Clinton, DeWitt, 17–18
Clinton, George, 15, 25, 45, 290
Clinton, Henry, 73
Clymer, George, 110, 183–84

INDEX

Cole, Catherine, 23
Coleman, John, 180
College of New Jersey, 5
College of William and Mary, 6, 29–30, 33
Columbia University, 149
Common Burial Ground, 260, 264
Concord, 88, 136, 155, 157, 185, 234, 247, 263
Congressional Cemetery, 27
Constitutional Convention, 8, 37, 52, 62, 80, 83, 93, 99, 115, 125, 128, 147, 150, 172, 180, 227, 229, 259, 280
Continental Association, 44, 47, 50, 64–65, 68–69, 86, 93, 97, 109, 117–19, 131–32, 147, 150, 153, 155, 260, 263
Conway Cabal, 144, 238, 243
Conway, Thomas, 242–43
Cornwallis, Charles, 73, 138, 228
Courthouse Grounds, 85, 256
Cowper, Basil, 246
Coxe, Tench, 60–63
Crane, Stephen, 64–68, 150
Cushing, Thomas, 262

D'Agnese, Joseph, 81, 86, 227, 256
Dana, Francis, 114
Declaration of Independence, 44, 85, 88, 102–3, 105–6, 110, 117, 122, 141, 143–44, 147, 150, 153, 161, 177, 180, 185, 189, 192, 217, 243, 250, 252, 256, 258, 269, 271, 282, 284, 290, 292–93
DeHart, John, 68–70
Dayton, Jonathan, 70, 151
de Kaleb, Johann, 71–74
Deane, Silas, 73, 155
Dickinson, John, 119, 184
Dorchester Heights, 135, 138
Duer, William, 75–79, 185, 239
Dunmore's War, 90

East Cemetery, 290
Edwards, Timothy, 114
Elbert, Samuel, 248
Ellicott, Andrew, 208
Ellsworth, Oliver, 166
Elmer, Johnathan, 221

Fauquier, Francis, 96
Federalist Papers, 5, 9, 123
Few, William, 37, 80–84
First Continental Congress, 44–47, 49, 64–65, 68–69, 86, 93, 97, 132–33, 150, 155, 197, 262
First Presbyterian Church, 64, 66
Fleming, Thomas, 234
Folsom, 270
Fort Moultrie Grounds, 195, 199

Francis, Tench, 60
Franklin, Benjamin, 62, 72, 109, 111, 128, 155, 209, 211, 240, 271, 277, 279
Franklin, William Temple, 128
Frederick, John, 110
French and Indian War, 49, 53, 125, 143, 149, 200–1, 232–33, 239, 292
Friends Burying Ground, 131, 133–34

Gadsden, Christopher, 126, 155
Gallatin, Albert, 15, 18
Gates, Horatio, 73, 242, 271
Genet, Edmond-Charles, 57
Gerry, Elbridge, 9, 19, 114–15, 165
Gershwin, George, 107
Grace Episcopal Churchyard, 75, 79
Grant, James, 241
Grayson, William, 31
Great Wagon Road, 200
Greene, Nathanael, 36, 82, 280
Green-Wood Cemetery, 44, 46, 147, 151
Gunn, James, 249
Gutzman, Kevin R. C., 15
Gwinnett, Button, 257, 259

Hall, Lyman, 36, 85–88, 257, 259
Hamilton, Alexander, 9, 11–13, 20, 31, 62, 78, 83, 111, 128–29, 149, 158–59, 166, 174, 176, 186, 204, 227, 280–81, 286
Hamilton, Henry, 55
Hancock, James, 11
Hancock, John, 114–15
Harrison, Benjamin, 155
Harrison, William Henry, 18
Harrod, James, 55
Hart, John, 69
Harvard College, 265
Harvie, John, 89–92
Hatcher's Run Estate, 40, 43
Hays Plantation Cemetery, 121
Henderson, Richard, 55
Henry Cemetery, 93, 101
Henry, Patrick, 10, 25, 55, 93–101
Hewes, Joseph, 49–50
Heyward Family Cemetery, 102, 105
Heyward Jr., 102–7
Hillegas, Michael, 108–12
Hollywood Cemetery, 28, 34, 89, 91–92
Holten Family Cemetery, 113, 116
Holten Samuel, 113–16
Hooper, William, 49–50
Hopewell Plantation, 201, 203
Hopkinson, Francis, 208–9, 218
Hopkins, Stephen, 261–62, 271
Houston, William, 37

GRAVES of our FOUNDERS

Howe, Tonert, 126
Howe, William, 234
Hull, William, 17
Humphreys, Charles, 117–20

Intolerable Acts, 69, 97, 132–33
Iredell, James, 121–24

Jackson, Andrew, 18, 169
Jackson, William, 125–30
Jay, John, 9, 152, 167
Jay Treaty, 173, 280
Jefferson, Thomas, 5, 7–8, 11–16, 24–25, 28–32, 34, 42–43, 56, 63, 83, 89, 92, 98–99, 119, 130, 163, 165–66, 168, 174, 183, 186, 209, 229
Jennings, Paul, 26–27
Johnson Family Cemetery, 121, 124
Johnson, William, 240
Johnston, Samuel, 121
Jones, John Paul, 271
Jones, Gabriel, 55

Key, Francis Scott, 175
Kiernan, Denise, 81, 86, 227, 256
King, Rufus, 20, 32, 115, 128
Kinsey, James, 68, 131–34
Kirschke, James J., 192
Knox, Henry, 128, 130, 135–40, 160–61
Kukla, Jon, 94–95, 97, 100

Lafayette, Marquis de, 30, 71–73, 130, 170–71, 173, 176
Langdon, John, 266, 270
Langguth, A. J., 228
Langworthy, 247
Laurel Hill Cemetery, 177, 182, 205, 210
Laurens, Henry, 127
Laurens, John, 127
Lawrence, Thomas, 284
Lee, Charles, 228, 241, 243
Lee, Lighthorse Harry, 243
Lee, Richard Henry, 115, 165
Lewis, Francis, 141–46
Lewis, Meriweather, 58
Lewis, William, 127
Lexington, 87, 136, 155, 157, 185, 234, 247, 263
Lincoln, Abraham, 16
Lincoln, Benjamin, 73, 126–27, 129, 197
Livingston, Robert, 14, 143
Livingston, Philip, 144, 147, 178, 194, 239, 243
Livingston, William, 68, 70, 147–52, 239
Logan, Benjamin, 55
Lord Dunmore's War, 54
Louisiana Purchase, 14, 28

Lovell, James, 114
Lynch, Thomas, 153–56
Lynch, Thomas Jr., 153, 156

Madison, Dolley, 13–14, 21–27
Madison Family Cemetery, 5, 21
Madison, James, 5–20, 23–25, 27, 29–32, 54, 100, 165, 229, 280
Magaw, Robert, 171
Magruder, Allan Bowie, 58
Marbury v. Madison, 167, 276
Marion, Francis, 202
Marshall, George C., 163
Marshall, John, 30, 92, 163–69
Martin, John Plumb, 157–62
Martin, Josiah, 49
Martin, Luther, 172
Mason, George, 9–10, 56
Mathews, George, 248
McHenry, James, 170–76
McKean, Thomas, 177–82, 184–85
Meigs, Josiah, 37
Mercer, James, 143
Mercer, John Francis, 172
Meredith, Samuel, 112, 183–88
Middleton, Henry, 155
Miller, Maria, 219
Mitchell, Samuel, 25
Mobley, Joe A., 47, 49–50
Monroe Doctrine, 32
Monroe, James, 10, 14–16, 20, 25, 28–34, 163, 165, 242
Montagu, Charles, 155, 198
Montgomery, Richard, 67
Montpelier Plantation Cemetery, 274, 276
Moore, Jonathan, 85
Morgan, Daniel, 202
Morris, Gouverneur, 189, 192–93
Morris III, Lewis, 189–94
Morris, Robert, 8, 77–78, 112, 127, 129, 185, 208, 218, 283, 285–86
Moultrie, William, 104, 156, 195–99
Mount Hebron Cemetery, 211, 215
Mount Vernon Cemetery, 224, 226

Napoleon, 14, 16, 18
New York, 17, 27, 30, 34, 44–45, 61, 73, 75–78, 82, 84, 127–28, 135, 137–38, 141–52, 154, 158, 160, 180, 189–92, 238–44, 280–81, 292
Nicholas, William Cary, 19

Ogden, Robert, 179
Old Haverford Friends Meeting House Cemetery, 117, 120
Old North Cemetery, 269, 272

300

INDEX

Old Stone Church Cemetery, 200, 204
Old Tennent Churchyard, 220, 223

Parson's Cause, 95
Patterson, William, 151, 167
Penn State University, 182
Pendleton, Edmund, 9
Pendleton, Nathaniel, 37
Penn, William, 112, 119, 131
Philadelphia, 7–8, 10, 17, 22–24, 50, 60–63, 83,
   87, 97–98, 104, 108–9, 111–12, 115, 127–28,
   130–33, 142, 155–56, 158, 169–70, 172, 176,
   179, 181, 183–87, 192, 205, 207–8, 210–12,
   214, 216–19, 221–22, 224–27, 229, 242–43,
   247, 252, 262, 264, 271, 276–80, 282,
   284–86, 292–93
Phillips, William, 42
Pickens, Andrew, 200–4
Pickering, Timothy, 166, 174, 185, 287
Pierce, William, 37, 83
Pinckney, Charles Cotesworth, 15, 165–66, 192
Pine Hill Cemetery, 265, 268
Pinkney, William, 31
Pope, John, 58

Quincy, Josiah, 155

Randolph, Edmund, 9–10, 98, 165
Randolph, John, 20, 25
Randolph, Peyton, 97, 262
Read, George, 179–80, 184–85
Read, Jacob, 229
Riker, John, 30
Rittenhouse, David, 205–10
Robbins, Karen, 176
Roberdeau, Daniel, 211–15
Roberts, Owen, 125, 127
Robertson, Donald, 5
Rock Creek Cemetery, 35, 37
Rodney, Caesar, 178–79
Rogers, Robert, 234
Ross, Betsy, 216–19
Ross, George, 218
Rossiter, Clinton, 8–9, 83, 229
Ross, John, 217
Rowan, John, 58
Ruggles, Timothy, 178–79
Rush, Benjamin, 144, 171, 258
Rutledge, Edward, 155, 199, 258
Rutledge, John, 155, 203

Saint Anne's Churchyard, 153, 156
Saint Paul's Episcopal Cemetery, 80, 84
Samuel Meredith Monument, 183
Sandy Point Cemetery, 157, 161

Scherger, Marion, 204
Schuyler, Philip, 76, 241
Scott, John Morton, 149
Scudder, Nathaniel, 220–23
Second Continental Congress, 7, 40, 42, 50, 69, 87,
   89–90, 97, 103, 133, 144, 150, 156, 211
Shipped, Edward, 282
Shirley, William, 240
Shockoe Hill Cemetery, 163, 169
Smallwood, William, 52
Smith, James, 184
Smith, Jonathan Bayard, 224–26
Smith, Ralph D., 38
Smith, Robert, 16, 69
Spaight, Richard Dobbs, 227–31
Stagg, J. C. A., 7, 20
Stamp Act, 95–96, 143, 153–54, 177–78, 184,
   251, 262, 284
Stanly, John, 230
St. Ann's Church of Morrisania, 189
Stark Cemetery, 232
Stark, John, 232–37, 271
St. John's Episcopal Churchyard, 68, 70
St. Thomas Jenifer, Daniel of, 172
Stiles, Ezra, 36
Stockton, Richard, 69, 145
Stratham Cemetery, 287, 289
Sullivan, John, 266, 271

Talleyrand, 165
Tallmadge, Benjamin, 174
Taney, Roger, 169
Tarleton, Banastre, 202
Taylor, John, 54
Tecumseh, 17–18
Telfair, Edward, 246–49
Temple Inn, 40
Thomaston Village Cemetery, 135
Thomson, Charles, 184, 262
Thompson, Ebenezer, 270
Thornton Family Burying Ground, 250, 255
Thornton, Matthew, 250–55, 271
Todd, John, 23
Toppan, Vhristopher, 270
Transylvania Purchase, 275
Treaty of Hopewell, 204
Treaty of Fort Stanwix, 54
Treaty of Paris, 53, 56, 128, 138, 243
Treaty of Sycamore Shoals, 275
Trinity Church Cemetery, 141, 145, 151, 243, 277,
   281
Trumbull, John, 145
Trumbull, Jonathan, 292
Tryon, William, 81

United States Constitution, 5, 9–11, 31, 35, 37, 62, 80, 111, 123, 147, 151, 165, 170, 172–73, 176–77, 181, 185, 192, 199, 204, 227, 229, 277, 280, 286, 288
United States Mint, 205, 209–10
University of Delaware, 170, 182
University of Georgia, 37, 39, 83, 88, 259
University of North Carolina, 229, 274, 276, 281
University of Pennsylvania, 208, 226, 277
University of Princeton, 207, 220, 224, 226

Varnum, James Mitchell, 158

Walker, John, 31
Walton, George, 37, 248, 256–59
Walton, John, 247
War of 1812, 5, 17–18, 32, 67, 174–75, 226, 286
Ward, Artemas, 137, 262
Ward, Samuel, 260–64
Warren, James, 213
Washington, George, 8, 11–13, 25–26, 28–31, 42, 55–57, 66, 73–74, 91, 98–100, 111, 121, 123–25, 127–30, 135, 137, 139–40, 144, 155–56, 158, 160, 165, 168, 170–74, 176, 180, 183, 185–86, 192, 209–10, 213, 216–19, 229, 234, 238, 241–43, 283, 288, 292–93

Washington, Martha, 129
Wayne, Anthony, 57, 185
Weare, Meshech, 270
Webster, Daniel, 16, 253
Wentworth, Bennington, 251
Wentworth, John Jr., 265–68
Westminster Hall and Burying Ground, 170
Whipple, William, 253, 268–73
White, Henry Clay, 37
Wilkinson, James, 57–58, 168, 242, 271
William and Mary College, 42, 164
Williams, John, 274–76
Williamson, Hugh, 277–81
Willing, Charles, 282
Willing, James, 285–86
Willing, Thomas, 282–86
Wingate, Paine, 287–89
Witherspoon, John, 7, 69, 145, 221–22
Wolcott, Oliver, 167, 290–93
Wolcott, Oliver Jr., 293
Wolcott, Roger, 290
Wythe, George, 10, 164

Yale College, 35–37, 147, 190, 290
York Pennsylvania, 42, 91, 104, 114, 144, 221, 242–43, 248, 266–67, 293

www.ingramcontent.com/pod-product-compliance
Lightning Source LLC
Chambersburg PA
CBHW020639230426
43665CB00008B/237